Being Black not much has changed

By Sally S. Eko
Nee Braimah

APPRECIATION

Sincere thanks to Mr. Nat Womble who suggested some language structures, made some corrections and gave advice.

DEDICATION

To All Descendants of Mother Africa wherever you may be.

Preface

I have always wondered why black people my race, have to be at the bottom of societal ladder in most part of the western world. I came to the western world in 1975 and my impression of the west before I left Africa was that it is a just society where people have a better standard of living and all people are equal.

I never knew the color of human skin makes a difference. In Africa where I came from people are people and the color of the skin does not matter. Even among Africans, we joke about each one of us being different but not superior to one another.

I was surprised when I saw that black people I saw in America were not enjoying the same standard of living like the white people. They were not even living together. This was a shock to me because I thought after slavery the black people were on equal footing with the whites but I was wrong. This observation made me uncomfortable. I did not experience any personal act of discrimination but I realized people make you feel you are different the way they interact with you. As a student at the University of Illinois at Champaign –Urbana, anytime I got an 'A, in a subject I was over praised by the instructors, as if it was not expected. The atmosphere made me feel different.

I was made to feel different and began to wonder whether other people thought black people were lesser beings. I also noticed that black people work in low paying menial jobs than whites. I used to question myself was that by design or accident. When I graduated from college, I got a job as a teller with a bank in New York City. I then told myself to go back home to Africa in order to be able to utilize my qualification in the area of my studies-Finance.

Since then I have always been concerned about the plight of black people in comparison to other people on earth. We are all humans but different in respect to our environment. The environment molds people. The sunny environment makes you worry less. Sunshine inspires happiness and joy. The sun helps vegetation and there was always plenty of food to eat. The environment was clean and healthy because there were no slums. The land was vast and people had enough for farming and shelter. When the sun sets, the moon brings illumination at night. The evening time is for story telling right under the illumination the moon brings.

If you observe humans, no matter our location on the planet earth our needs are the same. The most important need dear to every human is to have progeny to carry on life and enjoy the environment and be happy. African people have the same aspiration.

Unfortunately, a cold continent lies directly above Africa. People in a cold continent would not be as happy as people in hot continent, cold climate creates gloomy surroundings. This explains why summer is a month of fun and more out- door activities in cold continents. People in cold continents worry about the cold that comes after summer and they had to find ways to create lights to illuminate the gloomy long cold periods. They do not get adequate light from the sun so they had to be indoors most part of the year. They do not get much moonlight neither since the reflection of the sun illuminates the moon. Staying indoors most part of the year creates moody countenance because you see the same things most of the time.

Necessity is the mother of invention as the adage goes. People in cold countries had to find solutions to the cold problem by inventing electricity for light and the invention of light led the way to other many great inventions.

In order to improve the condition nature set them, they ventured to other places and lands. This adventure gave them the opportunity to see different places, learned, copied, and adopted what they saw. They took samples of what they saw during their adventures and used them to improve themselves and environment

Black people did not need light then since nature provided over twelve hours of light each day. The invention of light was the beginning of invention that changed the world. Many inventions like steam engines followed to make movement easier in the cold environment.

Their leaders wage enormous powers over the people. They created large armies to wage war against their neighbors who had what they did not have. They were able to take lands and resources to expand and improve the lives of the people. The leaders own everything and the people work for their keep. The Soldiers had powers too since they brought the bounties. The leaders were able to dispatch people to other parts and were able to conquer the people they met due to their improved technologies and expert in warfare.

It was through one of these adventures that they stumbled over West Africa and since then life in West Africa and Africa had never been the same again. They had taken over Americas from the natives and need labor to clear the land and develop it. They saw blacks to be stronger and can stand the harsh environment than the Native Americans hence they began shipping blacks to the Americas to work without pay. The gun technology gave them edge over Africans who fought with only bows and arrows.

The lives of Africans then were simple. They traded among themselves and Arabs from the Arabian Peninsula. The vocations of the Africans then were farming, animal rearing, mining, making agriculture implements, black smiths, and gold smiths. There were weavers of cloths, baskets, mats, and thatch for roofing. Some Africans were settlers who lived within City States with kings as heads others were nomads. The advent of slave trade and colonization changed African people way of life. They had to jettison their way of life and learn that of their captives. This trend

still continues today and has serious impact on the direction of black people in the world. The black person puts in more efforts now for the basic existence and yet he or she still trailing behind in terms of wealth and other comfort of the modern world.
The way forward is for the black man to find his position on earth and try to help himself instead of the illusion that other people would do everything for him. Black man or woman, remember all humans are competitors competing for the same finite resources. We are all here to establish ourselves on earth, how then do you think someone would make you have an edge over him or her. Think about it.

All humans that encountered one another have been copying from one another since time immemorial. Black people need to copy the good things other people are doing to make them live and enjoy life better. Black people should see themselves as integral part of the human community; have equal rights to the world resources and be actively involved in the world affairs. The idea that black people are only workers and not producers is a wrong fallacy that has become an accepted norm.

Black people should develop the Continent of Africa for modern jobs, conducive and safe environment, and shelters improved. If the Continent of Africa is developed ,such that people are able to meet their aspirations there would not be need for people fleeing Africa to places where they are not welcomed. Thousands of black people die unnecessary every year when fleeing current abodes to places of better economic conditions.

Africa is a beautiful continent with resources and it is up to the sons and daughters of Africa wherever they are to make Africa equal among the continents of the world. The old ways of doing businesses in Africa need improvement to be efficient and effective. Famine has no place in Africa. Africa is a land with tropical green forest where many animals live and survive. There are numerous rivers running through Africa. The belly of Africa contains precious and rare metals that have created wealth for other continents and their people. African leaders should let peace return to Africa and leaders that care about the people should emerge and lead Africa to greatness once again.

BEING BLACK NOT MUCH HAS CHANGED

Then, Now, and a Way Forward

TABLE OF CONTENT

Chapter One

Slavery and the Black Race

The natural state of humanity is freedom. Slavery was a degrading servitude created by man to satisfy his greed and lust. Slavery was an institution that destroyed a person's identity and made him/her lose dignity and pride. Slavery affected a person's psychic and being. In essence, slavery was a degrading and inhumane system man created to use another human being to satisfy his ego.

What made the slave different from the slave master? The predicament of being a slave as can be imagined could destroy any man. Slaves rebelled struggled, fought, hated, loved, prayed and came to the point of even doubting their Creator due to the inhumane treatment from their masters. The slaves who came from Africa have been believers in the Supreme Being so they lived and hoped they would someday be free. They waited, served, cared, loved, contributed, made, provided, and they remained slaves.

The slaves improved the life of the master through hard work while their life expectancy dwindled. Their strength made it possible for the ideas of the masters to become a reality. Their labor made it possible to create the free world that exists today. Yes, their labor was free so wealth increased; the poor became rich and the rich richer, yet the slaves had nothing but their strength. Aristocratic and middle class families emerged. Even the Europeans, who were serfs and slaves before Africans were enslaved became aristocrats and wealthy while the African remained nothing but a slave.

The impact of slavery to the wealth of Europe and America was unprecedented in their history. Slavery turned Europe from a warring continent into rich and industrialized continent. Slaves provided the free labor needed to work on sugar, coffee, cotton and other raw materials plantations in North and South America to feed the new factories springing up in Europe and America in 16th century.

These Africans made the free market enterprise possible because their labor was free; therefore, cost of production was low. The encounter with Africans changed the world because they were adaptable, healthier, and stronger and served the world with their labor on plantations that eventually led to the industrial era.

The African experienced cold climate for the first time. Oh Heavens! How horrible and devastating that experience was. They were cold, freezing cold, frost bitten but strong. They survived, because they were healthy, and stronger. Their minds wondered back to Africa anytime they wore those garments that protected them from the cold. In Africa, they adorned their body with cotton garments and ornaments that glitters in the twilight sun.

The African had to change and adapt to the new environment in order to live. As Charles Darwin, the famous biologist wrote, "it is whoever, that adapts to changes that survives and not the strongest", in his essay "On the Origin of Species."
Notwithstanding, millions of Africans died from being over worked and not from weakness. They lost their names and identity. They became a number, and eventually were given names by the slave masters.   Their mental faculty was incredible, and began to adjust to their new environment for survival. Africans learnt the language of their masters and gradually lost their mother tongue. They were clever, versatile, and created their own version of the master's language. They were unique in every sense of the word. They were the source of the new changes and were very valuable and indispensable, but their contributions were not recognized.

The Africans increased in population despite abuse. They ran away sometimes but could not go back to Africa because home was thousands and thousands of miles across the Atlantic Ocean. The Africans came from different places on the continent of Africa. They could have come from any of the following empires that flourished in Africa between 1235AD-1400AD: Shonghai, Mali, Jolof, Kongo, Bornu, Oyo, Benin, Kaabu, Lunda, Kong, Banama, and Wassoulou, the Aro-Confederate, the Asante–Union, and the Sokoto Caliphate.

The slave trade continued after the fall of the above empires into the rise of the following kingdoms in Africa: Ashanti, Oyo, Borno, Benin, Igbo Confederate, and many more city-states in Africa. Just like most places in Europe around the same period, people were fighting one another for supremacy and Africa was no exception. Unfortunately, the Europeans arrived in Africa around this period of internal rife and chaos, and it was very convenient for Europeans to meddle in the commotion and they took advantage of the situation. The Europeans had a superior weapon the gun and cannon that killed instantly.

The Arabs had been active in slave trade across the Sahara Desert for over thousands of years before the arrival of the Portuguese merchants in the early 1400 to the coast of West Africa. The most probably part of West Africa they arrived at are now, Senegal, Gambia, Guinea, Gold Coast now Ghana, Mali, Bight of Benin, Slave Coast now Nigeria, West Central Africa, South East Africa, Angola or Zimbabwe.

Towns were raided, people kidnapped, and the captives were sold and forced on a journey they did not plan for. Their hands and legs were in chains, and then they were packed like canned sardines on slave ships. They were debased, starved, but surprisingly survived, but not all survived millions died and their bodies thrown at sea without remorse from the Europeans. The ship owners threw the more courageous and aggressive slaves who resisted their condition, and the sick into the sea to perish. May the souls of those who lost their lives on this horrible journey be blessed and rest in perfect peace. They are remembered anytime any one says what a beautiful world. The world is beautiful because millions of slaves worked to make it possible.

Several books and literature are available on the participation of some Africans kings in trading war captives and prisoners from other African empires and kingdoms to the Europeans. The participation of greedy African kings, warriors, and merchants in slave trading is shameful.

No human suffering could equate the humiliation and degradation African Slaves encountered during the time the Triangular Atlantic Slave Trade lasted. The route of the trade transferred goods from Europe to Africa, human cargo from Africa to America, and wealth and raw materials from America to Europe. It was one of the most callous endeavors in human history.

The heinous past had been forgotten by the major operators the Arabs and the West, but not by the people whose history had been distorted, and progress stalled. Black people and Africans have not forgotten the horrors of slave trade that dispersed their race. The idea or thought that gave birth to the slave trade still exists. Things have changed but not very much for black people.

After more than four centuries of hard labor, degradation and torture that Africans in America endured gracefully and gallantly; at last some humanitarians who realized these people were as human as they fought vigorously on their side for freedom. Africans in America became free after more than four centuries of servitude, abuse, and dehumanization.

There were countless slave revolts anywhere slavery was enforced. The most successful slave revolt was the Haitian

Revolution-1791-1804. Toussaint L'Ouverture led the slave revolt; he died in exile in France in 1804. Hence, Haiti became the first black republic in the Western Hemisphere.

Other slave revolts that took place in the New World are as follows:
America

1712- New York Slave Revolt – Twenty black slaves killed nine whites and seventy black captured and then jailed by the Americans. Twenty-seven of the seventy convicted and twenty-six burnt at stake and one executed on a breaking wheel.

1733-1734- Slave insurrection in St John. These slaves were kidnapped from Asante in Africa and revolted against the owners and took over the Island of St. John in the Virgin Islands. This rebellion was one of the earliest and longest.

1767-1822-Denmark Vesey- There was an allegation that he was planning a rebellion to take over Charleston, South Carolina. The life of slaves meant nothing to the community. Vesey was executed by the community along with many others without evidence of the accusation. The allegation turned out to be false.

1776-1800-Gabriel Prosser an enslaved blacksmith led a rebellion in Richmond, Virginia in the summer of 1800. Militias got wind of the plan and executed Gabriel Prosser along with twenty –seven other slaves.

1811-German Coast uprising on the Mississippi River- The uprising resulted in the killing of two white men by slaves and in revenge ninety- five slaves were executed. The heads of the executed slaves were displayed on pikes in public places. The reason underlying the revolts was over work and difficult working conditions.   There were many blacks in Mississippi then, the ratio was five blacks to one white.

1815-George Boxley- He was white, and had sympathy for the slaves and wanted to form an escape plot for the slaves, but a female slave leaked his intentions to take over Fredericksburg and Richmond, Virginia. He escaped to Ohio and Indiana

1939- Stono Rebellion – These Africans were from Kongo Empire in Africa and revolted for liberty. This happened in South Carolina by the Stono River. They seized ammunition and weapons at Stono River Bridge armory and killed about twenty-five slave-owners. The militia captured about eighty slaves and beheaded them.

1831-NatTurner's Rebellion-NatTurner planned the rebellion in Southampton County, Virginia. In the uprising, the rebels killed about a hundred whites and the rebels captured were executed.

1839-1841-Amistad a Spanish Schooner travelling along the coast of Cuba was captured by a group of Africans who themselves were kidnapped in Africa and sold into slavery. These people could not speak in English but Mende language. (These slaves might have come from the area of present day Sierra Leone and Liberia).   They appeared before a Court in Connecticut, informed the court that they were neither slaves nor property. The thirty-five Africans returned to Africa by the help of slave abolitionist who were working to stop the heinous trade at that time.

1841- Madison Washington- One hundred and thirty-five slaves aboard a ship called Creole en-route between Virginia and New Orleans, was seized by nineteen slaves on board the ship. The leader of the slave revolt was Madison Washington. The revolted slaves after seizing the ship directed it to Nassau in the Bahamas.

1941- New York Conspiracy- Poor whites and blacks set fire to Lower Manhattan and Fort George. The militias caught the conspirators and burnt them at the stake

South America

1600- The following notable slaves in Panama ran away into the forest and nearby mountains to form resistance army against the Spanish slave owner: Felipillo, Bayano, Juan de Dioso, Domingo Congo, Anton Madinga, and Luis Mozambique. They enlisted many recruits from slaves who resisted slavery. They founded communities and organized guerrilla wars against the Spanish powers that enslaved them. The Spanish massacred thousands, but the fighting continued until the Spanish crown conceded to treaties granting the Africans life without violence and incursions.

1655-1695- Zumbi: Zumbi was the leader of slaves who resisted slavery and ran away to form their own settlement called Quilombos in Brazil around 1655. He formed an armed unit to defend Quilombos and the people against the Portuguese power. A Mulato betrayed Zumbi to the Portuguese who captured and beheaded him in 1695. The Portuguese displayed Zumbi's head in public to serve as a deterrent to other slaves who might be nursing the same ambition. Brazilians of African descent still remember Zumbi as a notable leader up to present time.

1760-Tacky's War-Tacky was a community chief in Africa before his enslavement by the British to Jamaica. He organized a rebellion against the enslavement of African people against the British. They took over the plantations and killed the white owners. Tacky continued to fight, but, in the end, the British killed Tacky. Most black Jamaicans believe they came from Tacky's community in Africa. .

1763-Cuffy alias Kofi a slave captured from West Africa led a revolt of more than 2500 slaves against the Dutch slave owners in Guyana. Cuffy's deputy, Akara killed him after a

16

dispute over the governance of Guyana. Kofi presently has a monument erected in his honor in Georgetown, Guyana.

1795-Tula, a slave, led an uprising of fifty slaves in Curacao and freed many slaves. Tula told the plantation owners that they no longer want to work for them. The owners had to run away. Tula demanded three things after the slave owners appealed to him to stop the uprising.
(i) An end to collective punishment
(ii) An end to labor on Sundays
(iii) Freedom to buy things from any seller of their choice
With his demands refused, he started a guerrilla campaign, poisoning wells, and taking foods. Another slave betrayed Tula, and on March 3 1795, Tula was executed.

1816-Bussa Rebellion- Bussa was born a free man in Africa. Bussa was kidnapped in Africa and sold into slavery. He was sent to Barbados where he gathered 400 slaves to rebel against slavery. Bussa and his men fought the slave owners, and he died in battle. Prior to the slave revolt of 1816, slavery had existed in Barbados for 124 years. In 1999, Bussa was honored as the First National Hero of Barbados.

1801-1832- Samuel-Sharpe- Samuel Sharpe was a slave Baptist priest in Jamaica who organized a peaceful general strike across many sugar plantation in western Jamaica for the emancipation of slaves in 1831. Reprisal by the white plantation owners led to rebels burning crops, but the slaves did not attack the owners. Sharpe and many slaves were hanged in 1932. Sharpe was honored with a National Hero in Jamaica in1975. He is on the modern Jamaica dollar bill.

For over four hundred years the greatest insult to black people called slavery persisted and no one raised a voice against this inhumane treatment but the African slaves who revolted and rebelled.

In the eighteen century, during the era of *Enlightenment* in Europe, emerged the abolitionists who criticized slavery for

17

violating the rights of man. The Quakers a religious society of friends founded in England in the seventeenth century agitated for the abolition of slave trade. In 1787, the Quakers and others formed a committee for the abolition of the Trans-Atlantic Triangular slave trade system. Despite the fact that anti-slavery sentiments were common by the late eighteen century, they had no immediate effect on the centers of slavery- the West Indies, South America and southern United States.:

Due to numerous revolts by African slaves in the Spanish and British colonies and the demands of various abolitionists, the British Parliament passed an act on March 25, 1807 abolishing slavery throughout the British Empire, but slavery continued until 1833. The importation of slaves from Africa was banned in British colonies in 1807, the United States in 1808, West indies in 1833, and the French colonies in 1851.

The following are some of the notable slave abolitionists who fought tooth and nail to ensure this callous trade stopped in Europe and the Americas:

Britain
William Wilberforce (1759-1833) was a British parliamentarian, and philanthropist, an Anglican, and a strong supporter of the Quakers for the advocacy of the abolition of theslave trade. He headed the parliamentary campaign against the British slave trade until the eventual passage of the Act of 1708. He moved to North America to continue the anti slavery campaign.

Thomas Clarkson (1760-1846) was a leading campaigner against slave trade in the British Empire. He wrote an essay on the evils of slavery. "Is it lawful to enslave the un-consenting?"

James Ramsey (1733-1789) was a ship surgeon, priest, and abolitionist. He worked on a slave ship and witnessed the living conditions and inhumane treatment slaves experienced on a ship. He decided to work for the abolition of the slave trade. He wrote an essay, "The Treatment and Conversion of African Slaves in the British Sugar Colonies in 1784" This essay had tremendous influence on British abolitionists. He moved to the West Indies and helped slaves gain freedom.

Granville Sharp (1733-1789) was a fervent campaigner for the abolition of slave trade in Britain. He formulated plans to settle blacks in Sierra Leone. He was a great defender of African slaves in Britain. In 1769 Sharp published an essay, "*The Representation of Injustice and Dangerous Tendency Tolerating Slavery*" He studied the English laws on individual liberty thoroughly and proved that the English law does not condone slavery in Britain. He challenged many slave owners in the court of law whereby many African slaves in Britain became free men.

Olaudah Equiano (1745-1797) was an African boy captured in West Africa and sold into slavery in Britain in mid seventeen century. He went through the hands of several owners before he bought his freedom. He became active in debates on the abolition of slave trade in Britain. He wrote the horrors of being a slave in his autobiography.

North America
Anthony Benezet (1713-1784), an educator who convinced people that slave owning was not consistent with the Christian doctrine. He advocated that British ban on slavery should be extended to America. He taught in Germantown school in Philadelphia in 1742. He added night classes for slaves in 1750 and founded the Negro School of Philadelphia in 1770. He established the society for the Relief of Free Negroes Unlawfully Held in Bondage.

William Lloyd Garrison (1805-1879), was the editor of a newspaper called the *Liberator* and he formed the American Anti-Slavery Society. He promoted immediate emancipation of slaves in North America. He joined the Quaker Genius Universal Emancipation newspaper with Benjamin Lundy also an abolitionist. They worked together towards the emancipation of black people.

John Greenleaf Whittier (1807-1892), was a Quaker poet and ardent advocate of the abolition of slaves in North America. He published the anti-slavery pamphlet *"Justice and Expediency* in 1833"

Harriet Beecher Stowe (1811-1896), was an author and ardent slave abolitionist. She wrote the novel, *Uncle Tom's Cabin* in 1852, depicting life of African Americans under slavery. The novel was widely read, and made the political issues of the 1850s on slavery available to millions of people in Britain and America. Her novel energized anti-slavery forces in American North, while provoking anger in the South-the slave states.

Frederick-Douglass (1818-1895), was the first African American nominated as a Vice Presidential candidate in the United States. He ran on the Equal Rights Party. He believed in the equality of all people. Garrison's speech at a meeting of Anti–Slavery Society, Bristol, in 1841 inspired Douglass He contributed immensely to the abolition of slavery.

James Mercer Langston (1829-1897), became the first black lawyer in Ohio in 1854. The first black elected from Virginia to US Congress. He founded the Ohio Anti Slavery Society in 1858.

Arthur Tappan (1786-1865), was a successful entrepreneur, he believed in saving souls than making money. He and his brother Lewis founded the American and Foreign Anti Slavery Society in 1840. He provided a lot of financial support to the operation of underground railway. (*Underground railway was a 19th century slave escape routes to free states and Canada. The abolitionists aided*

20

the escape with financial support, logistics, lodgings, transportation, and food. The free- states were mostly in American Northern states that freed slaves could live without fear or harm. Over 30,000 slaves gained their freedom over the time the underground railway lasted.)

Harriet Tubman (1820-1913), was an African-American, a nurse and, guide in the American Union Army, and an abolitionist. She escaped from slavery when her owner hit her with a heavy object on the head and suffered a traumatic head injury. She aided over seventy slaves to escape through the underground railway.

Abraham Lincoln (1809-1865), was the sixteenth president of the United States, opposed the spread of slavery in the American west. He opposed to the expansion of slavery in the United States He gave the right to vote to former slaves through three significant amendments to the constitution of the United States. These are, the 13th, 14th and 15th amendments. President Lincoln issued the Emancipation Proclamation of 1863 and promoting the passage of the 13th amendments to the United States constitution. These events of Lincoln abolished slave trade in America.

France

Jacques Pierre Briscot and Abbe Gregoire were members of the Society of the Friends of the Blacks and they campaigned fervently in France and her colonies for abolition of slave trade. France, in the First Republic, 1794 abolished slave trade and re-established it in 1799 under Napoleon. In the Second Republic, France abolished slave trade around 1848-1852.

No capital, no land, and no compensation was provided to the freed slaves to start life all over again in a foreign land. Some opted to go back home to Africa because there was no place like home. Those people settled in Liberia, Sierra

Leone and, southern part of Nigeria. Some also settled in Cameroon, Ghana, and Senegal.

Some stayed back because where was home after four centuries, they participated and contributed to make these places great nations so they stayed back and call it home. They stayed back because they knew they were strong, intelligent, resilient, adaptable, versatile and survivors. They scattered over North and South America notably United States of America, Brazil, Columbia, the Caribbean Islands, Jamaica and many pockets of South America where they have mixed with the original people and Europeans that it is difficult to set them apart as former African.

They labored on cotton, coffee, sugar and other plantations. They labored in the coal- mines, gold mines and other mines in the industrial revolutions. They built roads, harbors, railroads, houses, factories in short they did all work that required labor. Due to over usage their life expectancy became lower.

The African people identity was lost overtime. They called the Negros, which meant black, an Italian word. They detested this name because it was derogatory. It was demeaning, disgraceful so they fought to change it. They accepted to be called, 'black'. Black became their strength, pride, and power. Due to unguarded rape of African women by white men, mixed children were born and the culprits shamelessly denied these innocent children their birthrights. Suddenly, blacks became of many shades; light, brown, bronze and fair.

In most places in Africa, names given to children came from the social-status of a family or the circumstances of birth. Sometimes, names given to babies mostly come from the good feelings and joys a child brings. In other places in Africa, names were chosen from ancestral names or the day of their birth, especially in Ghana.

As time went by the goodness in black people was apparent, but they refused to reckon with it due to inherent greed. Blacks used their imagination to initiate many products to make life convenient but unfortunately, you were not given the deserve recognition.

The black population increased despite the initial set back due to deaths and purposeful elimination. Millions of Africans died during the triangular slave trade that is from Africa and finally the Americas, and its Islands popularly known as the Caribbean Islands.

Blacks have been brain washed not to love Africa, the beautiful continent of their ancestors. They blame Africa for their woes because, she allowed her children to be enslaved, and her resources used to develop other continents. People in other continents live a better life than Africa.

The Europeans called Africa the Dark Continent while exploiting and degrading the continent. Europe cannily took Africa resources to develop Europe leaving Africa undeveloped. The resources taken from Africa by Europeans manufactured into goods and sold to Africans at exorbitant prices. The black person spent the money from hard work to buy products from Europe that kept people in Europe employed and live better lives

Africans were strong then, they learned the cultures of their captors beside her own. Africans lost their empires, their kingdoms and had to adapt to new cultures and way of life. It is sad, that Africans are now the poorest people on earth who need aids and assistance, inspite of the fact that is richest of all continents in resources.

This is an irony. Why should it be? What is wrong with my race? It has become a fashion for artist to use Africa to boost their image by staging concerts to raise money to help Africa. Where does all this money go? Where do these "fundraising proceeds" go because no change has happened in Africa? Most Africans in this twenty-first century still do not have electricity, portable drinking water, and roads. These are basic necessities for a modern life.

The black population is highest in Africa, but black population is systematically decreasing through the Acquired Immune Deficiency Syndrome and unnecessary wars of greed and ineptitude. HIV and AIDS have inflicted a very high percentage of black Africans and some black people in Diaspora. HIV and AIDS are the worst and deadliest affliction in human history. These lethal diseases are transmitted, by blood and bodily fluids. What is going on?
This situation is alarming. The disease has been spreading like hay-fire in South Africa since 1995. South Africa black people endured a lot during apartheid, should this same people carry the scourge of these deadly diseases? South Africa got its first Black President in 1990 and HIV and AIDS among the black people was the first problem they faced. On average this disease has been killing black South Africans than a raging war.

This is worse than genocide and yet the world is not talking enough. The black world population is not doing enough either. Black leaders in the world are not doing enough to combat these diseases. If this trend continues, the population of black people would significantly reduce. AIDS is prevalent in South Africa, what happened? According to findings and statistics by the United Nations, sixty percent of Black South African is HIV positive.

What is the origin of the HIV? It is scary. It is heinous. This disease killing thousands in Africa makes one wonders whether there is a conspiracy to make the black race become endangered species. The black race is the least in population in relation to all peoples of the world and if sixty percent of blacks in South Africa carry HIV, there should be concerned that black people are becoming endangered human specie

A very large number of Africans died in slavery, and now HIV and AIDS are killing black Africans by the millions and yet not enough efforts are in place to address the problem. No insinuation but the human community should rise and be active in making medication for HIV and AIDS accessible. Whoever, or whatever, is behind this should note that this is a disgrace to the human race. Human beings fight for animal conservation why not the conservation for human beings whose strength and sufferings changed the world. This disease is a result of the new civilization. Human beings are probing too deep into nature. HIV/AIDS might have been accidentally been created and no one is taking responsibility due to the deadly outcome.

Human beings are over exploiting one another. Europe depends on African resources even in the twenty first century. European countries depend on African resources to run their factories but have not been concerned about the development of the people who work hard to produce the resources.

Slavery and colonization changed the history of black. Black people have not changed their economic dependency on former colonists. Whatever happened in the past cannot be altered but the future can be determined and changed. Sitting on the fence watching events go around without active participation would not help. All people are owners of this one world and everyone should participate in its progress. Black people should stop the dependency syndrome and get actively involved in the goings in the world.

This is a period of great fear and every human community is fighting for the preservation of its race. It has happened in the past and could reoccur in the future. Some group of human race no longer exist, even if they do their number is not significant.

Chapter Two

The Effects of foreign encounter and teachings on Black culture and tradition

The continent of Africa was like paradise on earth. The climate, soil, mountains, hills, rivers, streams, valleys, and forests; in short the vegetation was just perfect. Africa was the envy of the world between 13th to 14th centuries. There were gold, iron, and copper mines in most part of the continent. There were no major volcanic eruptions on the continent and no turbulent weather situations on the continent of Africa in the 14th centuries. With the exception of occasional earth tremors, Africa was paradise on earth.

People of different skin pigmentations inhabit the continent of Africa. The Berbers in the North are light skinned and the dark skin people lived in the lower Nile Valley to the East, Central, West, and Southern part of Africa
The richness of African gold spread to Europe around the 14th century. Mansa Kankan Musa a ruler of the Mali Empire went on pilgrimage to Mecca with a large entourage and they carried gold dust and nuggets. He loaded the gold dust and nuggets on large caravans, and was extravagant with the gold, bought many luxury things on his way back to his empire. One memorable thing he did for his empire was a university he built in Timbuktu in 1337. Word of his pilgrimage spread in Europe, that he spent so much gold that the value of gold fell on the Egyptian market.

Famine had struck Europe early in the 14th century causing millions of death over an extended period of years. The famine was devastating such that people resulted to cannibalism, infanticide, old- people voluntarily refusing food hoping the younger generation surviving.
After the Great Famine, came the Black Death, and it lasted around 1338-1375. The Black Death was the deadliest pandemic in human history, it spread quickly over a very large population, and the result was death. It killed millions

of Europeans and in the same period, the French and British were embroiled in warfare that lasted hundred years.

The long hundred years of wars from 1337-1453 among English and French dynasties added more hardship to the people. The hundred years of warfare was a time of military evolution, weapons, tactics, army structure and the definition of war changed; gunpowder and guns technology improved at that period. Europe developed warfare to a high level from fighting with bows and arrows and cavalry to using guns and, standing armies. Due to internal conflicts, the famine, plague, and many years of warfare, the fortunes of most countries in Europe declined. The need to explore other areas with riches was imperative and Africa was that place

The Mali, Ghana, and Songhai empires in Africa flourished around the 13th and 14th centuries from trading with Egypt and the Arabs from the Arabian Peninsula. The empires had rules and regulation on how people treat one another, lands divided amongst the people, and fixed exchange for common products. By 1352, Mali Empire had a thriving civilization comparable with the Muslim and Christian worlds of that time. The quotation below from an Arab Architect amplifies the goodness in black people in Mali Empire, *"The black people possess some admirable qualities, they are seldom unjust, and have a greater abhorrence of injustice than other people .There is complete security in their country neither traveler nor inhabitant in it has nothing to fear from robbers or men of violence"*.

Justice was the rule in African Empires in the 13th and 14th centuries. The rulers in Europe and elsewhere ruled iron handedly and cruelty and ruthlessness towards the people were rampant. The peasants and serfs in Europe mistreated by their rulers and owners, therefore, it was no surprise that the European explorers, merchants, and missionaries that came to Africa treated African people brutally. Brutality was the way of life for the ordinary person in Europe at the time.

The kings and aristocratic society did not have any value for the peasants, the poor, and serfs.

The proximity of Africa to the Iberian Peninsula made it possible for the Europeans to venture into Africa and amid rumors of the richness of the Mali Empire. A narrow piece of land connected African to the Iberian Peninsula in Europe before the construction of the Straits of Gibraltar. It was easy then for people to move from North Africa to Europe and Europe to Africa.

Europe did not know about the rest of Africa until the expedition of Portuguese explorers organized by Prince Henry the Navigator of Portugal in early 14th century. The explorers stumbled upon black Africa by accident and since then Africa had never been the same.

The gun technology made it possible for the explorers to capture the people at the coastline of Africa and established settlement along the West Africa Coast in 1445. Europe, burdened with wars, poverty, fighting among the royal houses, diseases, and famine; it was therefore great opportunity to find a land so rich and the people peaceful.

The explorers saw the possibilities of trading and making profits and wanted to know the source of the African gold. The gold wealth of Africa reported in several books and records indicated that 50% of the world's gold was coming from Mali Empire in the 14th century.

The Portuguese first captured Cape Verde in 1444. Between 1444 to1446 as many as forty vessels sailed from Portugal to Africa and bringing back gold and slaves from Africa to Europe. Gold and slaves began arriving in Portugal and the influx of gold permitted the minting of Portugal first gold coins in 1452.

The report from the Portuguese who became rich after their exploration to Africa spread over Europe like wild fire and every nation in Europe rushed to Africa. They entered into treaties with people who cannot read nor write and in the process took over most lands in Africa. The Europeans who came to Africa replaced most African leaders with some Africans of lesser status who appreciated their intervention and in so doing disrupted the ruling houses in Africa. This caused dissatisfaction among most African communities and wars broke out making it easier for the Europeans to get more slaves to ship to the Americas while the Africa economy collapsed.

The black race was very hospital and accommodating and people from Europe took advantage of this virtue and came to Africa to scramble for resources, and free labor. They destabilized the residence economy.

The Portuguese first built settlements on the coastlines of Africa and made Portugal prosperous from gold and copper taken from Africa and sold Africans as slaves. The British fought the Portuguese and took most of their holdings in Africa. The French being an archrival of the British came to Africa and took over most part of northern, part of West Africa and South West Africa and part of Central and East Africa. The incursion made European countries with African territories prosperous and became the envy of other countries in Europe.

There were resistances across Africa. The different African people had its own military system but did not have gun power. Africa was not prepared and the continent became colonized by Europeans.

Europe began to see prosperity while empires in Africa started losing powers. The French, the English, the Danes, the Dutch, and the Germans came to Africa to partake in the colonization of Africa to get resources for their factories. The Europeans took over the continent as if there were no inhabitants before their arrival. The nations in Europe were fighting among themselves over Africa and American continents. The European countries partitioned Africa and Americas continents among themselves.

The Spanish, Dutch, French, and British rushed to Africa and imposed their rule upon the people through the power of the guns and cannons. Initially, the relationship between Europeans and Africans was trade and the spread of Christianity, but the underlying factor was to take the African resources and hard-working people to develop Europe. This incursion of Europeans into Africa destroyed and derailed the growth of empires and destabilized the booming economy of Africa.

After the fall of the Mali and Songhai empires, some scrupulous and greedy rulers took over the reign of power in most part of Africa and they reigned with terror. These later empires in Africa connived and collaborated with the Europeans and engaged seriously in the slave trade. The Dahomey, Asante, Bambara, and Oyo empires established themselves as warfare empires that exchanged war captives and kidnapped people for guns and rums. The most notorious was Dahomey, the rulers engaged in human sacrifices to their gods and it was easy to go on war expedition capturing people and selling them to the Europeans on the coast.

The Portuguese could not venture into interior of Africa because of great resistance from the people and the new crop of African rulers captured people from interior of Africa and sold them to the Portuguese on sea coast of Africa. Oyo Kingdom warriors captured the notorious Dahomey king and the people supported Oyo because of the cruelty of the king to his people. In view of the large sums of money the European were paying to the kings to buy slaves; rampant raiding of people grew all over Africa to capture people and sell them into slavery.

While African kings and merchants in the 15th century were busy selling their people to Europe, Europe on the other had started taking care of its people, utilizing the resources and the slaves from Africa to develop Europe. Africans slaves and resources gave Europe a huge leap in development and they never looked back.

The encounter with Africa changed the way of life of the Europeans. They entered a new age of development. Europeans once a warring people began to mint coins and engaged in serious economic ventures. They reduced warfare amongst themselves and each European nation made large expedition to Africa.

The expeditions and explorations of Africa started by the Portuguese were later taken over by the Spanish, Dutch, French, and English. The Italians and Germans were having internal struggles so they joined the race to take possession of Africa late.

Due to possession of firearms the European explorers subdued the Africans and colonized the enter continent with the exception of Liberia and Ethiopia. They imposed a new way of life on the people with conditions. The French rule Africa directly while the British ruled indirectly. The French accepted the Africans as French provided they gave up their culture; the British did not accept equality even if an African adopted the British way of life; the French allowed racial marriage but the British did not. The Portuguese allowed racial marriage but thought they were superior.

The beginning of the 16th century saw a great revolution in every aspect of European life. The discovery of the Americas brought more prosperity to Europe and the economy was growing. New commerce, international finance, ocean-going trading fleets, and entrepreneurial bourgeoisie grew at astronomical rate. The flow of gold and silver from the Americas brought more prosperity to Europe. These developments led to the building of capitalist economy and widely use of money. The development of cannon had a great influence to the rise of centralized nation states in

Europe leading to the decline of the feudal system. European Nations fought one another, took land and possessions, and annexed them.

The discovery of America meant more slaves needed to work on the land. Britain merchants transported over 2.5million African people to the British sugar plantations in the Caribbean between 1690 and 1807. The harsh environmental conditions killed many slaves, and the slave merchants had to replace them quickly because the sugar economy depended on labor. That meant more people had to be forcefully taken from the Africa continent to the sugar plantations that fed European industries. The African people, later called slaves were forced under the threat of guns to the Americas by the Europeans to replace the indigenous Americans who died of diseases of the Europeans, massacre, over worked, and hard labor. The African was stronger, healthier, and not easily vulnerable to diseases.

The African was working on farms in the tropical land and therefore could work in the Caribbean and Virginia plantations in the Americas. Without any knowledge of where they were heading the Africans were lured, forced, drugged, and carried on ships like goods to the new world.

The beginning of the Triangular Trade was the worst injustice that ever happened to any human being. Africans were deceived, degraded, tormented, abused, and used. No human race was perfect, there were people who felt they were been oppressed by the African kings and queens so these people betrayed their people and captured and kidnapped fellow Africans and sold them to the Europeans who came to Africa under the disguise of spreading Christianity.

The spread of Christianity in Africa in the 16th century did more harm than good. The Christians particularly the Protestants persecuted in Europe found Africa peaceful and they pinched their tents. The Christians destroyed

32

everything African and imposed their culture and way of life. They taught the Africans who accepted their religion only to read the bible. The missionary looked the other when the slave trade was going on by the merchants they came with. The Europeans changed the existing institution and installed traitors of African culture as leaders.

Before the incursion of the Europeans into the interior of Africa, black Africans were cultivating the rich lands around them to produce food, rear animals, making implements and ornaments, carvings from woods and weaving cloths from cotton. There was a market economy in Africa. People were selling and buying among one another. There was specialization of labor. Families and clans had vocations they specialized in and these occupations passed from one generation to the next generation, a practice common at that period.

In most African societies, clans and families were synonymous with their vocation. Vocation was very important in African societies and specialization by family or clan was an important aspect of the African life. Unfortunately, the introduction of westerners into African societies destroyed this culture. The African man or woman believed in hard work and the only way one could live a better existence was through hard work.

The system of market economy practiced in Africa collapsed with the incursion of Europeans into Africa. Africans are capitalist and had practiced the system for centuries. They believed in people working to cater for the family. Colonization of Africa by the Europeans had devastating impact on the existing civilization.

The Europeans introduced crops they found in the Americas that cannot do well on temperate soil in Europe to Africa. The people of Africa began growing these crops at the detriment of their own food crops. The new crops: cocoa, coffee, and sugarcane shipped to Europe and processed into the new taste of sugar and chocolate Europeans suddenly developed due to affluence, and fed factories that had sprung up in Europe from the new wealth derived from slave trading and plunging of Americas and Africa resources. Cocoa was cultivated all over Africa and part of South America, not forgetting the extensive sugar plantations in the Caribbean.

African people worked under cruel and harsh conditions to cultivate the cash crops for Europeans merchants. The European traders shipped Ivories, coffee, timbers, iron ore, copper, gold, and shrimps from Africa to Europe. The colonialists named African countries based on the abundant produce or resources in a colony, for instance Ivory Coast-ivories, Nigeria –Slave Coast, Cameron-shrimps, Gold Coast- gold.

The Europeans waged wars among themselves to have bigger controls of lands in Africa. Despite the fact that the Portuguese were the first to have colonies in Africa, British and French had more colonies by fighting the Dutch and Portuguese and taken away their colonies. This act of taking over each other's possession through gun power explained how greedy and gullible the Europeans were. They used divide and rule methods to govern African territories, whereby people with different way of life were put together under a leader who was from another group of people. The method the Europeans employed to govern the colonies was not by accident, it was intentional to breed discord among the peoples.

The French employed paternalistic method whereas the British adopted autocratic method. Belgium ruled the Congo Basin very ruthlessly. They did not consider the people of Congo to be humans based on the way they treated them. The treatment of the people by King Leopold II was too harsh and brutal. There was massive transfer of wealth from Congo to Belgium during Belgium occupation.

The colonists intentionally created territories by alternating; that is the French would take a certain part then the Britain or French or Dutch or German or Portuguese and the various European language were imposed on the people to create more chaos and misunderstanding among the people.. This method deepened the language barriers, distorted and destroyed relationship. Neighboring countries needed interpreters if they needed to discuss concerns.

The English settled in east Africa and parts of West Africa, Danes, Dutch and later English settled in South Africa. The French, the English, had adjacent territories in order to increase confusion among the Africans who do not speak same languages and had different cultures.

The Europeans took over the continent as if there were no inhabitants before their arrival. The nations in Europe were fighting among themselves over Africa and American continents because of African resources. They partition the continents among themselves. They set an agenda to partition Africa through the Berlin Conference (1884-1885) organized by Bismarck of Germany to regulate European colonization and trade in Africa. Everything the European did at that was for their own benefits; they saw resources they needed and lacked and they grabbed them without conscience.

The main causes for the scramble for Africa are as follows:
(i) Europe was in a long depression.
(ii) Europe had deficit balance of trade
(iii) Europeans countries that had African territories had increased economic power and wealth.
(iv) Europe also found market for their surplus manufactured goods.

Britain started investing in Africa and was profitable due to cheap labor and abundant raw materials at cheap prices. Europe needed raw material like copper, cotton, rubber, tea, and tin for the industrial revolution that had just started in the middle of 18th century. In 1886, the Europeans rushed to South Africa for gold and diamonds that were in abundance. They dealt ruthlessly with the indigenous populations particularly the Khoisan people. The Khoisan people resisted the encroachment on their lands and resources and fought gallantly and vigorously but eventually succumbed to the power of the gun. The European almost extinguished the Khoisan population.

Slavery and eventual colonization of Africa had affected the life and history of Africans. Africa lost millions of people to Europe and America and millions killed in the process. The resources of Africa were freely taken during colonization and the process is ongoing nothing has changed over six hundred years ago. The Africa continent, the people, and resources are still under the control of the invisible hands of Europeans.

The European brought their religion that was not well accepted and practiced in Europe to Africa and condemned African religion. Africans practiced religious belief based on the Supreme Being through many smaller gods. By the time Christianity was being imposed on Africans, part of Europe was practicing paganism and witchcrafts. Not everyone in Europe was a Christian, there were pagans, atheist, witches, and wizards but similar beliefs were condemned in Africa.

Islam had already spread in most part of Northern, Central and Northern part of West Africa before the arrival of Europeans. Introduction of Islam into some parts of Africa by Arabs was readily accepted because it reinforced the existing belief in the Supreme Being. Africans believed that a Supreme Being created everything on Earth and in the Sky above long before foreigners introduced Islam and Christianity to the continent.

The Europeans incursion into Africa was the way a bandit or a thief comes into a house at night well prepared and caters away belongings while the owner of the house looked on. Europeans began to name places as if the people of Africa did not have names for their territories. This is why most towns in Africa have two names the indigenous names and the names used by the Europeans. People speaking the same languages, same culture, and in some cases related were divided into different territories by the Europeans. The over lapping of people and their cultures are still present in Africa.

The decision taken to divide African into territories without respect to their culture and custom is the underlying cause of most conflicts in Africa today. Most conflicts in Africa in recent times were the result of these ethnic overlap and the artificial border created by the colonial masters. Nations split into two countries by the colonialists. For instance, there are Yoruba people in Nigeria and Benin Republic, likewise Hutus in Uganda and Rwanda. There would never be peace unless the leaders in Africa unite so that there would be free movement of people across the continent the way it is in the United States of America. Any American can become a resident in any state in America.

There is currently restricted movement of people in Africa by various governments and this creates internal stress and tension. There is restricted freedom of movement within a confined space called country in Africa. People moved freely in Africa before the scramble for Africa and conflicts among various people was minimal.

African politicians should look into coming together to form a union. A political union of Africa does not stop current leaders from being in charge it would only make them better leaders by being responsible to the people they lead. This would allow Africa to bargain favorably for their commodities in the world market.

The United States of America consist of fifty states with diverse people from different background, race and culture and have existed for over three hundred years as a union and still waxing stronger as a unified entity. The United States of America is a perfect example of how diversity empowers a nation and people. African countries could learn from the United States of America.

Africans have not been able to resolve the issue imposed on them more than five hundred years ago. The strategies employed for the colonization of Africa is still effective. The continent has not been able to reverse any of the apparatus used to hold down the progress of Africa. The people of Africa still speak the foreign languages imposed on them as their official language in this 21st century. Europeans hold on Africa is as current as it was five hundred years ago. Africa is the supplier of raw materials to the factories of Europe and Europeans still determine how much they pay. The products from European industries exported to Africa are sold at exorbitant prices, while, the imports from Africa are bought cheaper.

The method the Europeans employed to govern the colonies was not by accident, it was intentional to breed discord among the peoples. The French employed paternalistic method whereas the British adopted autocratic method. Belgium ruled the Congo Basin very ruthlessly. They did not consider the people of Congo to be humans based on the way they treated them. The treatment of the people by King Leopold II was too harsh and brutal. There was massive transfer of wealth from Congo to Belgium during the colonial period. .

Europeans divided territories in Africa among themselves in such a manner that neighboring countries were under different authorities and spoke different European languages. That is, the French would take a certain part, then the Britain or French or Dutch or German or Portuguese and the European languages spoken imposed subsequently on the people in the territories. This method really deepened the language barriers among African countries. Neighboring countries needed interpreters if they needed to discuss concerns. One country spoke French or Portuguese while the next one would be speaking English. Africa looks like a jigsaw puzzle of European languages.

The whole of Europe was under the Holy Roman Catholic Church before the Protestants broke away from the Catholic Church. After the collapse of the Holy Roman Empire, emerged the British Empire, German empire and the United States of America who spread their influence internationally.

Every nation in Europe was trying to control one another through fighting and looting at that time, particularly, British, Germany, Italy, France, and the Netherlands. Therefore, it should not be surprising that force and war was the only means Europe could sustain it superiority over the lands they took over in Africa and the Americas. Britain at its height of imperialism controlled a quarter of the world through colonization.

The Britons innovated and invented many machines during the height of their imperialism, and had more understanding of mathematics, physics, chemistry, biology, electricity, and metallurgy. This new knowledge and developments led to industrialization era in Europe and later spread to the United States of America. The industrial revolution put more hardship on African people because of more demand for labor and raw materials. The

The Triangular Slave Trade was the worst injustice that ever happened to any human being. African people were deceived, degraded, tormented, abused, and forced to work. Some African kings collaborated with the Europeans by involving in slave trade; these kings betrayed their people by authorizing capture of innocent people, and kidnapping fellow Africans and sold them to the Europeans who came to Africa under the disguise of spreading Christianity and trade.

The spread of Christianity in Africa in the 16th century did more harm than good. The Christians particularly the Protestants persecuted in Europe found peace in Africa and pinched their tents. The Christians destroyed everything African and imposed their culture and way of life. They taught the Africans who accepted their religion only to read the bible. The missionary looked the other when the slave trade was going on by the merchants they came with. The Europeans changed the existing institution and installed traitors of African culture as leaders.

Other African kings like King Alfonso of the Kingdom of Kongo protested over the enslaving of his people to the Pope. He voiced out that the Europeans allowed into his kingdom were to spread Christianity and not to enslave his people. There were constant warfare between Africans and Europeans. The Europeans lived mostly on the coastal towns; they could not move inwards to settle because of resistance from the people. This distrust of Europeans by Africans persists as of today.

After the discovery of the Americas, Europe went through transformation in the 16th century that ushered in the modern science and philosophy, inventions, music, literature, arts, and, painting. In the same century of great achievements, European nations were tearing each other apart through series of wars for dominance on one another. These wars lasted over thirty years, 1618-1648.

Despite the improvement in the economy and way of life in Europe, the nations of Europe fought over control of colonies in Africa and the Americas. This period was the most bloody in European history because competition to take large colonies was fierce. Britain who had large colonies by defeating the Portuguese, Dutch, Italian, and Spanish was more prosperous.

The black labor built and sustained the new capitalist economy. The contribution of black race to the capitalist economy has been forgotten. Black peoples' contribution to capitalism is not included in modern economics. Can you quantify the labor of millions of blacks who worked without payment on plantation farms and the mines? The black man and the peasants built all the streets and iconic buildings in Europe and North America through free labor.

Suddenly prosperity came to Europe and America once again and the problems of famine, diseases, and poverty because of the past. The new wealth carted from Africa was so huge that serfs and peasants in Europe became bourgeoisies and aristocrats. Europe became lively again after the discovery of the riches and people of Africa.

Necessity is the mother of invention. The African environment was never harsh and life depended mostly on the basics of life; food, shelter, water and procreation. Europeans realized that the technological development in Africa was at the rudimental stage, and they were at a more advanced stage and they took advantage of the gentle people they encountered.

The technological achievement in the 18th centuries in Europe changed the people of Europe. The short African people (pigmies) in the Congo Basin were at a point in time displayed in cages in London and New York for spectators to see. Short people called little people are in every race not only in the black race.

There is diversity in humans just like other mammals. Creatures survive in their comfortable environments that would nurture and sustain them. Every creature blends with its environments and uses the resources in that environment for survival and continuity.

Black people have abundance of melanin to protect them from the scorch and ultra violet trays of the sun. The complexion and hair texture of a black person aid survival in sunny environment. The texture of the black person's hair is able to hold moisture to cool the brain in the hot sun. A silky hair creates heat in cold climate to protect the brain from intense cold. The vegetation and food in your environment sustain and keep you alive. Your environment gives you comfort and it has all that will make you live and procreate. The environment is rich with the food and resources the people need.

Black Africans encounter with Europeans changed their course of life. They had to learn new languages and ways of life imposed on them. They were brainwashed to the extent that they do not have faith in themselves any more. They do not appreciate their skin color. Products invented in order for them to bleach the color of their skin. There have been several propaganda designed to make them feel inferior due to the color of their skin and unfortunately, they fell for it. They bleached their skin to change their color and they become uncomfortable in their sunny environment. Black people have been having skin cancer because they do not have enough melanin the natural protection against the sunlight anymore.

Europe was able to advance technologically despite many centuries of wars amongst themselves because the changes were a continuation of the same process. Nobody imposed different cultures on them and if there was any; it was a continuation of the same principle and therefore did not change the existing cultures. If one studies the trend of development of Europe from being a warring and poor nations in the 13th -17th centuries to the richest economy of the world today; then one would understand that when one nation move into a new era the rest copy or wrestle power from one another.

Europeans found solution to their economic problem in the 14th century through the discovery of rich Africa that had abundant gold, copper, and other valuable resources. European then built war ships equipped with cannons to invade weaker African nations. They moved great wealth and people from Africa and other countries they colonized to develop Europe. The discovery of America also brought enormous wealth to Europe.

If Africans had been ruling themselves there would have been continuous development of its past. You can improve on an environment and culture when there is continuity. Africans have not been able to take significant strides in development due to the discontinuation of the original process and imposition of other cultures and ways of life. The traditional culture and development in Africa halted through European invasion and had not improved upon ever since. The cottage industries Africa had in the 14th -16th centuries are still running without improvements. How can a people move forward without improving upon the past? Human beings tend to improve on their past in order to advance forward.

The educational system of read, write, and, perform arithmetic imposed by the Europeans was to facilitate their mission. They were amazed at the level of African intelligence and therefore, limited their exposure to the kind of education that would arouse their curiosity to probe further. The intention of the minimal exposure to education was to create consumers of their products while they on the hand, engaged their people in production to keep them employed and improved their way of life. Yes, they succeeded. Africans have become perpetual consumer of European goods and neglecting to improve what their ancestors started to make life better for the majority of the people.

It is an irony that most descendants of Africa in Diaspora have the notion that Africans on the continent gave them away, what they did not know was that Africans on the continent also worked on plantations and in mines for the Europeans. Black people story is the same everywhere. Just like bees in a colony, black people worked while the European enjoyed the outcome

The Africans left on the continent were not free either they lived under the oppressive rule of the Europeans. They worked on farms to cultivate cash crops to feed the new factories and industries, and mined gold, copper, tin, iron ore, and diamonds for Europeans.

The age of enlightenment began in Europe in 17th century. It was a movement based on values, whereby the people began to reason and question the powers of the kings and nobles. Europeans began to use reasoning and philosophical thinking to assess situations rather than warfare. This new movement, the renaissance, ushered in the industrial revolution, and significant development to Europe and its peoples.

It was during this period that America declared their independence from Britain. The American Declaration of Independence and Bill of Rights, the French Declaration of Rights of Man and of the Citizen came out in this era. Intellectual and philosophical development, freedom for common people, self- governance, natural risks, natural law, liberty, individual rights, and common sense were outcome of the enlightenment era. This era was a departure from theocracy, aristocracy, and the divine rights of kings, which hitherto was the basis of European existence.

The following principles and ideologies evolved in the 18th century; republicanism, liberalism, naturalism, scientific methods and modernity. This was a period of freedom for people in Europe peasants and serfs. They could gather and discuss concerns and found solutions through reasoning.

The Quakers and various Abolitionists evolved in this period. They reasoned that slaves were humans too and should be free. The work of the Abolitionists, coupled with determination, and steadfastness of the slaves themselves, manifested into setting slaves freed in Europe and it reached the Americas eventually.

The black man was never at ease being a slave; he struggled on the day of his captivity and on the ship until the day he got his freedom. The black person had been in constant search of who he is or was. If one looks at history of Europeans and Africans before the fifteen century the difference in civilization was not there, it was at par.

In the modern world, trading between Africa and other countries is through imports and exports. Africa imports items that do not have effects on improving the life of the citizens. Africans imports foods they can conveniently produce on African soil. Africa imports used clothes, used cars, dried fish, expired medications, and things that the west considers dangerous for its citizens. Africans have become perpetual consumers of Europe surplus and a dumping ground for the left over from the West and East.

Why did the African nationalist fought for independence from Europeans? Is it to continue in the same servitude to the colonists? Africans have become so dependent on the west to such an extent that they cannot feed themselves but wait for aids and grants from their former masters. The situation is getting dire unless sons and daughters of the black race start thinking of the preservation and revival of the dignity of the race.

Africa has large vast land and water flowing across and yet the people cannot produce enough food to feed themselves. This time it might not be wars or enslavement that would reduce black population but diseases that the cost of cure would be out of reach for the black person. Currently, the devastating disease HIV/AIDS is killing sons and daughters of black people more than anyone else.

The generations of Europeans are continuously enjoying the fruits of the labor of their ancestors from the 14th century from the discovery of Africa and Americas. The policies and strategies used then are still in place and will continue to operate. Africans have to realize that they are not a continuation of the European continent. Africans still look up to Europeans to solve their problems. The funds that African leaders should invest on food production are spent on importation of weapons to destroy one another. When will the leaders of Africa put their people first?

Did the African nationalist fight for independence so that Africa would be dependent on foreign countries? The following black nationalist; would be turning in their graves by the way African leaders have reversed the role of Africans to be beggars from their formal colonial masters. Marcus Garvey, Dr. Kwame Nkrumah, Jomo Kenyatta, W.E.B. Du Bois, Joseph E C. Hayford, Booker T. Washington, Mojola Agbebe, Edward W. Blyden, Henry Thuku, Nnamdi Azikiwe, Sekou Toure, Patrice Lumumba, Awolowo, Ahmadou Bello and many more.

Africa is economically, the poorest of all continents. It is time for Africans to look inward and find solutions to the predicament of its teeming populations. Our ancestors long before us were progressive people, and progress can still come the way of Africa if Africans want to advance forward economically.

This is the 21st century and Africans still live the lives of the fifteen century. Current Africans leaders are not on the path to move Africa forward. The rulers of Africa are a continuation of the colonial masters because ever since independence African countries have become poorer and poorer.

Nelson Mandela and many freedom fighters were jailed in South Africa for making demands for equality and respect for African people in South Africa. Mandela spent twenty-seven years in jail and continued to fight for the freedom of South Africa's people from oppression under the apartheid system. The struggle for freedom continued unabated until his release in the 1990s. He became the first black president of South Africa in 1990

The Europeans are humans like us and they solve their problems themselves. The solutions might not be palatable for the rest of the world but they do solve their problems. Despite all the different ideologies in Europe and America, they act together when it comes to the protection and defense of their citizens. African leaders on the other hand put self-interest first over the citizens. People of Africa can only move forward if the African elites and governments redefine their current strategy and focus on the development of the people.

Patriotism is not strong among Africans because few elites and their cohorts manipulate power and, resources. Nothing motivates the masses to want to sacrifice their lives for their various countries. On the contrary, the citizens in the west are ready to lay their lives for their country due to the great sacrifices their forerunners made to leave them the comforts that has become the envy of people from other human race.

Patriotic people will lay down their lives or do anything for their community or country. Patriotic tendency arises when people realizes that the rulers would protect them no matter the circumstances. African leaders are yet to prove themselves as leaders and protector of the people. All the various wars going on in Africa have been on struggle for political powers nothing more or less. The innocent poor sons and daughters of Africa are on the battlefields fighting wars that do not make any impact on improvement of their livelihood.

Since the first coup-de tat in Ghana in 1966, over seventy of such senseless coups have occurred on African continent between 1963 and 1997. Millions of people lost their lives or limbs and yet the countries they died or disfigured for is poverty stricken as ever. The ironies of these wars are that the same Europeans who enslaved Africans five centuries ago are the same people manufacturing weapons that Africans leaders and governments buy to kill Africans. The elites of Africa and their collaborators keep on sucking Africa dry and portray Africa to the outside world as people in need of help for survival.

African politicians and elites should provide the basic amenities - water and lights that the rest of the world take for granted and the populace will not notice their greed. Politicians are greedy everywhere but service to the citizens overshadow any inadequacies on the government. The populace will be busy worrying about their families and how to provide a more comfortable and convenient life for them rather than look the way of the politicians.

Europeans are still exploring the world as they did centuries ago. The Europeans are a group of people who are never satisfied. They are continuously searching for answers to many issues and problems. The west, realizing that the rest of the world is not as inquisitive as they are; have taken it upon themselves to be custodian of this earth.

Despite independence for most of the colonies, the presence of Europe is still as apparent as they were centuries ago in Africa. They still have possession of most animal reservation they established and are still in control. The west does anything it wants without question from anyone and no one tells them what to do.

Europeans have invented many good things that create conveniences like, railways, airplanes, ships and even spaceships, medication, and many more but at what cost to humanity. The life expectancy of many people had improved from advanced medicine, but at what cost to other people. There is a scary practice going on lately called human spare parts. Yes, human spare parts are available to replace parts of the body for some people. The reason provided for this inhuman advancement in surgery is that the parts are from people at the point of dying. Since the world is advanced technologically, they should be able to save the lives of dying people whose body parts are sold in order to save others. Egocentricity, vanity, wealth, personalities, and greed rule the world today.

Africa educates the people with the scarce resources but does not create jobs for the educated individuals. These educated Africans leave Africa and go to Europe and America in search of work. The purpose of education is to live a better life and contribute to the society. In essence, Africa supplies educated cheap labor to the west just like it supplied labor for the industrial revolution in the 17th century. Has anything changed? Nothing has changed in Africa.

Africans leaders should stop being stooges of the west and find solution to the poverty and diseases that have become synonymous with Africa. African leaders and politicians should develop new ideology that revolves around and improving the lives of the people they govern.

Africa seriously needs infrastructure and basic amenities like water, and light so that the people can move from the current state of poverty and misery. The government and the educated have all the comforts of the modern life, but what about the farmers, the artisans, the laborers, the elderly, and the poor. Majority of the African population live in the villages and rural areas and do not have portable water to drink not to talk about electricity.

African governments and elites can afford to provide basic amenities and infrastructure if they decide to improve on the current condition of Africans. Particularly in the 21st century, technology has greatly improved to aid in installing machineries to build water dams and power. Africa has abundant sunshine and African government should invest in solar technology to provide electricity instead of acquisition of weapons.

The Sahara desert can be solar energy development station that can supply electricity to most part of the continent. The leaders of Africa enjoy political power but do not think about improving the life of their citizens. If leaders of Africa care they can team together to generate solar power from the heat the Sahara absorb from the sun. Indeed, this could lift Africa from the status of Dark Continent to Lighted Continent.

After the freedom from slavery, segregation was in America as a means to delay the progress of the freed black people. Separation of living areas and public facilities existed until late 1960s. The aspect of the past segregation is evident in residential arrangements whereby black people are concentrated in certain areas than others.

There was even segregation on the war fronts, particularly in South America. Black soldiers were in the fore where large casualties normally occurred. The practice of putting black soldiers on the fore in South America in the past reduced the black population in most South American countries.

Blacks never gave up. Their homes burned, lynched, killed, beaten, disgraced, and embarrassed but they continued with the struggle for freedom. Many brave blacks laid down their lives so that the generations after them would be better and respected and enjoy all that is available to other people. Revered Martin Luther King Jr., Malcolm X and many more expressed themselves about the situation of blacks in the late fifties so that black people could have rights and be dignified human beings.

While blacks in America were fighting for Civil Rights, African blacks were also fighting for their self- governance, equal rights, independence, and unity for African people. Enemies infiltrated and some blacks were involved in the killings of their own brothers and sisters.

There was even segregation on the war fronts, particularly in South America. Black soldiers were in the fore where large casualties normally occurred. The practice of putting black soldiers on the fore in South America in the past reduced the black population in most South American countries.

The Europeans that came to Africa lived like Kings and Queens; most did not want to go back to Europe because they could never enjoy the lifestyle they adopted in Africa in Europe. They had servants, and house cleaners that attended to all their needs. Some of the Europeans eventually made Africa their home but treated African people with utter most disrespect.

Due to misrule from the Europeans during the colonial period and the fact that European countries enslaved African, the new African government were aligning themselves with the then Soviet Union. The Soviet Union did not directly participate in African Slavery so it was natural for the African Nationalist to have trust in them and tried to adopt socialism immediately after independence in the sixties. The new African states were practicing capitalist/socialism.

The west could not handle this fearing that the Soviets would control their source of resources and market. They infiltrated Africa with intelligence gathering and toppled those African leaders who were moving towards socialism. They did exactly what they did four centuries ago during the beginning of the slave trade they armed African soldiers to over throw the young governments all over Africa.

The Belgians who were the most brutal of the colonialist did not want to leave Congo due to the rich copper mines, so they sided the opposing nationalists and there were several civil disobediences in the Congo region, and in the process, the first African pro- independence leader Patrice Lumumba was assassinated. No sooner, the military in Ghana overthrew Kwame Nkrumah, the first Prime Minister of

Ghana and his administration in 1966 while visiting Vietnam, he exiled to Guinea where he later died.

Series of military coups followed the newly independent African states in the 1960-mid1980s. The joy of independence was short lived. There were coups followed by counter coups. The men trained to protect the territorial integrity of their countries wrestled political power and became rulers instead of security keepers of their fatherland.

The African military tasted power and wealth for the first time and would never let go. The reserves the colonial administrators left Africa after independence meant for developmental purposes were used to procure ammunitions from the same colonialists. What an irony. The military and their western masters are behind the current predicament of Africa.

There is no system operating in Africa currently. The constitutions made by the first African leaders had been replaced by many others. There have been so many changes in governments in the past fifty years. New governments brought their own set of policies and jettisoned that of the predecessor. Without continuity of good governance, there cannot be progress. Stability in a polity ushers in progress.

America is moving forward because they operate on the constitution established by the founding fathers over two hundred years ago. They amend the constitution and do not change the underlying principles. That is the beauty of America and western civilization. The western civilization is premise on continuity. The west established a system of government that is constant, sturdy, and superior for any individual to tamper with.

The first African presidents or prime ministers never had the chance to execute their plans and programs. The military were impatient; they saw power and wealth and could not wait. The first coup in black Africa occurred in 1966, just nine year after the first independence from colonial administration. What can any government do in nine years particularly in a place starting its independence from foreign domination for the first time?

Unfortunately, the military could not govern any better because they did not have any plans. Their main purpose for staging coup was power and aggrandizement. The military failed African people. They created the present image of Africa. The military dragged African to wars for power at the neglect of the people and country. The military still hold on to power in pockets of Africa. Their regime is the most violators of human rights and most corrupt. The rate of ignorance and illiteracy is quite high in countries that are under military rule. They rule by fiat and do not have regard to the people. They convert the wealth of the country into their own. The military has no place in governance unless they become civilians. The military have the tendency of perpetuating themselves in power.

Dictatorship creates fears, mediocrity, mistrust, and ineptitude. The end of dictators creates chaos. An example was former Czechoslovakia after the death of Tito and Ivory Coast after Houphet Boigny. People lived in fear under such rulers and their death releases built up pressure and hatred that cumulates into chaotic environment. Human beings by nature yearn for freedom to run their lives. People also believe in rules and order for safety but not at the dictate of an individual

Most countries in the modern world are under republic principles; that is governance is by the people and the people contribute and decide who rules them. The period of a few individuals dictating the affairs of nations are over and African leaders should be part of this new world order. Democracy is the name of the game and if well practiced; anyone who has the interest of people and country at heart would get a chance to rule.

The western world took control of Black Africa again when they had their stooges in the name of military Generals as Head of States. Africa had not been able to execute its Independence and reap the benefits since the progress in the west is dependent on African resources and market. A peaceful and organized Africa might create problem for the industrialized world probably. The west cannot and could not keep its eyes off Africa's people and resources.

A peaceful and organized Africa would make the world better and happy. There would be less African risking their lives to move to Europe and America. These Africans, who are frustrated by the way and manner African leaders govern, leave Africa to find greener pastures and peace overseas would find comfort in their own back yard if African leaders incorporate human development into their strategies. Diseases and poverty would be something of the past if the peoples of Africa are exposed to proper education that enables them to improve themselves rather than the education that teaches them to be consumers of western products.

The west is delighted the way African leaders have ruled Africa since independence, because it seems to justify their perception that, the west is superior to Africa and Africans cannot rule themselves.

That perception is not true because black people have proved over, and over, and time and again that, they are equal with all human races. The leaders leading Africa have not done much to direct the people to the current reality of the world. African leaders have to redirect their style of leadership in conformity to republican principles. The world copied a lot from Africa and made them their own therefore it is all right if African leaders copy the principles that make other nations better.

By the way, capitalism is the natural way people had been trading for thousands of years. Capitalism just resurfaced in England in the 18th century. The English modified capitalism through the financial system they created. Merchants across the Sahara and elsewhere had been pulling resources together in order to trade in the years past in Africa. There is nothing like pure capitalism; government has to intervene in the free market to curb human nature of greed and uncontrolled exploitation of the poor by the affluent.

The concept of capitalism is excellent because it allows for individual developments, releases entrepreneurship, innovation, and creativity but it also leaves room for exploitation if the system is unchecked. Governments exist to protect people from themselves. There is nothing like absolute freedom, absolute freedom would be anarchy.

Moreover, people have different talents, some people will always move ahead and some will trail behind. No matter how hard some people try, they would be poor. For this reason, there should be governments to assist the poor, the disabled, and the elderly poor since the resources on this earth belong to all humans and creatures.

Everyone on earth determines to enjoy life and pass on a better place to the next generation and generation yet unborn using the same finite resources available or take possessions of other people resources to maximize their own enjoyments. Why then should anyone allow blacks to have what would benefit them? This is what some African leaders have been asking the western nations to do.

These leaders talk about transfer of technology from the west to Africa. The only way Africans can move forward is to lift themselves up towards self- determination, initiative, and progress. African leaders are the only ones who do not have faith in the people they lead. The moment they get into leadership, they assume that they are not part of the lot. Africa is the only continent that does not control its resources and destiny.

No African leader has come up with plans and strategy to curb diseases and poverty, and entrepreneurs are not encouraged to improve what they do to be able to create employments. The aspirations of the leaders are to be in power and transfer the power to their next of kin without regard to what the people want. Africa is the only place, in this day, and age, where governments exist for themselves and not for the people.

Nothing has changed in Africa, dependency on the west by African leaders has grown to such an extent that, the west is expected to provide guidance and direction for Africa to rid itself of poverty and diseases. Just recently, the president of France uttered that Africans are not ready to rule themselves. Do you blame him for saying the obvious? How do we interpret that?

It is time African leaders realize that it is their responsibility as leaders to improve the situation in their respective countries by creating a better future for their own children yet unborn. The people may look ignorant and accept whatever the leaders do for fear of their lives but providence always prove these leaders wrong because the horrible way they administered always live after them.

A military sergeant who took power in Guinea started killing his own people recently when the people demanded why he reneged on his promise not to seek reelection. This is only a sergeant a low rank in the military, what experience did he acquire in the military to make him a head of a country. This could happen only in Africa. What happened to the constitution of Guinea?

African soldiers should be discouraged from staging coup to change governments by an agreement among African leaders. Part of the agreement should be to send troupes to defend the constitution of affected country. If this idea is implemented, there would be stability in Africa and would attract investment funds that would aid developments. Most countries that developed have long history of stability.

Entrepreneurs move their wealth into stable environments. In order for African nations to attract foreign investments, there must be political stability on the continent. Entrepreneurs operate to make profit and increase their wealth. There are more investment funds in the world now but none is coming to Africa due to political instability and lack of basic infrastructures.

How could the world respect Africans when the leaders and military behave as if there are no laws that need to be honored or respected? If the military respect the law, country and people there would not be a coup. The military in Africa takes the people for granted because no one stands up to them when they take over power the way they do.

African government and leaders have taken the people of Africa for a ride for too long and it is time the leaders begin to respect the people and give them their rights. The people of Africa have had it with the leaders who rule without regard to the progress of the people. The African is a hard working individual but cannot make changes without the support of the government who is the custodian of the people's resources.

Happenings in other places in the world is available to Africans now by way of the internet services, people have more awareness and are observing the way other people are living, and they deserve and want the same.

There are many brilliant and fervent Africans in Africa and in Diaspora who are willing and ready to bring better changes into Africa. Who else can have African at heart if not Africans? Who else can be proud of Africa if not Africans? There are some westerners, who would assist to improve Africa if Africans make genuine gestures in improving their current predicament.

Africans struggled to get political freedom and should put the same effort in having economic freedom. After over five centuries of deprivation of their dignity and resources, it is time Africans take responsibility for their economic progress. Africans were never a warring people in the past but have suddenly been killing each other for political positions in the 21st century.

The world changes every minute and Africa cannot continue to move at the current rate. Africans cannot compete with the rest of the world but should develop and improve the lives of the people in education and creating stable environment that allows people to use their initiative to improve themselves. The current situation in Africa is very chaotic and dire. Development cannot happen in a chaotic and unstable environment.

Currently some leaders in some African countries are fighting over election results. What happened in those countries happens in the west all the time, but the politician in the west put the country, and people first and resolve political differences amicably. The losing party is definitely hurt but there is always another chance ahead, and this is the beauty of democracy in the west.

African leaders do not understand what democracy means. They keep on fighting after every election and innocent poor Africans are killed because somebody wants to be president and wage power. This is really an irony. They clinch to the seat of government as if it has been ordained to them.

Africans need change for the next generation to be better and became equal in the human community. The people of Africa are tired of being third class citizens in this world. It is not in everyday conversation but if you are from a third world country, you do not need any genius to interpret your rank in the world as a person. Africans were enslaved and became freed and now drowning in political and economic enslavement by theirs leaders.

The development in the west was possible because the people of Europe stopped fighting one another and became stable, and began to concentrate on what was important, and that is the development of the environment and people. The western leaders put a lot of planning and executed the plans for Europeans to be where they are today.

There is not much change going on black Africa. There is no system in place to change things around for the better. The leaders of African travel to every part of the world and see the way people live; yet they have not made any concrete effort to improve the lives of their citizens.

Some African leaders do not let their children acquire education in Africa because they know the educational system they have in place is not equipped to educate people to be inquisitive and creative. They send their children to Europe and America to be educated. Why should it be that way? What is good for the goose is good for the gander. These leaders could create an enviable education in their respective countries and train their children in their own country instead of draining the coffers of their country to train their children overseas.

African countries have hospitals managed and operated by African nurses, personnel, and doctors but not good enough for African leaders. Whenever Africa leaders are sick they shamelessly fly overseas for treatment. These leaders could equip their hospital to any standard in the world if they make the health of the citizenry a priority. Medical education is universal, people in other countries are involved in researches to improve on medical education and practice just like in other facets of life.

What are African leaders doing to get their people out of the predicament of poverty and misery that seem to have no end? The images of Africans on western television are that of hungry, poor, and melancholy people. The African before slavery looked healthier than present generation of Africans. What is wrong with the leaders of Africa?

Africans have acquired the education that lifted the west from poverty and misery but Africans have not been able to apply the western knowledge to improve their lives. Most Africans that study abroad do not want to go back to Africa to contribute to the development of their respective countries but rather stay back doing odd jobs that have no relevance to their education.

African leaders should involve the citizens in decisions making. African leaders should realize that, the people make government work. Until all hands are on deck, the few current leaders of Africa would not be able to make the right decision for the people. People's involvement in their governance is what democracy is all about. Many systems of governance are practice in the world but democracy is the only system that allows people participation to choose their leaders and be involved in the political process.

Plans and system from foreign countries had not worked in Africa and would not work in the future. You cannot implement a culture of a group of people, developed over centuries and impose it on another group of people, and think it would work.

Several international agencies have tried to solve African problems by using indicators developed with parameters from advanced economy, but they did not achieve the expected result. The plans that might work would be to study the people's environment, culture, laws and perception. It is like asking a cat to be a tiger or a tiger to be a cat. There is no scientific studies to prove this, but by observation of black people who had lived under western culture for over hundred years still want to relate to their African culture. Culture is not determined only by the environment but by the totality of a people.

Africans keep tagging along the rest of the world and the governments have not been taking decisions that would improve the economic standard of their citizens. Africans have to determine ways to improve their economic and financial situation

Africans need to look inward to build themselves out of the current poor economic situation. All the developed countries looked inward when development started and they satisfied their internal demands before looking outward. The steps African leaders have taken so far have not helped improve lives in Africa but rather make Africans depend more on the rest of the world. The leaders of African look up to the rest of the world as a baby looks up to the parents. What is wrong with the leaders of Africa? Why are African leaders treating their people the way they do.

African countries have been operating on the past system laid down by the colonial powers and have not made significant changes to detach themselves from the past. Africans can solve the current situation if they realize how far behind the people are in relation to other people on earth. Africans can change for the best if the leaders and elites put the right foot forward by deliberating on the good of all instead of the selfish attitude that have bedeviled African leaders.

People in other countries are now taking ride to the moon. Africans have not learned to live comfortably in this world let alone a ride to another planet. Have African leaders thought seriously about the situation facing their people? African leaders act to please their foreign collaborators who aid them to siphon African resources and wealth to their respective countries. These same people turn around and pity Africa for their misery and diseases.

Africans people are ready to improve themselves because they love life but the leaders are the hindrance. African leaders kowtow too much to external interferences than their own people. African leaders are the only leaders in the world who have no regard for their citizens. If the leaders care about the people of Africa, Africa would be moving at par with the rest of the world. People created the west and east; Africa could be better if the leaders make it a point to improve the current situation in Africa.

Africans travel all over the world to work to improve the lives of their family and in most cases are under employed. Obtaining a university education means securing a job related to your field of study with good pay and comfortable life. That is not the story with most Africans who travel abroad; with university degrees, they do menial occupations and drive taxi -cabs in the western world. They obtain their degrees from the west but getting employment in their chosen fields becomes a hurdle. With bills to pay and family to care for, they end up hanging their diplomas on the wall and perform jobs that do not require higher education.

Being under-employed, is prevalent within black people. Africans keep on piling degrees upon degrees but find it difficult to apply the knowledge to make impact in their societies. Knowledge without application is a waste

Could the reason be that blacks do not have businesses of their own that would employ them readily, or other people do not have faith in their ability or capability or nothing has changed?

These Africans cannot go back to Africa because they do not earn enough to provide them with sufficient funds to pack and go back to Africa. Going back to Africa becomes indefinite postponements. How many people from the west leave their country and travel elsewhere to be under-employed?

The rich Africans do not have faith in African experts. They often employ foreign professionals to manage their businesses and ventures. The west trusts anyone of its kind but Africans find it difficult to trust one another. This mistrust is one of the reasons the west continue to make use of Africans and African resources. Africans distrust one another this makes it easy for foreigners to take advantage of them. There is power in unity and Europe and America are example of the power of unity. People progress when united for a common purpose of improving the lives of everybody in the polity.

Long years of sojourn in foreign lands change people and when they return to their respective countries encounter social, political, and environmental shock. Frustration sets in as they face problem of assimilation into their own society. The system in Africa is different from anything anywhere in the world. The individual is on her/his own. There is no public support for individuals without jobs or unemployment benefits. If you are lucky to get a job, there is also the problem of the African bureaucracy. It is therefore very essential that African leaders open up to the people they rule to build Africa for the future. It takes the whole people to bring changes and not a few. A dedicated few can initiate a change and educate the larger society about the benefit and progress the new change would make in their lives. The people of Africa are anxiously waiting for leaders that would lead them to economic freedom.

The perception of most people in the west about Africa is animals and people running wild in the jungle even among the enlightened and educated folks. The thought of Africa brings nothing to the mind of the westerners than animals and people living in the jungle. This great interest in animals in Africa is part of the scheme to control everything on this planet.
They have all sorts of conservation organization to preserve animals in the African forest but when they needed lands to develop and build sprawling estates in America and most part of the west they did not think about the animals, they destroyed the buffalos, wolves, foxes and most of the exotic animals in the American forest.

Africans currently live in crowded towns, villages, and cities. Should Africans decide to live in sprawling estates in the future should the preservation of animals take priority? Africans are kind hearted and believe every creature has the right to live on earth and would always make room for other creatures

There are different groups of people in Africa and their physique and cultures are different, just as the people and cultures of Europe are different. The Europeans have grouped African people into four distinctive sects as follows:

Bantus are in Sub-Saharan Africa, Central Africa, East Africa, and South Africa. These people migrated from southeastern part of Nigeria and Cameroon, according to a research conducted by Joseph Greenberg and Malcolm Guthrie.

Berbers are indigenous people of North Africa. They spread from west of the Nile Valley to the Mediterranean Sea down to the Niger River. Notable people of the Berbers were Roman Emperor Septimus Severus, Saint Augustine of

Hippo, Ibn Battuta and Pope Miltiades and currently, soccer star Zinedine Zidane. North Africa was part of the Roman Empire and people moved freely, mingled, and inter married.

Tuaregs are the inhabitant of the interior of the Sahara of North Africa. They spread over to the following countries, Niger, Mali, Algeria, Burkina Faso, and Libya. They are mostly nomads.

Pigmies are the little people of Africa. They are in Central Africa Republic, Southern border of Angola, Rwanda, Burundi, Uganda, Democratic Republic of Congo, Botswana, Namibia, and Zambia. They have various indigenous names they prefer.

Nilotic people live in the Nile valley of Africa. They are mostly in Southern Sudan, Uganda, Kenya, Southern Egypt, and Northern Tanzania. The Maasai people of East Africa are part of the Nilotic people.

Nubians are mostly in Sudan, East Africa, and Southern Egypt. They live close to the Nile River. They are mostly farmers of date palms. They are darker than Egyptians in North of Egypt.

There are populations of European stock in Africa who now call Africa home. There are Arabs mostly in North Africa and Indians mostly in East and Southern Africa.

African established Schools and University in order to acquire knowledge and use the knowledge to improve their situations, but the education Africans acquired had not helped in developing Africa. It benefits the west because these educated Africans are great consumers of western goods. This explains why Africa has not been able to progress despite the large number of educated elites.

The only way African can benefit profoundly from the acquired knowledge is to apply the knowledge into the traditional way of doing things. The Japanese and Chinese did the same they transformed western knowledge into their own languages and applied them. Japan and China are a par with the west. For instance, the nomads in Africa should be able to benefit from animals scientists and veterinarians. The scientists should assist the illiterate nomads scientifically to promote large productivity and have stable ranches instead of roaming animals around as they have done thousands of years gone by. The nomads have been rearing animals for centuries and assisting them with modern techniques would boost their stock and increase meat production.

Subsistence African farmers should have access to agriculture advisory services from agricultural experts, in order to improve farming in Africa. This would improve the lives of farmers and food production increased so that Africa can minimize dependence on food importation. Every country should be self -sufficient in stable food production particularly in Africa where there are acres and acres of land. There are many rivers in Africa that African farmers could use to irrigate farmlands where they experience scanty rainfalls.

Do you know what Europe did when it was having famine problems in the 16th century? The rich took lands from the peasant farmers and turn subsistence farming into large plantations and the peasants had to work on the farms of the rich for wages or crop sharing. African elites should not take farmland from the peasants without appropriate compensation, the rich or elites can compensate the subsistence farmers for their lands to develop large mechanized farming for food crops. An individual farmer cannot afford the farming machineries, but cooperatives or leasing companies can make purchase and lease to farmers.

Africans have wealth of resources and human power and yet they keep looking up to Europe and America for aids. These countries Africans look up to have their own internal problems and cannot solve the whole world problems. If Europe moved from poverty to prosperity, why has it been difficult for Africa to solve its problems?

The same knowledge educated Africans acquire is use in making all the things we import. Africans should put their hands on deck and work together as a people to lift the people of Africa from poverty and misery. The west cannot continue aiding Africa as the world economy changes and every country tries to be responsible for its people. Africa should be self -sufficient at least in food production because it has the resources and labor to do so.

Africans do not have the capability to engage in modern warfare, because warfare has advanced in technology and Africans should use their resources to build amenities instead of investing in arsenal. A large percentage of the human race could be eliminated in an instant should any global war break out. There are nuclear war- heads, missiles-that can travel thousands of miles, not to talk of biological weapons. There are fighter planes called drones that operate with remote controls. War does not solve human problems but creates fears and distrust among the human community.

Africans need to develop so that the life of degradation would not become permanent. We have billionaires, millionaires, doctors, engineers, scientist, pilots, actors, lawyers, technocrats, and men in all facets of human endeavor and yet our contributions go unrecognized because we as a people have not been able to develop our people. We do not protect our children. We do not value our children. Our elites have it all but majority of black people are still suffering. Majority of black people are at the bottom of the poverty level.

The rich exploit the poor to be rich through owing resources and paying the poor meagerly for just existence. The rich countries want to continue being rich while exploiting poor countries for their resources. Africa has highly educated Africans to change Africa from a poor continent to the envy of the world but unfortunately selfishness and greed has eating deep into the fabric of African leaders and elites.

Countries are judged not by how many millionaires they can boast of but how many citizens are gainfully employed and living in decent accommodations and having basic amenities. Americans and Europeans measure the level of achievement of their governments by the low level of people who are unemployed. The ideal number is 4% unemployment that each leader in the west strives for when in power. African leaders need to think of how to improve the life of their citizens in order to gain respect the world population.

In 2007, a Nobel Prize winner, scientist, James Watson an American, said in Britain that, Black people are less intelligent than white people. He added that, *he was inherently gloomy about the prospect of Africa, because, all our social policies are based on the fact that their intelligence is the same as ours, whereas all the testing says not really.*
He went on to add that, *he hoped that everyone was equal, but countered that, people who have to deal with black employees find this not true.* Continuing his statement further, he stated that, *there are many people of color who are talented, but don't promote them when they have not succeeded at the lower level. There is no firm reason to anticipate that intellectual capacities of peoples geographically separated in their evolution should prove to have evolved identically. Our wanting to reserve equal powers of reason as some universal heritage of humanity will not be enough to make it so.*

What do you make of Mr. Watson's assertion? If a man of his caliber is making that statement in the 21st century, can you imagine what was about a black person in 16th century?

You see what needs to be done is for black people to take charge of their own destiny and not rely on others so that people like Mr. Watson would not have the nerve and audacity to say and write degrading statements about black people. Mr. Watson has observed that despite all the ill treatments his race has meted on black people through the ages, the black still depend and trust the same race that enslaved them. Mr. Watson should remember that their current state of development was possible because of the encounter with black people in 14th century where they plundered their resources and their labor to develop and got out of diseases and poverty that plagued Europe in the 14th century.

The African continent has resources and people who are waiting for leaders who would take them away from poverty and hopelessness. Black people are not war- mongers and vindictive people, but that does not stop us from enjoying the fruits of this earth. Mr. Watson had the confident to say what he said, because when he left that meeting and stepped out a black-man met him to polish his shoes, a black-man worked on his sewage, probably, a black person works in his house as steward. We allow ourselves to be talked down to, because we have become addicted to material acquisition to always need money to buy things we do not need and others get rich from our uncontrolled consumptions.

There are still more work to be done by black people all over the world to be able to get our rightful place in the human community. The educated Africans should detach themselves of foreign influence and be creative to benefit their people in view of the unique situation black people now find themselves. African intellectuals have done many researches in many fields of studies that need entrepreneurs and investors. These researches and findings are stuck on the shelves of the various universities in Africa. The black scientists do not market their findings as such nobody hears about them. Black people should be aggressive as other people when it comes to the world affairs. All the hard work these scientists do become inconsequential if the results sit on top of shelves in the university faculties.

The black man has served the west for so long; and yet never appreciated. The black man needs to move forward, enough is enough. The black race is too reserved. They accept all the negatives things they say about them. The children and grand- children of the colonial masters are continuing in the same foot- steps of their ancestors; they treat black people with contempt. Everybody feels he or she is superior to the black person, no matter the black person's economic standings. Attitude towards Africans are that of someone needing help and pity. They have the notion that Africans live among animals even in this twenty-first century, the age of the internet and fighting drones.

Actually, it is a mere propaganda to make the African or Black person feel like a lesser being? Aids, the disease that started among homosexual in the1980s in the western hemisphere has spread widely in Africa and has become synonymous with Africa. Alas, Africa now is the home of Aids particularly Southern Africa. When South African blacks were struggling under apartheid, they did not have aids. Now after the struggle of over five centuries is over for them to take charge of their destiny suddenly surfaced HIV and Aids.

Black Africa needs to wake up to its responsibility. In the 13 century when Europe was in the same predicament as Africa is currently facing, they mobilized themselves to find solutions. The learned, the rich, and, the royal came together and started rebirth, enlightenment era, industrial revolution, re construction, the world wars for the new order to the present time. Black people, now is the time to develop Africa and to create employment for the people. There is unprecedented large unemployment rate in the west and a vast number of unemployed are blacks. What does that tell black people who depend upon labor employment for livelihood? Is it not time to start being creative and use ingenuity for survival? Black people can be producers and not only workers.

People have booked their seats to travel and tour the moon soon. Who knows what could happen next? The estimate to travelling to space would cost about $1billion dollars. Nuclear weapon ownership is growing; despite propaganda for non-proliferation of nuclear weapons, global warming is becoming a threat. What are black people doing as co resident of the planet earth to safeguard the planet earth? The black race cannot continue sitting on the fence for other people solving the earthly problems.

Black people are not strongly involved in the decision processes on earth or protect themselves from abuse by other people and accept all decisions made by others without questioning. Some fewer people are using more of the earth surface and populations of all people continue to grow and if black people especially those in Africa do not protect and take care of the environment it could be taken away from them without knowing. Many Europeans are buying lands in Africa particularly in Central Africa. The world is for all of us but some people are using a larger portion than most of us.

Black people have to wake up and improve themselves and participate in the world around them. We have sat on the fence for too long. We should also take charge of things around us. We can do it, what is holding black people back? We assume that what others changing the world for the good of all but no, we are giving a share only when it is convenient and gainful to the provider.

Let our voice be heard and our actions be noticed, get actively involved in the developments in the world. Black people are full member of the human community. We need to improve ourselves and change the way we view the world. We need to direct your resources towards the development of our environment for our benefit and others who believe in us.

We operate in a market where the purchaser determines the price of our produce. You work hard and spend your earnings on things you do not need. You accumulate goods, which later become trash because you do not need them. You spend all your earnings and borrow more to spend on consumables. You work all the time to pay for things you have bought that you do not need. It has become a virtual circle. You do not save for rainy days or you do not earn enough to save for rainy days. You do not save period. Since you do not save, you cannot have wealth. You look poor and exist in poverty.

Black people are the hardest hit anytime there is a disaster or calamity because the only source of livelihood is our earnings and most of us do not save for rainy days. Do you remember the Katrina hurricane that hit the Gulf Coast of the United States in 2005? Do you remember what you saw and what happened? You see, we live in uncertain times and uncertain events do happen, so we should readdress the way we currently live, be prepared for future uncertainty by putting some money aside. Nothing is guarantee these days.

The name black reflects nothing but poverty. There is poverty because some people are too greedy. We have the resources, and our labor, that entrepreneurs depend on to become rich. The resources in Africa are finite and there would be none when Africans need them with the rate they are mining and giving them away. Africa relies on exporting its natural resources instead of adding value prior to export.

All we do is to consume products made by other people. We have turned into a consuming object. We are now bigger and less healthy than before. Our physique, that was slim, slender, strong, and healthy suddenly, adapted to the new food and environment. Our generations began getting bigger particularly those of you in North America. Those in the Caribbean were able to maintain their slim physique because they continue to eat tropical foods. You now have several diseases like diabetes and high blood pressure. You may dispute this, but have you bothered to research on the food you eat whether they agree with your biological make up? You are what you eat.

You are addicted to buying and accumulating things. You have been dissipating your energy working and using your money to buy things that do not improve your life but rather make others rich, live in the best place, and train their generation to continue living the good life while your generation lives in perpetual poverty. Your acquisition instinct is so large that you borrow to buy then work and pay later. You have to change this trend. You have to start putting some money aside now so that your generation will not continue to be the lower working people.

Everywhere in this world, the black man or woman perform the menial jobs even with university education. The black man is out there serving at hotels, on the beach, security guards, sewage workers, miners, janitors, chauffeurs, waiters and many more. Are you on earth to be your brother's servant?

You have changed situations around before, remember, you were enslaved and you came out of it victorious. You fought for your freedom for over centuries but you finally became free. You can change your economic situation. You developed your own music from African rhythm and you gave birth to jazz music. You developed calypso in South America. The sound of calypso is nothing but African beats and rhythms. You invented many things to make life easier for everyone but never given the credit for them.

Your lifestyle is unique. You are an amazing being, despite the abuse you still came out without losing your dignity. You have proved in so many ways that you have excellent qualities. You are marvelous and great whenever you have the opportunity you shine.

You are patient, enduring, accommodating, humane, and gregarious. You are not greedy and selfish; you provide the balance to make living worthwhile. Years of mistreated has taught you to be tough when the need be. You have more goodness in you. You fought when you had to fight. You fought when enough was enough.

You educated yourself when they deprived you of education. Blacks built schools and institutions. You were seen as a threat and they did all they could to break you but you were resilient. Laws were enacted to stop your progress but you moved on despite. You are free but you cannot be free from the law, so they said. They incarcerated you by any trivial offence. Most of your males prevented from acquiring knowledge or professions that could make them sustain a family and women became bread- winners for their families. You became a society where the woman heads the family. Your women are strong they kept the fort safe.

Your womanhood has always been strong. These women were the queen mother back in Africa. These women advised the king makers and the men came to them for advice concerning nationhood. Therefore, it was not new for black women to take charge and keep fort. The women kept the people together. When the black man was incarcerated, or could not get a job it was the black woman who kept the family together. Without these strong and intelligent women there would not have been us. It is sad that human nature forgets. Why should some musicians debase black women in their songs?

These musicians have forgotten that without the black woman there might not be many of them living. If anything at all, the black woman deserves praise and admiration, and not scorn or relegation. The black woman stood strong where men could not dare. The black woman started the changes. She dared and refused to give up her seat. She said enough is enough. She started it, our men and women understood, and supported the change that was long overdue.

Rev. Martin Luther Jr. in the 60s took over the struggle for civil rights in peaceful demonstrations. Eventually he paid the ultimate price for our struggles. He died but the struggle continues. We are still moving towards the promise land Rev. Martin Luther King Jr. preached about but we are not there yet. Many obstacles need to be hurdled before final destination. You are getting close but you need to make more strides. You need to think of your children yet unborn.

The set up was not meant to make you any better than a worker in a termite colony. You have made big strides but you need to do more. You have very good leaders who have been outspoken and standing up for any injustices being done to you. You do not appreciate the work of these people but if not for them, who will stand for you.

Politicians stand for everybody but few leaders stand for you. They leave their families to fight for your rights. Please do appreciate them when they stand up for you.   Some of these leaders went to jail for you, some paid the ultimate price for you. They fight for your rights all the time if not these rights would have been abrogated. Nothing has changed and things hardly change.

Do not antagonize or blame anyone, but start believing in yourself. You have dignity. You have a beautiful color love it. Your hair is not nappy, it is natural; the color and texture complements the tone of your skin. You can manage the hair if you pay attention to it. It is very flexible. Take good care of that hair. In the 60s people tried to copy your hair- style, the Afro hair do but they could not because it is unique. On the other hand, you can make your hair straightened, braided, curled, or afro. You have the best but nobody promotes it. You have to promote what you have. If you say, your hair is beautiful others will say it is beautiful. You short change and under estimate yourself a lot. Your color is beautiful and you have different shades.

Some black people even dispute who their ancestors are. You have been brain washed to detest your fore bearers. Your ancestors were not created salves rather were enslaved. Your ancestors fought when they were captured; but did not have guns as their captors so they were enslaved only through the power of the gun by force. They did not just succumbed; they fought fiercely for their freedom. They decided to live so that their generation can survive. You are free but you still behave as you are still under bondage.

Black people have been told many negative things about their ancestral continent Africa that make some detest having any connections with Africa. The black Africans were not the first people to be enslaved by another people; the Jews were enslaved in Egypt for thousands of years and gained their freedom and became leaders of their masters.

The Jews suffered immensely in Europe but look at the Jews today they control the financial power of the world. The Jews are scattered all over the world just like blacks but they always make the best of their situation and accept every Jew as a Jew no matter their economic standing in life. There are twelve tribes in the Jewish people according to the Bible but they do not allow the division to mar their purpose of being free, strong powerful and rich.

The Jews love themselves and black people could emulate this oneness of the Jewish people. The Jews do not hear what people say about them but concentrate on their goal of being a people with determination. People who held power over them at some periods in their history mistreated the Jews, but they believed that one day they would be on their homeland. Most Jews do not live in Israel, they do not even go there, but they are contributing funds, resources, technology to make Israel a great nation. The Jews remember the land they left.

Keith Richburg in his book 'out of America' wrote many negative things about Africa. An excerpt from that book is as following: **'thanks God for bringing his nameless ancestor across the ocean in chains and leg irons and for being American. I have been there, I have lived there and seen Africa in all its horror. I know that I am a stranger there. I am an America, a black American and I feel no connection to that strange and violent place.'** Keith it is unfortunate that you experienced Africa in a negative way. Every year millions of Europeans troop to Africa to visit despite your observation or feelings about black people ancestral home. Despite the under developments and all its horror it is the most natural and peaceful place to be. Africa is natural and it is moving towards modernity but slowly and carefully.

On the other hand, Pete O' Neal and his wife Charlotte Hill have been living in Africa for the past twenty- five years. They live in a village in Tanzania, which they have transformed into a modern place. They assisted in connecting electricity, portable water and attract tourist to the remote village. They are among the respectable people in the village. They taught their neighbors electronics, carpentering, food preservation, and have introduced them to poetry, music, and foreign dances. Though he was a former member of a group that struggled for equal rights for blacks in the United States of America, he realized his dreams in Africa.

Keith, what is your own contribution towards your ancestral home? Your criticisms of Africa does not matter, that continent has helped all continents developed and it has been neglected and abused by those who used her; a better person is one who sees something bad and contributes to make it better. The Europeans have said it over, and over again, that they do not need any mixture in their race. An atom of a black blood in white is black.

Europeans who left Europe due to religious persecution, felons, and poverty still pay tribute to Europe. Despite all that, they still assist and love Europe. An example is America's involvement in the two world wars and the war of the Falkland Island. After the world wars, America contributed great amount of wealth to rebuilt Europe. America is ready to fight their last drop of blood to defend Europe because it is their ancestral home. Your past is your past no matter what. You can change everything but not the blood that runs through your veins.

Therefore, Keith instead of seeing all the negative things about Africa you could lend a helping hand to make improvements on the continent. It is good to know that you know how your ancestors got to America. It was no fault of theirs. They fought gallantly for freedom.

What they portray about Africa is a deliberate attempt to continue to make people of African descent not to love Africa and help its progress. You are not inferior to anyone. If not for the discovery of African people, the current world would not have gotten the benefits they now enjoy. The labor of African slaves built the modern world. The west had ideas but the Africa slaves had the strength to implement the ideas.

Europe before encounter with Africa was embroiled in wars, have endemic disease, poverty, famine, fighting among themselves, and authoritarian rule by nobles, knights, kings, and queens. They did not have the strength to develop the New World as seen today if not for the labor from slaves. After the development of America into a country, many immigrants came from Europe to enjoy the new wealth. The population of blacks was more in the Americas during developments but millions of Europeans moved into the new world. Europe and America owe their current development to Africa and they should reciprocate. You will think they will realize the havoc they have done to the psychic of black people in Africa and across North and South America.

They talk about guinea worm, malaria and now HIV and Aids. Guinea worm is water borne disease found among people who drink untreated water. The world health Organization knows that guinea worm is water borne but have not made provision of potable water a corner stone of its fights against the disease. The World Health Organization treats diseases and not causes of the diseases. Treating the causes of the diseases would eradicate diseases and this would result in the wellbeing of the people. Some of the funds used to procure medication to treat the disease should be channel into provision of potable water projects and guinea worm disease would be history.

The investment in medication benefits the pharmaceutical companies, and investment in water project would be a one-time project while treatment of guinea worm is an ongoing venture, creating jobs and money for the companies.
Black Africans should not expect anyone to help take care of them. They should start to be responsible for themselves and their people. Black people should take the initiative in improving the lives of their less privilege.

Malaria is transmitted to humans through mosquitoes. Mosquitoes breed in stagnant waters, wet bushes, pools, and ponds. Why are mosquitoes in extinct in most part of the world and not in Africa?

According to an article by Thomas C. Nchinda of the World Health Organization, Africa accounts for 90% of malaria cases in the world. It was estimated that 300 to 500 million cases of malaria was recorded in Africa in the last decade. Each year in Africa, about 1.5 to 2.7 million deaths result from malaria of which 90% are children under 5 years of age. What an alarming statistic. When the malaria eradication program began in the 1950s, the malaria endemic Africa was not included. Why?

79

Malaria is a tropical disease, and it kills many Africans each year and as such, Africans should take the lead in eradication of malaria because it is their debacle. We as people do not value our own life. Insecticides alone if properly used can reduce incidents of malaria drastically. Spraying of ponds, pools, and stagnant waters frequently could destroy mosquito's larvae. Eradication of mosquitoes should be a concern of black people because this tiny insect carries the malaria parasites that kill millions of black people in Africa.

Eradication of malaria is a project Africans should have embarked upon sooner; but they assume it is the duty of World Health Organization. The incident of malaria borders more on cleanliness. If covered drainages are use in Africa the way it is done in the western world, there would be fewer places for mosquitoes to breed. Africa has open drainage systems and these are fertile places for mosquitoes to breed. Some governments in Africa have stated constructing covered drainage, which is a good step in the right direction.

One Nigerian politician, whose political agenda to eradicate mosquitoes in Nigeria was always ridicule and never won an election. His fellow politicians made fun of him. He has been using the eradication of mosquitoes and other pests as his priority if elected. He had the best agenda, but never won elections. He would have saved thousands of lives. That is politics in Africa. The politicians prey on the ignorance of the electorate. Politicians in Africa prey on the ignorance of the majority of the electorate and canvass for votes without agenda that benefits the majority.

The gains of the sixties for all black people all over the world are slipping away gradually. Military men who seized power from the first African Nationalist leaders sent Africa into deeper economic problems. Most of these former military leaders are now wealthy Africans and they should contribute to the continent that gave them their wealth. We have to bring all our people along to prosperity. The few of you who are affluent should let it be their responsibility to develop the continent.

When Moses was leaving Egypt he came along with all the Israelites, he did not leave anyone behind. That is why despite the suffering of the Jews in the past they have economic power. They see themselves as a people and any one of them would go all the way to help a Jew who is falling behind economically. That is what black people are not doing. There are enough affluent black people on the continent of Africa to assist in alleviating poverty and suffering. The affluent black people should create job opportunities where everyone could benefit. These rich Africa invest their monies in the west that does not need their investments. Africa is yearning for investments.

There are business opportunities in Africa where the rich Africans could invest their money with good yields. Propagandists who want the status quo to remain continue to portray Africa as unstable politically therefore bad for investments. The current political instability in Africa is a deliberate attempt to keep black people where some people think they belong. It is up to us to realize that we deserve a better life as any other human being. We stop just being a consumer and become a provider, an innovator, an initiator, an inventor and we would be able to improve on our lots. No human being should live in poverty, because there are adequate resources to make everyone have enough. .

Africans usually go with the flow. Africans accept anything that the west and east throw at them without question. We have become dependent on others to solve our problems. Others still use us the way their ancestors did four hundred years ago, except that, we receive wages that are not enough to cover basic living expenses and we supplement this with credits. We live on aids, loans, and grants. For how long would a people continue to live as under developed human? We spend more on consumer goods than anyone else does. They make most of these goods for us in order to make profits. Any time someone makes profit on you, part of your own wealth is gone.

It is only a black man who will have a college education and be doing menial jobs. You acquire knowledge but you do not apply them to your environment or your living style. The government or the entrepreneurs you have will rather stack their money in European and American banks rather than invest them to create jobs for African people. If they invest in Africa, they create job opportunity for Africans.

The west operates by the rich investing their money to create opportunities for people to work and have decent life while the rich in turn make more money and increase their wealth. Ever since the creation of legal tender in the 17th century, the British and other Europeans had been investing in the colonies and creating more wealth. Africans leave African countries every day to seek greener pastures all over the world. Africans have land and resources to change the current situation given people oriented leaders.

There should be a new orientation in Africa. Africa leaders love power more than the people they are supposed to govern. It is only in African countries that leaders in power do not respect the outcome of elections. They feel once elected the people would continue electing them. African people know the difference now they want improved way of life not the status quo of disease and poverty. The average African wants to live like the leaders too. With increased number of people having formal education, reality is dawning on the people that they hold the power to elect leaders through their votes.

Diamonds and many rare minerals are taking from Africa to Europe as was done five hundred years ago but the continent of Africa continues to remain undeveloped. Africa should not be a poor continent because it has abundant resources that are highly valued but continue to be the least advanced of the six continents.

African leaders have betrayed their people for too long. Ironically, nobody in the west realize there are rich Africans, because if there are what are they doing to reduce poverty and diseases among their people. Not everybody in the western hemisphere is rich or comfortable but they all enjoy the use of clean water and lights. Africa leaders have not make Africa a place the people in Diaspora would long for. The western negative propaganda about Africa is part of the problem; what efforts are we as Africans making to change this perception.

Europe and America developed through their own initiative and Africans should do the same too. You have all that it takes. You should start with basic infrastructure first then investors can come in and invest. You can start producing food by assisting the hard working but neglected African farmers. African governments need to assist African farmers.

Do you know how much assistance the governments in the west give to their farmers? You see the western system of governance is very complex. The system of government in the west is premise on free enterprise. It does not mean there is no government assistance. Governmental hand is everywhere despite the entrepreneur system in the west. The government prop most businesses by being the largest consumer and by way of subsidies, grants, and credits. The governments subsidize farmers heavily if not nobody will be able to buy food. If farmers put all their overheads on food production, it would be too expensive for the average person. The food stamp system in the United States helps the poor and the farmers. The farmers receive subsidies for their produce and the poor consumers receive food stamps from the government to buy food produced by the farmer.

African government could start by assisting farmers and providing them with advice and techniques to meet the current standard in the global food markets. Production of sufficient food is the bedrock of every government but African governments rely on importation of food they could produce locally. African countries have the potential to produce enough food to feed their population and even export surplus. There are millions of people of African descents in North and South America, who would be interested in African food if well prepared and packaged. Food production aspect of development is vital for the survival of any nation, but sadly, it has not been a priority to African governments.

A nation is only a nation if it can put the people to work efficiently and effectively. It is only in Africa that governments do not see employment of their citizenry as their major responsibility. In most instances, they do not have records of occupation and vocation people do to sustain themselves. African governments do not see provision of employment as the essence of governance. The employment of citizenry is the focus of governance in the current world.

African people about six centuries ago worked on plantations in the Americas to develop Europe and America. Now Africans leave Africa and go to Europe and America to work with the skills and specialized knowledge acquired in Africa. We leave Africa undeveloped because the politicians are not doing the right things to make life comfortable. Our contributions and efforts are vital to uplift Africa, its people and her descendants. African people and descendants in Diaspora make sacrifices to develop Africa so that your children's children can relax in the sun and enjoy instead of working all their lives just like you, the parents. Stop living like you are strangers and visitors on earth.

Doctors, nurses, professors, bankers, lawyers, architects, accountants, computer programmers, scientists, surgeons, pharmacists, chemists, biologists, engineers of Africa descents make your impact on Africa. We are a laughing stock, we are not respected due to our under development of our ancestral home and the fact that, we condemn our continent instead of contributing towards its progress. If we are clever, we should develop our part of the world instead of rushing to developed places in the world.

African politicians need to provide the people with basic needs of the modern world like portable drinking water, lights, and improved infrastructure. African politicians practice many ideologies: Marxist, Capitalist, Socialism, Maoist, and mixtures of others. There has to be stability and continuity in a polity for the country to progress.

We have mastered the European cultures very well but we cannot use them to improve ourselves. It is not our fault because it is not easy to use someone else's culture and ideas. Right now, we can go back to the past and study the remaining ruins of our cultures or study the way Africans who stuck to the past do things. This way, we can make improvements and build upon them and new ideas would come forth. Africa leaders should be people oriented and develop their people.

The family was the center of everything in Africa but it has now changed. Affluence is measure in Africa by the number of imported luxury cars and how many personal houses they have built. It is when black Africa respects the people once again would they be able to move forward. Your systems need to be re-structured.

The many coups after most Africans countries attained their independence from Europe derailed progress. It was part of the Cold War strategy, the west felt African leaders were moving towards communism and they might lose control of Africa indefinitely. Africa is the market place for European products and raw material center for the industries. The industrialization in the west depends on resources from Africa. Therefore, the fear of losing the market and resources to the Soviet Union prompted the financing of some African military men mostly trained in Europe to topple

African nationalist leaders who fought for African independence from European domination.

The dream of the nationalists to educate Africans, develop Africa into a modern continent was killed by military men with the aid of the west after less than a decade of independence. Retrogression set in, since these military men trained to defend the territorial integrity of their nations do not have the ability to lead nations. They did not have any plans to develop Africa, but to enrich themselves with the resources of the African people. These crops of military men and their collaborators in the west are to blame for the under development in Africa today.

The nationalist did their best to secure Africa's independence from foreign domination. The new African military leaders who came to power in the 70s, called themselves revolutionists, but nothing changed for the better in Africa if not worst. The only thing that revolutionized was their wealth they all shed poverty off themselves and suck their countries dry.

Africans still follow the same system set up six hundred years ago to produce raw material for factories in Europe. They produce the 'cash crops' like cocoa, coffee, sisal and many others while neglecting improvement on food production. Most African countries rely on a single commodity export as the main source of income for their economy and this makes them dependent on the up and down in the economy of the importer countries.

Africans need to develop an economic systems based on the needs of the people in addition to the exports. We cannot even feed ourselves. Africa with its large land mass cannot produce enough food to feed its population. We export our mineral resources and produce at prices determined by the importer. The importer processes the mineral resources into finished goods and sells back to us at exorbitant prices. The importer becomes richer and the exporter poorer, while the resources of the exporter are depleting. They build houses and mansions on their land to live in while advising us to conserve our land for the changes in the climate, while our people live in over- crowded and unhygienic environments.

We can change the current situation in Africa if we focus. We focus by being genuinely interested in the uplifting of our people. Unfortunately, people who do not want change hold wealth in most black Africa. They trade in finished products from the industrialized countries. The farmers who produce the cash crops also have wealth and own most land. The only way Africa can move forward is when the elites, the educated, and the illiterates work together as a people who want to make life better for themselves and the generations yet unborn.

The educated Africans cannot continue the way things are and look down upon the illiterates, but the illiterates own more wealth. The illiterates control the local economy in Africa. Illiterate in the sense of western education, they are knowledgeable on how things work in their favor. The educated Africans should involve the illiterates in the new Africa to bring everyone along to build trust and consensus. If everyone is involved and see the benefit of the changes, no amount of external pressure would make them waiver.
African languages should be part of the means of communication so that everyone whether literate or illiterate will understand one another. The countries that are controlling most development in the world today used their natural language. The English, the French, the Japanese, the Germans, and the Chinese use their own languages and these make communicating easy among all the people. America developed its own English!

The illiterate Africans do not trust the African elites because they behave just like the colonialists. They speak the languages of their colonial masters that Africans who do not have opportunity of formal education do not understand. These elites behave like strangers to their own people therefore trust that is vital in establishing a relationship is lacking. The elites live in reserve areas away from their people. These elites provide water, and lights and good infrastructure in their residential area and neglect the areas of the illiterates, blue- collar workers, and semi- educated. The world sees Africans in the eyes of the illiterate Africans not the elites.

The western media sees nothing good on Africa to report except diseases, refugees, and the poor and of course the animals. This propaganda about Africa and the people would never vanish until Africans begin to take charge of their own destiny by making life better with the involvement of every one. Africans have to value themselves as important and deserve all the comfort in this world as well. We work hard but we have not been able to enjoy much comfort. We have become the poorest people on earth. African countries take loans from the World Bank with huge interest charged and have created huge debt liability with nothing to show for it.

The United Nations Organization was set up to aid Europe recover from the devastation of the two world wars. The Western nations do not have any intention or plans in developing Africa if they do Africa would have emerged from the present predicament of poverty and diseases. Therefore, it is in the hands of black people to develop Africa. Africa should be your pride.

The World Bank as an agency of the United Nations established at the Breton Woods Conference in the United States of America in 1944 to regulate the international monetary and financial order. It established the international trade exchange rate. After the Second World War, they rebuilt Japan, Germany, France, Britain, and extended large loans to China, Korea, and India for their development. The World Bank excluded African countries from the generous reconstruction arrangements after the Great Wars. The west should have helped African countries since they took resources from the continent during colonization and Africa soldiers fought on behalf of the colonists during the two world wars. Everyone takes from Africa but no one gives back to Africa. These same people point fingers to Africa and mock her and the peoples for under developments.

In 1971, the American Dollar became the international medium of exchange replacing the gold standard. The World Bank lends money to countries to help in economic developments. Majority of these poor countries are in Africa. The World Bank uses one standard to measure all countries, but countries are not the same in terms of needs, resources, or economic developments. The World Bank demands that all countries taking their fund had to devalue their currencies and adopt the free market economy. The shock therapy is an economic policy introduced by the World Bank to the borrowing countries to liberalize their markets, reduce government control of their economy to allow free market to evolve. The governments had to loosen control on prices, stop subsidies, sell state assets, and float the currency so that value of the currencies would be determined by the market.

The strict measures can work in some countries but not all. Countries that have framework of laws, regulation, and established practice were able to benefit from the shock therapy. It failed in Africa because Africa has not even started to implement real governance let alone have laid down policies. Africa had just gotten independence from the colonialist and was trying to sort itself out in the new responsibility when the military sponsored by the west derailed the progress of the young African countries.
The program laid emphasis on the growth of the Gross Domestic Product and not sustainability of the growth given the economic indicators of these countries.

The World Bank has now made water privatization a pre-requisite for loans. Portable water is a serious deficiency in Africa. If provision of water is privatize in Africa, how would the poor farmers obtain this vital resource for irrigation, and consumption?

There is great disparity between Africa and the developed world. Africa has never been allowed to develop at its pace; the west still treat Africa as if it is a colony. The leaders of Africa due to greed and the personal benefit they derive have continued to sell Africa short in the eyes of the world.

Some Africans in Diaspora are ashamed to be associated with Africa. The progress in Africa has been too slow if it is moving at all. There are so many humanitarian organizations set up to redeem malnourished African children. People go to Africa to adopt children because their parents cannot provide for them. Do you realize how far behind Africa is in terms of progress? If a country cannot do the simplest things of taking care of its children, environment, providing water, and sanitation, it is an indication that the government does not have any policy statement for development.

The air around in most cities is full of pollutant from automobiles exhaust waste, waste from nuclear, green-house gasses, many creation of man from wanting to live a better and comfortable life. The carbon dioxide produced is getting more than the oxygen produced. People get tired easily in cities than in rural areas where the trees produce more oxygen. This means that living things are systematically destroying themselves by air pollution due to greed and the culture of acquisition of material things due to wants and not needs. Is this civilization? The beginning of this civilization introduced man to better of way of living and improved his environment, reduced the dissipation of his energy in search of his needs due to efficient transportation, communication and market systems but currently greed has taken over and products are brought to the market place to exploit the ignorant rather than improve his lot.

Africa has not started her industrial revolution and the air around is polluted. Who did that? Africa has to undertake her development now. We have to take the initiative. We have to harness our resources instead of feeding the factories in the industrialized world. Africans act as if the world cares about whether they develop or not. Africa is the control the developed countries use to measure how far they have developed. They world forget the fact that if not for free black labor they would not been where they are today.

The printed clothes Africans wear are either made in Denmark or Switzerland or Holland and staple food, rice is imported from China, and Thailand. Africans have become so dependent on imported goods instead of developing their local economy. Africans were enticed with the same goods six centuries ago and continue in the same process. Nothing has changed. Political independence is not the same as economic independent. African countries need to have economic independent in order to prosper and this is in their own hands.

Look around African countries, the resources that could go to providing infrastructures, education, water, electricity are diverted to importation of ammunition, food and clothing, used items the west cannot not use. Our children go to school under trees and unfit buildings and yet we spend money to buy food we could grow on our own soil.

The Africans have been weaving their clothes before colonization and they still do. The cloth weaving industries in African countries can be improved upon to meet modern demand, style and taste. Africa has a big artisan populations what are the governments doing to incorporate them into the modern system? Most of the raw materials used in manufacturing everything around you are from either your earth or forest. We should begin thinking about what to do as

91

people to improve our economic standing in the world. Most of you have education and qualifications that if applied can move Africa into a better position than where she is now. We need to start thinking about us, the future of our children and the ones yet unborn. We have helped the world while we remain undeveloped.

We are not given the recognition of the free labor we gave the world to build the current civilization. We laid the foundation for the world we have now. The world lay emphasis on capital and not labor and without labor, ideas and capital with not produce. The world needs all residents on earth including other creatures and features to make it a better place for continuous existence. Humans have taken over; some humans have taken over the administration of the world as if they are the only resident.

Chapter Three

Coping Despite Odds

We are marvelous. We have crossed many difficult obstacles. We become a renowned athlete, a musician, a politician, a doctor, a scientist, an engineer, an actor, an artist, a lawyer, entrepreneurs, and many more in human endeavor, but parts of us are still struggling. Our successes never called for celebration because what we achieved was not expected, it was not part of the plan.

We were different; no they made us felt different, probably out of fear because inwardly they feel our capabilities so they did all they could to dehumanize us. We are imposing, we have dignity, they tried to destroy the unique gift of the Creator to human, but they could not.

Jesse Owens (1913-1980) the Great Athlete won four Gold medals in the Summer Olympics of 1936 in Berlin Germany in the following events: 100 meters, 200 meters, long jump and was part of the 4*100 relay team. Adolf Hitler refused to shake his hands because of his racial bigotry and ignorance. Hitler believed his race was superior to that of Owens.

On the other hand, Owens was magnanimous, he said this about Hitler, quote, "*When I passed the Chancellor waved his hand at me, and I waved at him. I think the writers showed bad taste in criticizing the man of the hour in Germany.*' That was humanity and nobility at the highest point.

The president of the United States at that time did not honor Owens either despite the fact he gave America honor. Jesse Owens, was recognized by, President Dwight Eisenhower in 1955 with the honor, "Ambassador of Sports." Owens was honored by President Gerard Ford in 1976 forty years after the glorious feat in 1936 Summer Olympics,

Berlin, Germany. He later received many posthumous honors.

The black man's capabilities and enormous contribution to the development of the world has been forgotten. The new world was built on the strength of the black man he provided 'free labor' under the most inhumane situation in man's history.

None had been able to sing the way we do. Our music changed the world in the 60s; because we brought style into the way music was composed and sang.

A black-man was among the first expedition that went to the North Pole but he was not recognized.   Matthew Henson a black man and Hillary Peary reached the North Pole in 1909, but the credit went to Peary. Henson was posthumously, honored by the Explorers Club of New York in 1937, and a medal by the United States Navy in 1946.

Africans and Africans in Diaspora fought gallantly in both World Wars but were not decorated. Africans lost over two million men in the Great Wars, but were never praised by those who caused the war.
Dr. Arthur N. Lewin, and many historians have written on the contribution of African- American men and women in all American wars. They were major participants and fought bravely and gallantly.

The history of the Tuskegee Airmen was the most amazing how racism can blindfold a people. Initially, the government was reluctant to train them to be air fighters because of their race. Later they trained at Tuskegee Institute, a school established by Booker T. Washington a renowned black against slavery. These Tuskegee Airmen escorted American bombers past several attacking German fighters and did not lose any bomber to enemy planes.

One third of the Revolutionary War soldiers were Africans, including many of those in President Washington's personal entourage. Black men fought in every naval engagement, and were significant members of President Andrew Jackson's forces at the Battle of New Orleans.

Two hundred black soldiers fought in the civil wars often as shock troops in murderous engagements like the battle of Fort Wagner in which 13 black soldiers won the Congressional Medal of Honor.

The Buffalo Soldiers; mainly black-men formed the ninth and tenth Cavalry that patrolled the Western Frontier for over twenty years. In 1898, during the Spanish American War, the Buffalo Soldiers rescued President Roosevelt and his "Rough Riders ", at the battle of San Juan Hill.

In World War I the entire 369 regiment, "The Harlem Hell-fighters" won the Croix de Guerre, the highest medal for bravery in France.

In World War II, Doree Miller, a black cook in the air force, who was never trained to use anti-aircraft gun, shot down five Japanese planes at Pearl Harbor on December 7, 1941.

Despite discrimination meted to blacks throughout American history, they have always supported the nation, especially during periods of need like in wars. Black women also served the country with distinction despite segregation and bigotry.

We had brave and honest black men and women in the past and same qualities in the present. We have talents in all facets of human endeavor but our physical prowess, and features is what the world notices. Blacks are the best when it comes to outdoor sports like soccer, football, baseball, sprinting, running, tennis, boxing, and lifting.

The following list are notable black sports men and women :

Michael Jordan- a retired professional basketball player, now in business with great success.

Michael Duane Johnson- a retired United States sprinter. He won four Olympic gold medals in 1996 in Atlanta and crowned world Champion eight times.

Earvin Johnson Jr(aka Magic Johnson) - a retired American professional basketball player. He is an advocate for HIV/ADS prevention and a philanthropist.

Kareem Abdul- Jabbar- a retired professional basketball player. He is now an author, actor, and coach.

Muhammad Ali-is a retired American Boxer and three times World heavyweight Champion. He was a Gold Medalist in the light heavyweight division at the 1960 Summer Olympics. He is the greatest boxer of all time in the sense that he brought finesse into boxing. He was crowned "sportsman of the Century " ,by Sports Illustrated and "Sports Personality of the Century " by British Broad casting Corporation in 1999. He also received many honors. He currently has Parkinson, disease but that has not slowed him down in his many community and country duties. He is a humanitarian and a devout Muslim.

Arthur Ashe-(1943-1993) the first black tennis player to win at the U. S Open and Wimbledon. He won three major tournaments in his career. He was elected into the Tennis Hall of Fame in 1985. He served in the U.S. Army from 1966-1968. He contacted HIV in 1998 from blood transfusion probably during a heart surgery in 1983.

Althea Gibson-(1927-2003) was a tennis sensation in the 1950s. He won the French Open in 1956. She also won at Wimbledon and U. S, Open Championships. She was inducted into the Tennis Hall of Fame in 1971.

Venus Williams –dominated Women's Tennis in 2000. She won singles titles at Wimbledon, the U.S. Open and the Sydney Olympics. She the Sportswoman of the Year by Sports Illustrated in 2000.

Serena Williams- she was a four times winner of the Australian Tennis Open. She won the singles title at the 1999 U.S. Open. From 2002 to 2003, she won all four Grand Tennis Slam at once: 2002 French Open, Wimbledon, and U.S. titles, and the Australian Open 2003. She won the U.S. Open in 2008.

Every person in the world contributes to everything that the world enjoys today. Do you enjoy chocolate? Chocolate is made possible by the poor African farmer who work bare footed to plant and harvest the cocoa beans that is turned into chocolate after several months of drying in the sun.

Black farmers in Brazil, parts of East and West Africa grow coffee that stimulates and keep the people in cold climate countries warm.

Despite the horrible condition of discrimination, segregation, and colonization blacks contributed immensely to the field of science and engineering.   The following people of African heritage contributed their quota to the fields of science and engineering:

Madam Walker built her own industry to manufacture hair products in the 1900s. She gave an address at the National Negro Business League Convention in 1912 and this quote from her address is still relevant in the 21st century. *"I am a woman who came from the cotton fields in the South. From there I was promoted to the washtub. From there I was promoted to the cook kitchen. And from there I promoted myself into the business of manufacturing hair goods and preparation. I have built my own factory on my own ground.*

George Washington Carver- biologist – he discovered that peanut and soya beans are edible. Peanuts and soya beans are a multi- million businesses today but nobody remembers the black man who made that possible.

Julian Lavon Julian (1899-1975) was a black chemist who pioneered the synthesis of medicinal drugs from plants. He produced the drugs on industrial scale. He pioneered chemical synthesis of the human hormone, steroids, progesterone, and testosterone from plants steroids. His work laid the foundation for cortisone, corticosteroids, and birth control pills. He worked for Gidden Company for many years.

Du Pont did not offer him employment because of the color of his skin despite the fact that he was the most qualified among the candidates. After many years of contributing to Gidden Company, Mayo Clinic, Merck and Up John, he founded his own company Julian Laboratories Inc.1953.

He sold Julian Laboratories U. S. and Mexico factories to SmithKline and the chemical plant in Guatemala to Up John in 1964 and founded Julian Associates and Research Institute. He was inducted into the National Academy of Sciences for his contribution to the sciences in 1973.

David Blackwell – he earned his Doctor of Philosophy in Mathematics at the age of 22 from the University of Illinois. Despite his achievement, he could not secure a post to teach in other universities except a black university. After many years of teaching in a black university, he was hired by the University of California at Berkeley as a professor of Statistics in 1955. He co- authored the book, TheTheory of Games and Statistical Decision" in 1954. He received many honors in Mathematics and Statistics. He won the von Neumann Theory Prize in1979. He is retired and lives in California.

Benjamin Banneker- (1731-1806) was an astronomer, mathematician, surveyor and almanac author and a farmer. He constructed a wooden clock at age 21 that worked and made a replica of pocket watch. He published almanac from 1792-1797. He was a member of the surveyor team on Federal Territory that later became Washington D.C. He was a strong member of anti-slavery movement.

Edward Bouchet (1852-1919) was the first black to graduate from Yale in 1874. He got his Ph. D in Physics in 1876 also from Yale. He taught physics and chemistry in the Institute for Colored Youth for 26 years in a Quaker institution, Philadelphia.

Garret A. Morgan- (1877-1963) he invented a respiratory protective hood, hair- straightening preparation, and patent a traffic signal, he later sold the rights of the traffic signal to General Electric. He used his hood to save workers entrapped in a tunnel system filled with fumes. He received a Gold Medal of Bravery award by citizens of Cleveland, Ohio, however, his nomination for the Carnegie Medal denied due to the color of his skin. He established a newspaper called Cleveland Call.

Frederick M. Jones-(1893-1961) he invented refrigeration systems for trucks and railroad cars and this revolutionized the food industry. He built a transmitter for Hallock's radio station in Minnesota. He patented a ticket- dispensing machine. He had patents for the following equipment that are vital to today's living: portable x-ray machine, sound equipment, air conditioning units, gas-engines. He also developed an air conditioning system for military field hospitals and kitchens. He had over sixty patents to his name. In 1944, he was elected into the American Society of Engineers and in 1977 inducted into the Minnesota Inventors Hall of Fame.

Elijah McCoy-(1843-1929) was an engineer he studied engineering at Edinburgh, Scotland.   He invented an automatic lubricator for oiling the steam engine of locomotives and boats. He got his patent in 1872 in the U.S. for this feat. He had over 57 patents relating to lubrication, folding ironing boards, and lawn sprinklers. The invention of lubricators made the railroads saved time and moved faster. The lubricators are use on naval vessels, oil drilling rigs and mining equipment. He sold his patents rights to inventors due to lack of investments fund. He later formed his own company named Elijah McCoy Manufacturing Company. In 2001, he was inducted into the National Inventors Hall of Fame in Akron, Ohio.

David Blanding-an engineer with Boeing helped developed sophisticated electric actuators for advanced unmanned air systems, space vehicles and commercial airplanes. The actuators are use on the x-45 Joint Unmanned Combat System, the x-37space technology demonstrator and 787 Dream-liner. This new device replaced the traditional hydraulically powered actuators. He is active in Boeing educational program for minority students. He is a member of International Council of Aeronautical Sciences.

Mae Jamison- She is a physician, a dancer, engineer and an NASA astronaut. She resigned from NASA in 1993 and formed her company, the Jamison Group the same year. She established a foundation called the Earth We Share, a science camp for ages 12-16 to work and solve current problems in 1994. In 1999, she founded Biosentient Corp to develop a portable device that allows mobile monitoring of the involuntary nervous system. She is a strong advocate of science education. She is on the International Space Hall of Fame. She has received many honors to her name.

Adekoge Olubummo- (1923-1992) was a mathematician, and Physicist. He pioneered the establishment of the forum for Functional Analysis and its Applications.

Carter G. Woodson-(1875-1950) was an author, historian, and founder of the Association for the study of African American Life and History. He is
known as the Father of Black History. He was instrumental in founding the Associated Publishers in 1920, the oldest African- American publishing company.

Mark Dean –holds a Ph. D in electrical engineering from Stanford University. He is an inventor and computer scientist. He holds three patents of IBM personal computer. He became an IBM Fellow in 1997 and was inducted into the National Inventors Hall of Fame the same year.
.

Philip Emeagwali-a computer scientist, geologist observed bees in the making of their honeycomb and was able to use that knowledge to develop a super computer that used 65,000 processors, which perform computation at 31billion calculation per second. He won the Gordon Bell Prize in 1989 for programming the Connection Machine Supercomputer to help analyze petroleum fields.

Rosa Louise McCauley Parks-(1913-2005) On December 1955. She refused to give up her seat to a white passenger. The action led to resistance to the racial segregation that was the law in America. She became deeply involved in the Civil Rights moments. She received many honors for her contribution to the Civil Rights Movements.

Henry Sampson- is an inventor, writer, film- maker, and nuclear engineer. He received Masters and Ph. D in Nuclear Engineering from the University of Illinois Urbana Champaign in 1965 and 1967 respectively. He patented binder system for propellers and explosives and a case bonding systems for cast composite propellants. He co-patented a Gamma-electrical cell used in Nuclear Reactors. He also made films on early black filmmakers. He was in the Navy and earned Atomic Energy Commission honor between1965 to 1967. He won the Black Image Award from Aerospace Corporation in 1982.

Granville Woods-(1856-1910) worked in the railway and became a Chief Engineer of the Steamer. He was denied promotions he deserved, so he resigned and formed the Woods Railway Telegraph Company in 1884. In 1887, he patented the Synchronous Multiplex Railway Telegraph, which allowed communications between train stations from moving trains. He manufactured and sold telephone, telegraph, and electrical equipment. In 1888 Granville Woods developed a system for overhead electric conducting lines for railways. Alexander Graham Bell's Company purchased the rights to Granville T. Woods "telegraphony" enabling him become a full time inventor. He contributed greatly to the modern electric transit systems. By the time of his death in 1910, he had over fifty inventions patented.

Charles R. Drew- (1904-1950) a physician, medical researcher. He developed techniques for blood storage. He applied his knowledge of large- scale blood banks to save lives in World War II. He protested against the practice of racial segregation in the donation of blood of different races since it lacked scientific foundation. In 1943, he served on the American Board of Surgery as examiner. He died in a tragic car accident in 1950 on his way to a medical conference. He was honored posthumously with the Medical School in California named after him.

Lewis Latimer- (1848-1928) an inventor, a drafts man. He made significant contribution to the development of the light bulb. He patented in 1891 the Process of Manufacturing Carbons" an improved method for the production of carbon filaments for light bulbs. He was inducted into the National Inventions Hall of Fame for his work on electric filament manufacturing techniques.

Otis Boykin- (1920-1982) an inventor, engineer. He invented improved electrical resistor for computers, radios, televisions, and assortment of other electric devices. Among his inventions are variable resistor used in guided missiles and small components thick film resistor for computers. He is famous for the pacemaker.

Lloyd Quaterman–(1918-1982) a scientist specialized in fluoride chemistry, nuclear chemistry, and spectroscopy. He worked in many government departments. He was on team of scientists that worked on the Manhattan Project, in New York, New York. He received a Certificate of Recognition from the U.S. War Department in 1945. He also received a Honorary Doctorate of Science from St. Augustine's College in 1971.

Daniel Hale Williams-(1856-1931) was a surgeon and cardiologist. He performed the first successful heart surgery. He founded the Provident Hospital. He set standard for the surgical profession. He was named a charter member of the American College of Surgeons and was a member of the Chicago Surgical Society. The renowned musician Steve Wonder honored him with a song titled the "Black Man" from the album of songs in the Key of Life.

According to recent statistics, forty-five percent of the population in Latin America is believe to be of Africa descent. There are currently approximately 116 million people of African descendants in Latin America. Their ancestors were hard working Africans who worked on the sugar, cocoa, coffee plantations, and in the mines to dig for gold for the Spanish, British and Portuguese colonists. They fought gallantly in wars to defend the colonists and their properties.

The Spanish Colonists reduced the black population by letting them fight in the fore. They were never included in the population census so it was difficult to estimate their number. Without the strength and bravery of these Africans, the Spanish would not have been able to dominate the original inhabitants of South America.

Black people are relegated to the background in Latin America to an extent that, it is difficult to trace the contribution of blacks in the area of invention and science.

Despite all the unequal opportunities available for the black man in Latin America countries, they have been able to use their natural talents to bring fame to countries that do not even recognize their existence. They have brought their talents to the forefront in sports, athletics, soccer, music, dancing, poetry, and working hard to keep themselves going. Some notable among Latin America people of African descendants are as follows:

Ramon Carrilo-(1906-1956) was neurosurgeon, neurobiology, and public health physicians. He contributed valuable research about the brain cells. He contributed novel techniques for neurological diagnosis. He discovered the 'Carrilo Disease' that is cerebral scleroses. He exiled to Brazil due to political upheaval in Argentina. He became very sick, and in sickness and poverty, he produced work on philosophical anthropology.

Gabino Ezeiza alias Black Gabino-(1856-1916) was a musician, song- writer, and a poet. He was excellent with *payadores*. He did over 600 compositions.

Edison Arantes do Nascimento-alas Pele- a retired Brazilian soccer player. He received the title 'Athlete of the Century by the international Olympic Committee. He is also a member of the American National Soccer Hall of Fame.

Edgar Renteria- major Baseball player, his feat in 1997 World Series brought him into the limelight. He received Columbia's greatest honor. He has established a baseball training facility for young Columbians.

Joe Arroyo- He sings and writes about black life in Columbia.

Luis Murillo- was a former governor of Choco a predominantly black area in Columbia. He was outspoken for the black people and the Columbian government were not pleased with the way he defended his people. He was threatened and his family was clearly in danger so he sought asylum to be in the United Stated. He works with Lutheran World Relief in Washington.

Piedad Cordoba- she is a Columbian politician and a lawyer. She is currently a Senator in the Columbian Liberal Party. She is very outspoken against injustices to minorities. She became the president of the Columbian Liberal Party in 2003. There have been many attempts on her life. She is a strong voice in Columbian politics.

Papa Roncon- is a musician and a legendary symbol of Afro –Ecuadorian music.

Monica Chala- won Miss Ecuador Beauty Pageant in 1996. She is involved in uplifting the blacks in Ecuador.

The soccer team in Ecuador is predominantly black. The team qualified for World Cup in 2002. They serve Ecuador with pride and patriotism.

There are many black men and women, who are continuously contributing their best to this world to make it a better place for everyone. It is time the world recognize the contribution of blacks.

Jon Entine in his book, the "Taboo" tried to convince himself that blacks are capable only in sporting activities. Has he ever been to Africa? Well Africans are out door people due to the sunny environment. The black people physique is designed to withstand warm environment and very agile. The African body does not store much fat to create heat for the body for warmth since there is no need for it. The African climate is warm all year round and people have been spending more time out- doors, whereas in the temperate climate people stay indoors in the winter months in the past. Due to advancement in technology for the production of heat producing outer- wears people do not spend much time indoors in winter as it was in the past.

Blacks are not only excellent in sports but in all human endeavors. The only issue is that some people are greedy and take credit for what does not belong to them. Blacks have contributed immensely to human existence in all fields of human endeavor. This modern world would never have been possible without the black person.

The virtue of easy going and temperament of black people should not be interpreted as weakness. This is nature's way of balancing events on earth. If everybody is aggressive, greedy, aloof, and inconsiderate, can you imagine the kind of world this would be? Jon Entine should broaden his experiments and findings to appreciate black people's contribution to science, technology, and the way the world is now.

A recent example of display of high intellect was the wining of grand master of chess by a Zambian, **Amon Simutowe**. His was the third of such victory in the whole world. Chess is a game of the brain not physical.

Since time immemorial, settling conflicts through diplomacy had been the hallmark of blacks. What has happened to black people? We survived under segregation in America, apartheid in South Africa, and European colonization of most part of black Africa. Instead of using the freedom to unite among ourselves, we now see differences in one another that never existed in the past. Different groups lived in harmony except occasional internal conflicts that are resolved through dialogue rather than war.

In America, we did not let the relegation to the background set you back; we established schools, colleges, and continued to demand your civil rights and fought for independence from European domination in Africa. We began to move up. Our strength and bravery in the face of adversity threatened the establishment. They made laws to break us but we became stronger and determined. Jim Crow laws in America, apartheid in South America, and horrible colonial administration in Africa all designed to make the black person less human. The black man overcame all the hardships and struggles.

We fought without weapons but with our brain and determination and won. We persistently demanded our rights and acceptance as equal among men. We fought through all means possible. Sometimes we had to fight like them. We fought peacefully. We demonstrated peacefully, we marched peacefully and hatred of us increased.

There were two systems of laws the written and the unwritten. The rules changes adversely whenever it was in our favor. We were disgraced, embarrassed, and jeered. Miraculously our strength grew day by day. We were resilient we kept moving forward in grace. We were emancipated, voted and be voted for. We are now free in the world but we have not gotten economic freedom.

We are tolerant and forgiving. We have virtues that others lack and as such do not see the difference. We are not pragmatic, we reason deeply before we act. Our peaceful appearance, humble and calmly way we handle life make other people to under estimate us. We have demonstrated in many ways that aggression is not the way to go through life. We have not been aggressive in the way we pursue life and the aggressors have taken advantage of this to give us many labels. Nature balances everything. We are thoughtful and restrained; we weigh issues before we take decisions.

The world is currently going through myriad of problems and challenges due to many rushed decisions taken in the past. The rush to this era civilization in the last six hundred years is creating more problems in the world. The frequent earthquakes, tsunamis, and global warming are probable indications that the earth is being over stretched.

The rush to depend on petroleum and by- products is gradually changing the climate that sustains life. There is evidence of global warming everywhere. It does not require a scientist to know that the air around our atmosphere is changing. The quality of air in big cities at nights and morning is enough to explain global warming. The air is dense and thick at night but get lighter in the morning before humans begin their bustle and hustle activities. All humans do is to acquire and acquire material things as if life is forever.

There is the possibility that humans, through their greed would destroy this world with their inquisitiveness. Since humans began the scientific developments, they do not know when to stop because no major catastrophe had occurred beyond control. There is catastrophe looming but humans have refused to accept their inefficiency. The unusual recent Tsunamis' and Earthquakes are warnings for cautions.

Recently the moon was bombed to test for water and life existence. Humans can destroy but unable to create, humans make things but cannot create. The resources on earth are finite and cannot be replenished or recreated. Those who are advocates for global warming have foresights but the greedy ones are in denial because they want more like the proverbial Oliver Twist.

Life has been improving and getting better from the point of view of material acquisitions yet most black people struggle to get even the minimal. We have to work twice as much to be recognized. Skeptics always find something wrong in anything we do. These skeptics find a way to remind us about slavery that was a result of ignorance and greed.

They remind us of what they did to our ancestors in the past in various ways to stop us from progressing forward.

We are in every facet of American governments; we are in parliament and council members in the United Kingdom. We have been in control of Haiti since we landed in the Northern Hemisphere. We are in control of all former British Colonies in East Africa and West Africa once again. Our struggle ended in South Africa in 1990 when Nelson Mandela became the first black President of South Africa through an election. That was an achievement of great proportion. Black Africans now rule Black Africa.

Africans are portrayed as being incapable of governing themselves and improving the lives of the people. Africa has a well of well-educated people but unfortunately, the education is not reflecting on the people and the environment. Is it because what Africans learn is foreign or because they are not ready to make adjustments to improve on the lives of their own people?

The West does not see any progress in Africa because they do not want to see the strides Africans have made after independent from the colonial rules. African countries gained political independence, but still have long strides to make for economic freedom. Africa should not reject its culture but improve upon them. It has been a rough ride for Africans since 1492 when the Europeans began meddling in the affairs of African people.

African Countries at a glance:

Liberia.
Liberia got its independence in 1847 from the United States. Some freed American slaves, who wanted to move back to Africa, settled in Liberia by the United States of America in 1816. They named their capital Monrovia after the fifth president of the United States Monroe. There were

indigenous Africans when the Americans arrived but the two groups eventually assimilated. The African-Americans ruled Liberia until 1980 when the military took over power under Samuel Doe.

Charles Taylor took over power in 1989. Civil war broke out and instability put the economy of Liberia in shambles, thousands of Liberians died. Charles Taylor became president in 1997. His tenor was brutal, the economy deteriorated and became dysfunctional, and that led to a second civil war in 1999. International involvement to bring peace to the war torn Liberia offered Charles Taylor asylum in Nigeria. Charles Taylor is found guilty for the thousands of people killed in the recent Sierra Leone civil war by the World Court in Hague. Another election held in 2005 and a run off between George Weah, a famous soccer player and Ellen Johnson-Sirleaf, a Harvard trained economist ushered in Ellen Johnson-Sirleaf. She became the first female president of Liberia and of Africa. Liberia exports iron ore, diamond, rubber, and timber. She had embarked on many projects to heal the wounds of long years of civil wars.

Liberia has the following mineral resources: Rubber, iron ore, diamond, gold and mica. The agricultural exports products are coffee, cocoa, timber, palm kernel, and fruits. The main stay of the economy is the exportation of rubber, the minerals, and cocoa. The government should negotiate with these importing countries to establish some processing industries in Liberia to create jobs for the people instead of taking all the raw material to process in their own country.

The government of Liberia should have the development of the people in mind instead of kowtowing to foreign countries. These foreign countries leaders respect their people and every move they make is for the development of their country and people. The Liberia leader currently is a product of the west and she should implement program that is gear towards the improvement of the people and environment. The duties of a leader of a country includes to improve lives of the people, protect the people from outside and internal aggression and to defend the beliefs and culture of the people.

New developmental changes should come to Liberia so that people would be patriotic and any time anyone tries a coup the people would stand up and stop it. Coups are not the best to change political power. Democratic principle should develop strongly in Africa so that people would have a say on governance. The moment citizens are part of the political process they become aware of governance and protect legitimate governments.

Ghana

The oldest Africa country under British Colony to get its independence is Ghana and that was 1957. The area now called Ghana, was inhabited in pre –colonial times by a number of kingdoms like GA-Danmes on the eastern coast, the Asante Empire inland and the Fanti States along the western coast.

The Portuguese came to the coast of Ghana in the 15th century and the Dutch, Danes, British, and Swedes followed due to report of abundance of gold and ivory in the area. The name Ghana came from the Ghana Empire that flourished in the 10th- 13th century along the Upper Niger River all the way to present Mauritania, Mali, and Senegal. Ghana had plenty of gold hence the British called it Gold Coast. The Portuguese built the Elmina Castle in 1481 that later became the holding place for slaves en-route to North and South America.

Ghana has come a long way. Dr. Kwame Nkrumah was the first President of Ghana. He attended Lincoln University in Pennsylvania where he met Marcus Garvey and W.E.B Du Bois. They were involved in demanding freedom for blacks and decolonization of the African continent. When Nkrumah became the President of Ghana, he had laudable programs for the young country and the continent as a whole but the

111

West fearing that Dr. Kwame Nkrumah was moving toward communism assisted in the over throw of Nkrumah's government in January of 1966 after only nine years of freedom from Britain. Dr. Nkrumah spearheaded the formation of the Organization of African Unity. The overthrown of the infant government in Ghana started a domino effect in Africa.

Young military men supported by the West took over power from the African Nationalist all over Africa. There were series of coups in Ghana after the first coup of 1966. Flight Lieutenant Jerry Rawlings came to power in 1982 through another coup. In 1992, the government of Rawlings organized a democratic election and Rawlings was elected in 1992 and again in 1996. Ghana has been stable politically since 1992. The current President elected in 2009 is John Atta Mills. The leaders have not made major efforts to develop people, improve lives, and involve all people in the political and economic process.

Ghana still depends on exports of cocoa, coffee, timbers, and minerals: gold, diamonds, manganese, and bauxite. The exportation of resources where the price is determined and controlled by the importers would forever affect the progress of the country. Ghana should look beyond exports and invest in the development of the people so that people can be creative. The people of a country are the bedrock of development not trading where the vagaries in other countries dictates the price of commodities.

Ghana should form cartel with other cocoa and gold producing countries so that they the sellers dictate prices and not buyers. As long as the current trend continues, there would never be significant progress. The intellectuals and able body men and women that should stay and develop the country flee due to under development and lack of decent jobs and adequate necessities of lives. The Government should be concerned that their citizens had to flee and work

112

in another country and remit money. What hinders Ghana from sustainable development?

Cote d'Ivoire (Ivory Coast)
The area Cote d'Ivoire was home to the following African kingdoms before the arrival of the Europeans in 15th century: Kong, Abron, Baoule, Agri, Indenie, and Sanwi. It became a French colony in 1843 during the scramble for Africa by the Europeans. The system of rule applied to Cote d'Ivoire by the French was association and assimilation. The French made it a point to ensure that the French culture and language is enforced and that the French are superior to the local people.

France needed coffee, cocoa, and palm oil to boost its industrialization that began in 1800s and the Ivoirians' were the right people because they had well developed agriculture system in place before the advent of the Europeans. The French used forced labor system for the plantations. The people resisted vigorously but the French over powered them due to superior firearms

Ivory Coast became independent in 1960 and Felix Houphouet-Boigny became the president. He ruled from 1960 to 1993. There were two coups de-tat in Ivory Coast, 1999 and 2001 after the death of the president, Houphouet-Boigny. Disenfranchisement is what follows when a ruler who rules for so long dies. They become an institution and it is difficult for followers to give their allegiance to someone else. Civil war or chaos follows when such a leader dies and that happened when Houphoet- Boigny died.

Civil war broke out in 2002 and this uprising lasted until 2007. A peaceful agreement among the leaders of the rebel was reached in 2007 and election would be held in 2009. The French government never gave full independence to Cote d'Ivoire. They controlled the economy until 2006. The government of Ivory Coast should start development of the people. The people of Ivory Coast should start taking care of themselves instead of the illusion that they are French.

Ivory Coast leaders should involve the people in decision making to develop talents and move the country forward. Many talented Ivorian can move the country forward if the government has faith in the citizens instead of over reliance on France. The people of Africa are not an extension of France and the government should begin to develop the people through adequate and functional education. The educated Ivoirians move to France instead of spending their energy in their own country to develop it.

Sierra Leone

The early inhabitants of Sierra Leone were the Sharbro, Limba, Temine, Tyra Mende and Kono people. These early people used iron in the 9th century and agriculture was their main occupation due to the dense forest. The Portuguese reached this area in 1462 and named it Sierra de Leone meaning Lion Mountains.   The Portuguese built a fort on the coast in 1495 for trading. The Dutch joined the Portuguese later and became involved in the slave trade. The English joined the heinous trade in 1562. They introduced brutal means to the trade by using swords and guns to force people to get into the forts. They chained the captured people in the most inhumane way and shipped them off to the Americas.

In 1787, Britain settled London's black people in Sierra Leone. These people fought on the side of Britain during the American Revolution wars and were promised freedom by the British Some freed blacks from Nova Scotia and black Americans who escaped to Canada due to the brutally of slavery settled in Sierra Leone as well. The British settled more freed ex-slaves in 1792 and founded Freetown. The area became a British Colony in 1808. Fourah Bay College established in 1827 as an institution for English speaking West Africans became the center of education.

There were riots from 1935-1955 because of monopoly on mineral mining by the De Beers Company owned By Cecil Rhodes a Briton. The people also resisted the foreign domination and taxation. After over fifty–three years under British harsh administration, Sierra Leone became independence in 1961 due to demand of the nationalists and Milton Margai became the first Prime Minister. Margai died in 1964 his brother Albert Margai succeeded him. A bloodless coup occurred in 1967 and Siaka Stevens won an election that followed the coup. Since the first coup de tat, the country had witnessed over ten coups within a period of ten years.

A civil war broke out in 1991 due to corruption, instability, misuse of public funds and neglect of the masses, and ineptitude of government. Young children recruited to fight in the war without adequate training died in their thousands. The civil war continued for a number of years and the United Nations sent a peacekeeping force in 1998 supported by Union of African soldiers from various African countries. The same year, the rebel militants took five hundred United Nations peacekeepers hostage. This action protracted the war that created thousands of refugees who fled to Liberia and Guinea. The war ended in 2002 through the mediation of United Nation. An election held in 2007 brought in Ernest Bai Koroma, the current president of Sierra Leone.

Sierra Leone is rich in the following minerals: Diamonds, Bauxite, Rutile, Titanium, and Iron Ore. The mines are owned by foreign companies. United States and European investors own Sierra Rutile Limited, the major mining consortium. Logging is a common occupation but subsistence farming occupied about 52% of the population. A country with rich mineral resources, fertile land, and great natural harbor like Sierra Leone should never be poor. Many countries are rich from Sierra Leone resources while the citizens of Sierra Leone remain poor.

The new administration of Sierra Leone should put the people first. Citizens of a country want their government to protect them and make everyday living easy and pleasant. Sierra Leone resources are what industries in developed countries depend on to boost their economy and improve the living standard of the people. The leaders of Sierra Leone should begin to negotiate in their own favor for the exploration of the natural resources. The investors should invest in projects that would create jobs tor the country in the same way they help governments in their home countries. They should contribute to the development of the country where they make their money if they had not taken the initiate to do so.

It is sad when leaders who control diamond, gold, bauxite and other mineral resources say they do not have the capital. Who has capital?
Ownership of paper currency as capital is controlling the world economy instead of capital derived from resources and the productivity of people. This new view of capital is putting African countries at great disadvantage since they cannot even mint their own currency, even if they do their currency does not command international value.   Sierra Leone and many Africa countries hold the Ace card in the world but do not know how to govern.

The present African is even worse than their ancestors who allowed slave trade, at least hey resisted slave trade but the current Africans made themselves slaves. The educated Africans should be fully involved in the political process of their respective countries.   Africa has experts in all spheres of human endeavors; the only problem is trust; there is no trust among black people. Mistrust is the bane of the black race; and that is why instead of development with the vast knowledge acquired from the west and east, it is retrogressing.

If the leaders of Sierra Leone have plans to improve the lives of people of Sierra Leone, they have resources for it.

The achievement of good leaders is improved life of the people. Improvement of life is what the western governments do and that is why they are ahead in human development. In the west, everybody is important. If the leaders of Sierra Leone see the people as the most important resources they have then the country would move forward because everyone would see itself as part of the country and patriotic tendencies would come natural to the people and they would defend a government who provides and allow development and achievement of dreams.

The human development progress by the governments of the west is achievable in Sierra Leone if the government of Sierra Leone makes the citizens the centerpiece of governance. The west has good environments, stability, and concern for every citizen.

Senegal

Senegal was part of the old Ghana Empire that flourished in the 11th to 14th centuries in West Africa. The Mandingo and Jolof empires later occupied the area after the fall of the Ghana and Songhai empires.

The Portuguese came to the area in early 1400s and that ended the glorious day of the existing empires. The following Europeans followed the Portuguese; Netherlands, England, and later France. In 1677, France established a permanent settlement in Senegal on the Island of Goree. Goree was a notorious departure points for slave trade during the slave trade period. Senegal became a possession of France in 1840 and France established itself economically and militarily amid resistance from the indigenous population. France forced the indigenous population to cultivate peanuts for France.

In 1914, France allowed Senegal to elect a representative to France Parliament under the assimilation and association policy. A federation of Senegal and Mali formed in 1959 became independent in June of1960. Unfortunately, the federation lasted only two months. Senegal became independent in September 1960 and Leopold Senghor the Prime Minister. He was in power from 1960 to 1981 when he retired and handed power to Abdou Diouf.

Sene-Gambia a union between Senegal and Gambia formed in 1982 and dissolved in 1989. Diouf was defeated in an election in 2000 by Abdoulaye Wade. In 2004, Wade signed a peace treaty with separatist movement in the Casamance region. The separatist movement formed over twenty years, have been demanding the secession of Casamance from Senegal, due to economy and social neglect by Senegal governments.

The exports of Senegal are fish, chemicals, peanuts, cotton, and calcium phosphate. The majority of the population is engaged in agriculture. Poverty is a chronic problem in Africa because the leaders do not see themselves as the father of the nation. Programs instituted do not take the progress of people into consideration.

The average Senegalese is a hard working individual but they need support from the government to help them improve on the way they go about their business. The government should educate the people in the modern way of farming to increase productivity. The government should assist small businesses with loans and equipment for farming and fishing. The government should encourage businesses to aid the farmers by buying produce from the farms. This would make the farmers produce more and have funds to live on and improve their lives. Senegal has been a peaceful country but emphasis needs to be placed on human development to stop young adults from risking their lives by trying to escape to Europe on boats. Many of these young men die and some end up in prisons in these foreign lands.

The governments of Senegal should involve the people in the political process so that the development of every citizen becomes the goal. People who go abroad work for their livelihood and if work and decent environment are available in Senegal these people would stay and work in their own country. People make a country and the government of Senegal should work towards a better life for the citizenry. The French government aim is to provide job opportunity for every citizen of France. What is the goal of the government of Sierra Leone? Is Sierra Leone a colony of France? If no the government should focus on ways to develop the country and the people. The government impresses foreign countries instead of looking inward and finding solutions to poverty that has become an endemic.

Gambia

In the 9th to 10th century Arab scholars and traders came to the area now Gambia to trade in gold and ivory and educate people in Islamic education. Gambia was part of Ghana and Songhai empires that flourished in the area in 11th to 12th centuries. It became part of the Mali Empire at the beginning of the 14th century.

The Portuguese reached the area in mid -15th century and dominated the trade. The Portuguese sold the right to trade on the River Gambia to Britain in 1588. France and Britain fought over the possession of Gambia until the signing of the treaty of Versailles in 1783. Millions of people were taken from this area during the period of the Triangular Atlantic Slave trade. The people were forcefully taken and sometimes through raids or in war. Bathurst the capital of Gambia (now Banjul), was established in 1816 by the British. Gambia became a British Colony in 1889. Gambia troops fought with the Allies in Burma in World War II.

Gambia was the last of the British African colonies to be independent in 1970 and the first Prime Minister was Dauda Kairaba Jawara. Gambia is a small country surrounded on the mainland by Senegal and has a small coastline. The main export crop is groundnut/peanuts. Fisheries and subsistence farming engage over 70% of the population. The government should develop processing of the peanuts at home and then export. The processing plants would create jobs and hence more revenue for the people and government. The companies buying the groundnut should set up processing plant in Gambia so that the people of Gambia get more benefit from the groundnuts they export.

Groundnuts are processed and use in the production of food, creams, soap and in pharmaceutical products overseas. The pharmaceutical companies made huge profits and they should be investing in Gambia to improve the lives of the people who work to produce the groundnuts. It is time companies that depend on Gambia resources for their industries put something back in the country that supply the raw material.

Gambia has remained under developed and impoverished and yet these people work very hard to supply groundnuts to multi-million companies. The government of Gambia should negotiate for the development of their people. Poverty should be reduced by the government through engaging the people in employment and making them the focus of governance.   Gambia only has political independence and not economic power. The economic system Britain set up to feed its industries is still in operation.   A country can only progress when it is in charge of its economic independence.

Mali
Mali was part of the Ghana, Mali, and Songhai empires that flourished in the 11th to 15th centuries in West Africa. The empires were rich in gold, salt, and ivory. The various empires at that time participated in the trans- Sahara trading with North Africa and the Arabs. The present Mali fell under French control in the 1800s.

Mali became independent in 1960 and Modibo Keita was the first Prime Minister. He implemented socialist ideologies and nationalized most economic resources. Modibo Keita's government was over thrown in 1968 through a bloodless coup led by Moussa Traore. There were several coups in

120

between the election of Alpha Oumar Konare in 1992 as the president. Amodou Toumani Toure was elected president in 2002.

The main stay of the Mali economy is agriculture, cotton is the largest export. Mali is the third largest producer of Gold in Africa. It has deposits of kaolinite, salt, phosphates, and limestone in commercial quantities. In addition, Mali produces tobacco, rice, millet, corn, and vegetables.

Despite all the resources majority of the people in Mali are poor. The resources of the country are not used to the benefit of the people. The government should develop the people and the companies importing raw material from Mali could establish factories in Mali to create jobs for the people. These companies have been importing raw materials from Mali ever since the scramble for Africa but have not thought it fit to set up factories in Mali to engage the people.

The people of Mali deserve a decent way of living just like any other human being in any country. The leaders of Mali should be responsible to improve life and make their citizens enjoy a comfortable existence. The government should emulate the way of governance of their foreign political friends. These foreign governments make the people the main reason for governance. The politicians in Africa do not see the people as the reason for governance. They treat public property as personal and are in most cases not accountable to the people.

In 2005, the Mali government granted the construction of a railroad to the Savage Corporation based in Salt Lake City, United States of America. The health situation in Mali is very deplorable. Malaria, cholera, and tuberculosis kill many people every year. It is surprising the government of Mali has not been able to reduce the incidence of these diseases. These diseases thrive in dirty environment. These diseases could be eradicated if the environment is clean and people drink clean water. Please, you do not need technology to inculcate cleanliness. It is a matter of the government educating people on healthy living and the causes of most of these diseases. The government cannot continue to neglect the uneducated members of the society. These people form the largest member of the society and they produce food for the country.

The outside world does not see Mali in the eyes of the affluent but through the eyes of the peasants. Europe became a great continent when it stated taking care of the peasants. America is great became the environment is conducive for people to develop their talents for a better life and everybody has access to the basics of life: portable water, lights, and decent accommodation.

Malian tradition is passed on from generation to generation through *griots*; these are musicians who narrate stories from the past. Some famous Malian musicians are Oumou Sangare, Toumani Diabate, forka Toure and Salif Keita.

Guinea
Guinea was part of the Ancient Ghana Empire around 900AD. It became part of the following empires Mali, Sossou, and Songhai. These empires were displacing one another during that period. The Portuguese came to the coast of Guinea in the 15th centuries and began enslaving the people in early 16th century. The French colonized Guinea in 1890.

Guinea was the first French Colony to gain independence in 1958. Ahmed Sekou Toure was the first President. He adopted socialist ideology and was close to the eastern bloc, thus former Soviet Union and definitely, the western power did not appreciate that move. Sekou Toure died in 1984, and was succeeded by Lansana Conte. Conte died in 2008 after twenty years as president of Guinea. His tenor witnessed many public outcry due to corruption, neglect of the masses, and dictatorial policies.

Moussa Camera led a coup the same day Conte died and he is still the leader of Guinea.

Guinea is very rich in mineral resources such as bauxite has the fourth largest deposit in the world, iron ore, diamonds, gold, and uranium. Guinea has excellent soil, water, and climate conditions that can enable the country to develop large mechanized agriculture.

The mineral deposits in Guinea are jointly managed by the government of Guinea and the following foreign companies-The Compagnie de Bauxite, owned by Aluminum Company of America and Rio Tinto Alcan Inc, a Canadian company, the Bauxite de Kindo, and Russki Alumina, a Russian company. Alcon-Alcan has signed contracts with the government of Guinea to build a large alumina refinery with a combined capacity of 4 million metric tons per year.

AREDOR, a joint diamond mining venture consist of companies from Australia, British and Swiss consortium began exploration in 1984.. First City of Canada purchased the share of the consortium in 1996. Among the latest addition to foreign companies in Guinea is, Hyper-dynamics Corporation of America

The people of Guinea live under poor conditions despite the wealth of the country. The companies that mine the mineral resources in Guinea are multi- billion corporations but the wealth derived mostly from the mineral resources of Guinea has not trickled down to the people of Guinea. You see nothing has changed in the relationship of Europe and America with African people. The leaders of Africa still behave like their predecessors who did not have regard for their people and allowed enslavement of their people by Europe and America. These Guinea leaders negotiate the resources of the country to benefit themselves and cohorts.

The processing of these minerals can take place in Guinea to give the people of Guinea employment opportunity, instead of taking them to their country to develop. These corporations should train the people of Guinea to work in their companies to improve their standard of living.

Notwithstanding, the rich mineral resources mined and sold, the government has not made adequate provision for education of school age children. Only 40% of primary school age children attend schools. It is a shame that children would not attend school and a government does nothing. What kind of future does such a government envisage for the children who are not acquiring education? The people who rule Guinea do not have any plans for the development of the country and people. They rule for power's sake. Guinea has not witnessed any progress despite the natural wealth of the area. The country belongs to all people in Guinea and not the personal property of the rulers.

The foreign countries and companies these leaders depend on respect their fellow citizens and endeavor to provide secure environment for the people to develop their various talents. Why is it difficult for the leaders of Guinea to have the development of their people as their goal? The people of Guinea are hard- working people who should not live in poverty and misery. A leader is for the progress of the people in a nation. It is the reverse in Guinea, where the leaders live better while the larger population lives in poverty and in an environment, without basic things of life like portable drinking water, electricity, decent schools, and good accommodation. The leaders do not deserve a better living condition than the populace.

Guinea-Bissau
Guinea-Bissau was part of the Mali Empire in the 15th century. The Portuguese came to the area in the mid- 15th century and named the coastline Slave Coast because of the large population of people the Portuguese later turned into slaves. In 1956, the people rebelled for independence from

the Portuguese under the leadership of Amilcar Cabral. After long struggle, they unilateral declared independence in 1973. The international communities recognized Guinea-Bissau as an independent state in 1974, after the fall of Estado Novo of Portugal.

Guinea Bissau had been under a revolutionary mode of government since independence. The first multi- party election was held in 1984. There have been series of coups in Guinea- Bissau and these brought economic instability. Raimundo Pereira was an interim president until an election in June 2009. Malam Bacai Sanha became president in a runoff election in September of 2009.

The economy of Guinea depends on agriculture, fishery, cashew nuts, and peanuts. The long civil war has seriously affected the economic development of Guinea- Bissau. It is one of the poorest countries in the world. The merger resources of the country go into procuring arms to fight among themselves instead of developing the people. Power politics is a bane of Guinea-Bissau.

Equatorial-Guinea
Equatorial- Guinea comprise of a mainland (Rio Muni) and several islands in the Atlantic Ocean (Corisco, Elobey Grande,Elobey Chico, Annobon,and Bioko) and the capital is Malabo. The original inhabitants were the African short people. The Bantus migrated to the area between 17th to 19th centuries. The Portuguese colonized Equatorial Guinea in 1474. Portugal exchanged the islands of Annobon and Bioko with Spain in 1778 for land in the Americas. It was also controlled by the British from 1827-1843. It finally became a Spanish colony in 1900. The mainland and the islands united in 1959.

Presidents Obion and Francisco Macias Nguema ruled Equatorial Guinea with iron hands. These rulers did not have regards for their citizens. They neglected development and the country's revenue were used for their personal wants. Foreigners enjoy freedom than the citizens of Equatorial Guinea.

Cocoa was the main export of the country until 1996 when petroleum became the major source of income. The revenue of the country has increased dramatically but this increase in wealth has only benefited the few elites. Majority of the population of 500,000 are poor despite the annual per capital income of about $30,000. The president gives free access to international companies to operate the oil fields while neglected the development of the people. What kind of a leader has no regard for his citizens? The international community will always look the other way because they get benefits from Equatorial-Guinea that are more important than to be concern about how the leaders treat their citizens. The leaders of Equatorial Guinea should be ashamed of themselves for the way they treat the less privilege citizens. It is shameful, despite the revenue from petroleum majority of the people still lack basic amenities. The leaders are not the face of Equatorial Guinea it is the people.

Burkina Faso
The people of Burkina Faso were hunters in the 12th century, and they hunted with scrapers, chisels, and arrowheads. The Mossi and Yatenga kingdoms flourished in this area in the 12th century. Those kingdoms fell under the French and British expedition in that century. It became a French colony in 1896 after series of wars and fierce opposition from the people on foreign domination. The people eventually subdued by the gun power of the French.

In 1958, it became independent under the name Upper Volta. The first president was Maurice Yameogo. In less than seven years as sovereign state, the military took over power in 1966 due to civil unrest and misrule by the civilian government. Sangoule Lamizan became the Head of State under military dispensation. A bloodless coup in 1980 led by Saye Zerbo replaced the government of Lamizan. There was another coup in 1982 led by Jean-Baptiste Ouedraogo due to ineptitude of the government of Zerbo. There was another coup staged by Thomas Sankara in 1983. Sankara leaned towards Marxist and Leninist ideology, and he changed the name of the country from Upper Volta to Burkina Faso (meaning-the country of honorable people). A palace coup brought Blaise Compaore to power in 1987

Burkina Faso is rich in the following mineral resources-manganese, limestone, marble, copper, iron, pumice, salt, phosphate and gold. Despite the large deposit of mineral resources, 80% of the country's population is engaged in subsistence agriculture. The farmers rear livestock and cultivate sorghum, millet, corn, peanuts, rice, and cotton.

Formal education is beyond the reach of most people because it is very expensive. The government of Burkina Faso should take the responsibility of offering some public education to the people so that they can move forward in this knowledge world. The people are hard- working but the government needs to assist the people in what they do by proving technical support for farmers. The cotton producing countries should form a cartel like oil producing country so that they can dictate the price of cotton. Items made with real cotton are very expensive and growers of cotton should enjoy the same life style like the importers of cotton. The other solution to the country's poverty is to form partnership with companies that mine the mineral resources to set up processing plants in Burkina Faso to create jobs for the people. The government should be concerned about the development of the people.

How could one person be winning the presidential election for almost twenty years without any improvement in the lives of his citizens? . Is Burkina Faso practicing monarchy or democratic system? These sit tight leaders should be ashamed of themselves. The fact that they stay in power for so long means that they gagged the freedom of their people.

The people cannot oppose the power of the leaders or else they lose their lives. This is the reason progress is eluding most African countries. Freedom for the people generates more ideas that can benefit all people. The people of Burkina Faso work very hard but they are one of the poorest people on earth.

Togo

Ewe and Mina kingdoms occupied the area of present day Togo in the 12th century. People migrated from the countries of Ghana, Nigeria, and Benin to the area between the 11th and 16th centuries. The coastal area of Togo became a major trading post for slaves in the 16th century.

In 1884, a treaty signed in Togo Ville in Germany, made Togo a German territory. Togo became a German colony in 1905. After the defeat of Germany in the First World War in 1914, Togo became the French and British colony.   The part of Togo administered by the British became part of Ghana in 1957. French Togo became independent in 1960 under Sylvanus Olympia. A group of soldiers led by Etienne Eyadema Gnassingbe assassinated Olympia in a military coup in 1963. The soldiers did not give the young country any change to develop after the French handed political power back to the people of Togo. Three years is not enough time to judge the progress of a young country.

 Eyadema Gnassingbe ruled the country with iron hands for thirty- eight years and died in 2005. The son of Gnassingbe succeeded him and the reaction of the international community was condemnation with the exception of France, Senegal, and Nigeria. Faure Gnassingbe stepped down, but he won the presidential election conducted afterwards.

The economy of Togo depends on phosphate, limestone, and marble mining. Togo has a large cement factory that supply finished products to neighboring countries. Togo also produces cotton, coffee, and cocoa for export. Majority of the people depend on subsistence farming.

The wealth of Togo does not reflect on the indigenous population. The government does not offer the people opportunities to improve their lives. This scenario is common in Africa where the wealth of the nations are controlled and used by the ruling classes, with little or no attention to the predicament of the populace.

Why do the military disrupt legitimate government and take power in African countries. These military leaders set back the progress of their countries. They took power from elected legitimate leaders and rule on behalf of the colonial powers, whom the nationalist fought to gain independence. The case of Togo is a typical example where foreigners control the economy, while the citizens work under the foreigners. France kept Eyadema in power while the resources of Togo were purchased at prices that favor the buyer; France. The people never benefit from the wealth of the country from the government selling the resources of the country. The people live in poverty and continue to do what their ancestors before them did.

Now that Faure Gnassingbe, the son of Eyadema is the president, he should not continue to administer Togo in the style of his father because he did not improve the lives of his people. He was president for himself and the foreign power that perpetuated his rule. How do African governments in power feel when their people are rated as the poorest in the world even though these people work hard each waking day?

Benin
The kingdom of Dahomey occupied the coastal area of the present day Republic of Benin. The kingdom comprised of different ethnicities that run away from slave trade that was prevalent in the area in the 15th century.

Dahomey was a maritime military kingdom. They had an elite female military corps. The Europeans named them the Amazons due to their fearlessness and strong prowess. Eventually, the kingdom joined in the slave trade and it flourished for three hundred years. Dahomey lost its power by the middle of the 19th century to the French who took over the area in 1892.

Dahomey gained independence from the French in 1960. The first president was Hubert Maga. Mathieu Kerekou came to power through a military coup in 1972. He changed the name of the country from Dahomey to the Peoples Republic of Benin in 1975. Kerekou was defeated in an election in 1991 by Nicephore Soglo. Soglo lost to Yayi Bori in 2006 presidential elections.

The country has large resources but the wealth of the country has not tickled down to improve the lives of the populace. Benin has the following minerals in commercial quantities: Off shore petroleum, iron ore, phosphates, chromium, rutile, marble, diamonds, and limestone. The governments of Benin are not making adequate effort to educate the people. Western education has changed the way things were and in order for any people to progress in this 21st century they need to have educated people. It is through education that people can understand their own culture and learn from other cultures to improve themselves.

The government needs to embark on the development of the people. Not every country will be become industrialized like Europe countries and America. Benin should capitalize on the advantages of agriculture by assisting farmers and using modern technologies in agriculture. The government should subsidize the farmers, and businesses should buy the harvest from farmers and process them for sale and excess harvest should be stored in silos. The governments in the west subsidize their farmers heavily, and this is the reason a farmer in Europe or America enjoys the same standard of living like anyone else. Farming is the largest employer of labor and government involvement would make agriculture attractive and lucrative. There are markets for Africa food overseas due to a very large population of blacks in Diaspora.

The government of Benin governs with the same platform the French colonial masters established. There has to be positive changes in the way Benin governs the people in order to achieve progress for the people. The leaders of Benin have to involve the people in the business of government move the people and nation forward. The few elites and politician cannot do it alone unless the whole populace is involved. The colonialist left Benin over forty years ago but Benin cannot do anything on her own without involvement of the former colonial leaders. Why should Benin be looking backward after it fought for independence from France? The military leaders who came to power after the country's independence wanted power and not the progress of their nation.

These leaders have built mansions for themselves what about improvement in the abode of the ordinary person. There has not been improvement in the houses of the people particularly in the rural areas. The leaders live in mansions and enjoy comfortable lives comparable to Europe or America leaders and majority of their citizens wallow in object poverty.

The government should grant the people freedom to express themselves and be creative. Benin should learn from France the way it protects its people. It is all the citizens of a country, working together on a common front, that build a nation, and not the few elites and political leaders. The leaders of Benin should learn the development of people from the European Union and America.

Nigeria

Bantu migrants who spread across most central and southern Africa occupied the area of present day Nigeria. The Nok people who developed terracotta sculptures lived in the central part of Nigeria, the Hausa and the Kanem –Bornu Empires flourished in the Northern part of Nigeria in the 14th centuries. The Fulanis, led by Usman dan Fodio conquered the Hausa States in the early part of the 19th century. Usman dan Fodio spread the religion of Islam during and after the conquest. He also established the Fulani Empire in the conquered areas. The Europeans came to the Fulani Empire in 1903 and divided most of the empire among themselves.

The Yoruba kingdoms of Ife and Oyo were prominent in the South Western part of Nigeria down to part of Benin Republic in the 700-1400. The Yoruba people produced terracotta and bronze heads. Another kingdom is the Benin kingdom whose power lasted between 15th to the 19th centuries. The Nri kingdom of Igbo people, flourished in South-East of Nigeria around the 10th century.

The Portuguese colonized Eko, a coastal city in Nigeria and changed the name of the city to Lagos. The Portuguese traded in Lagos and engaged in slave trade. The British took power from the Portuguese, and moved into the interior of Nigeria and traded in goods and slaves in 1885.
Nigeria became part of the British Empire in 1901. The British united the Southern and Northern Nigeria in 1914. Slavery did not stop in Northern part of Nigeria until 1936.

Nigeria became independence from British rule in 1960. Three ethnic based political parties, The Nigeria People Congress based in the North, the National Council of Nigeria, and the Cameroon in South East, and the Action Group based in the West formed the government, and Nnamdi Azikiwe was made the Governor General. The country became a Federal Republic in 1963 and Nnamdi Azikiwe became the first President.

A series of military coups derailed the young country from 1966 to 1967 that cumulated into a 30 months bloody civil war with millions of people killed and thousands displaced. There was oil boom immediately after the war and this helped in the reconstruction of infrastructures destroyed during the civil war.

There was mismanagement of funds and misappropriation into irrelevant programs. If Nigeria's revenue accumulated in the 1970s have been invested in water and power amenities, Nigeria would have been an advanced developed country in Africa.

Despite the wealth from oil revenues Nigeria has not been able to provide its teeming population with good drinking water and regular power supply. Most industrial development depends on regular supplies of electricity and water.

The country returned to democratic form of government in 1979 but it was short lived due to corruption and ineptitude. The soldiers came back but they were worse than the politician they blamed and replaced. The military had ruled Nigeria for a longer period than the elected political leaders therefore the current situation in Nigeria is a result of military intervention in the young republic in 1967.

A military ruler who promised he would return the power to the politician ruled for eight years and he annulled the only political election adjudged by the world as being fair. This former president had not thought it fit to let the people of Nigeria know why he annulled the election. That is the kind of power African leaders wage over the citizens, they just do whatever they like and noone dare question their acts. The winner of that election Abiola died in prison. Shehu Yaradua was a very prominent Nigerian politician and entrepreneur, also died in prison.

Nigeria had its first military brutal dictator Abacha and he died disgracefully in power. An interim government held the mantle of power until an election in 1999. The People's Democratic Party won the election of 1999 and won again in 2007.

Nigeria is rich in both human and natural resources. Nigerians work hard and want to improve their lives and live a better life. The country had not had long periods of stability to develop sturdily since achieving independence in 1960 from the British. Nigerians are resilient people and with good and sincere leadership, Nigeria could be the giant in the sun it is aspiring to be. Nigeria has the potential to be a developed country but it lacks visionary leaders.

Nigeria's natural resources are; petroleum of high quality, natural gas, coal, bauxite, tantalite, gold, tin, iron ore, limestone, lead, and zinc. The revenue derives from the aforementioned resources are not use by the political leaders to improve infrastructure or provide basic amenities that all citizens can enjoy. The revenues from petroleum alone if well invested could bring significant changes to the country. Industries could be set up and jobs created if the leaders care about the people.

Nigerian has free education therefore more children have access to education; but the environment has not been conducive for complex industrial businesses that create employment opportunities. Lack of planned environment and system discourage people from investing in Nigeria.

The leaders do not encourage the development of the people. The leaders embroil themselves on petty matters that do not bring or encourage progress. Visionary leaders move a nation towards progress, but alas, Nigeria lack leaders who are genuinely interested in creating an environment that would aid people to develop their potentials. Nigerian leaders like most African leaders do not have interest in developing high standard of living for their citizens. Even when there are job or project opportunities, the Nigerian leaders would rather employ foreigners to do the job. African leaders have not understood the essence of governance. Nigeria needs a new direction where everybody matters.

The illiterates, literates and everybody should be actively involved in building a nation that would be able to support its people. Resources are available; what are lacking are leaders who would be able to bring out the patriotic instinct in everyone to make Nigeria a country to love and die for. A leader has to be selfless in order to lead a nation.

Nigeria has been involved in stabilizing the West African region by mediating in conflicts. Nigeria supported South Africa during the struggles for freedom from the then South African apartheid regime. Nigeria is a prominent member of the African Union.

Cameroon
Early inhabitants of present day Cameroon were the Sao civilization around Lake Chad and the Baka hunter gathering in the southeastern rain forest.
The Portuguese explorers came to the coast of Cameroon in the 15th century and named the area Rio dos Camaroes, (The River of Prawns) and this name from usage became Cameroon. Cameroon became a German colony in 1884. Fulani soldiers founded the Adamawa Emirates in the Northern part of Cameroon in the 19th century.
 After the defeat of Germany in the First World War, Britain and France split Cameroon into British and French Cameroon.

 In 1960, Cameroon gained independence from France under President Ahmadou Ahidjo. The southern part, the British Cameroon united with French Cameroon in 1961 and formed The Federal Republic of Cameroon. Ahmadou Ahidjo's ideology was planned liberalism. He used money from cash crops and petroleum to create national cash reserves, and he paid farmers and financed major development projects. The projects failed due lack of trained personnel to manage the projects and endemic corruption. Ahidjo ruled for twenty- two years, he stepped down from the presidency in 1982 and handed the power to Paul Biya.

 The presidency in Cameroon has enormous power because he controls all resources and has absolute authority. Cronyism and corruption had hindered progress in Cameroon. The people are mistreated with no regard whatsoever by the police. There is an unspoken tension in Cameroon between the Anglophone and the French speakers because of the domination of the body polity by the French speakers since independence in 1961.
Free education is accessible to most children and Cameroon has a very high school attendance. Cameroon has a higher per capita income but does not reflect on most people. The few elites enjoy the best of everything. Seventy percent of Cameroon population is engaged in farming. They produce the following crops: banana, cocoa, sugarcane, oil palms, rubber, tea, coffee, tobacco, cotton, peanuts, and rice. Fishing is predominant in the coastal regions.

 Europeans own and manage the logging industry in Cameroon.   Petroleum export is the main stay of Cameroon economy. Cameroon has the potential to be an industrialized nation but nepotism and lack of concern for the masses has not allowed the government to tap into the human resources and develop them for the country to leap into a better future.

Gabon
The early inhabitants of Gabon were the little people, the Europeans called the Pygmies. The Bantus took over the area through migration from the central part of Africa in the 14th century. The Portuguese arrived in the area in the 15th century and named it Gabon. The French reached the area in 1875 and colonized it.
Gabon became independence in 1960 and the first president was Leon M'ba. M'ba was a dictator and got the support of

the French due to their logging businesses in Gabon. M'ba died in 1967, and succeeded by Bongo.

Bongo followed the same dictatorial mode of governance like his predecessor. He died in June 2009. The interim president is Rose Francine Rogombe, the senate president.

Gabon depends on off shore oil exploration. It exports manganese, iron, and timber. It has a large uranium deposits.
The government of Gabon does not focus on the development of its people but rather rely on foreign nationals to manage most businesses and corporations.

Most African leaders once in power neglect their people and look up to the west. The western countries take responsibility of making sure everyone of their citizen has a job and live comfortably. Why do African leaders find it difficult to take a lesson from the west on governance?

Angola
The Khoisan hunters were the earliest inhabitants of Angola. The Bantu moved to the area trough migration from central Africa. The Bantus then dominated the area due to their skill in metal works, ceramics, and agriculture. The Portuguese reached the area in late 15th century. The Portuguese founded the city of Luanda in 1575. The Portuguese traded heavily in slaves and most were shipped to the European colonies in the Americas especially Brazil. The Dutch occupied Angola briefly, between1641-1648 when Portugal and Spain were embroiled in war in Europe.

Portugal regained control of Angola and signed treaties over the lands with Angola leaders who could neither read nor write. The Portuguese instituted harsh rule and control over the peoples of Angola. The Portuguese had been in control of Angola from the 16th century to 1975. The Portuguese occupied Angola for over five hundred years. What an exploitation of one people over another.

The nationalist of Angola stated agitation for independence from 1950 but it fell on deaf ears of the Portuguese. Black guerrillas attacked in 1961 and in the process the following nationalist parties sprung up- MPLA(Popular Movement for the Liberation of Angola) founded in 1956, FNLA(National Front for the Liberation of Angola) in 1961, and UNITA(National Union for the Total Independence of Angola) in 1966. The Portuguese never wanted to leave Angola because they were controlling the rich diamond mines and petroleum exploration.

Civil war broke out immediately after gaining independence from Portugal in 1975. The civil war became a bloody warfare that lasted twenty -seven years, from 1975-2002. The civil war claimed millions of lives. United States, Portugal Brazil, and South Africa supported FNLA and UNITA while the then Soviet Union and Cuba were supporters of MPLA. It was the third world war without the official title. There was a ceasefire in 2002 after Jonas Savimbi the leader of UNITA, was killed.

The president of Angola elected in 1992 is Paulo Kassome. China became the dominant power in Angola after the exit of the Europeans. What is wrong with African leaders? African leaders are so dependent on external assistance to such an extent that they do not know how to initiate anything on their own. It is time African leaders begin looking inward and use their own people to solve its problems. African leaders have not learnt from the past. It was the same naïve behavior that African leaders portray that made the Europeans to enslave the people in the past.

The progress of a nation is measure by the quality of life of the majority of the people and not by the few politician and their cohorts. The people of China are improving the life of their people while using African resources. Despite the wealth of Angola from diamonds and petroleum revenue, majority of Angola people live in poverty. Educating the people of Angola has not been a priority of the leaders. The world would never accord Africa the respect it deserves unless the people are developed and have good standard of living.

Mozambique

Bantu speaking people migrated to present day Mozambique in the fourteenth century from central Africa. They established agriculture and cattle rearing communities. They had iron making technology and made iron weapons for hunting.

The Portuguese reached the area in 1498 and established trading posts on the coastal areas. They ventured into the inland and searched for gold in the 16th century. The commodity gold was abundant and the area became lucrative to the Portuguese. Arab traders traded in gold and slaves with the Portuguese around the same period. The Arabs and Portuguese became wealthier while the Africans became poorer and dehumanized. The French and British arrived in the 19th century to trade. The Europeans used forced labor in the mines and on the plantations they established.

A nationalist movement the FRELIMO (Front for the Liberation of Mozambique) was born to address the inequality between the indigenous black population and the Europeans in 1964. Due to the political instability in Portugal in 1970, FRELIMO was able to take control over Mozambique. Most Portuguese fled Mozambique to Portugal in the face of warfare and confusion. Mozambique became independent in 1975 and Samora Michel became the president. No sooner, another militant group called RENEMO (Mozambique National Resistance) emerged with support from the apartheid regime in South Africa and Rhodesia under Ian Smith. The ideologies of these two groups of militants clashed and the young republic broke into a long civil war.

The civil war protracted between1977 to 1992. Millions of people lost their lives and thousands became refugees. Samora Michel died in a plane crash in 1986 while returning from a peace meeting from Zambia.

Joaquim Chissano took the mantle of power after the death of Samora. The country adopted market economy when Chissano assumed office. Chissano stepped down in 2004 after eighteen years in power and Armando Emilio Guebuza became the president.

Mozambique has large deposit of titanium. In addition they produce the following crops: cashew nuts, copra, sugar, cotton, tea, citrus fruits, and fishing. Yet, majority of the people of Mozambique live in object poverty. The people of Mozambique are hard -working people but the government projects do not include making life better for their people. They spend the revenue from the resources on things that do not add value to the people of Mozambique. The government spends a large percentage of the revenue that accrue to the country on ammunitions. The government of Mozambique has not accorded priority to educating the people, improving the environment, and offering basic amenities.

The 21st century is a knowledge age and people that are not acquiring knowledge are behind in the scheme of things in the world. The level of ignorance of people would be reduced, and living standard improved if they have access to basic education. The government should invest in the vocation of the citizens of Mozambique. The essence of governance is to keep the people productive. Productivity does not come from foreign investment. Internal activities if geared towards improving standard of living would increase the gross national product of a nation.

African leaders have the notion that they have to get external funds to improve their country. The western countries depend on the productivity of the people. The greatness of a nation is measure by the progress of the people and their wellbeing.   Mozambique leaders should try making the people the focus and they would be amazed at what the people of Mozambique can do.

Somalia

Different groups of people had inhabited Somalia, and the majority of the group had always been the Somalis for over 2000 years. Islam came to Somalia in the 7^{tth} century. Many city -states and kingdoms rose in the area between the 12th - 15th centuries. In the northwest were the Sultanates of Adal and the Ajuuran that flourished in the 14th -17th centuries.

Somalia resisted European colonization during the scramble for Africa in 1884 by the Berlin Conference charter. The great protector of Somalia sovereignty was Mohammad Abdullah Hassan, he fought vehemently for the autonomy of Somalia from any foreign domination.   The French, British, and Italians eventually dominate Somalia in late 19th century.

Somalia became independent in 1960 and Aden Abdullah Osman Daar, the first president. Ethiopian and Somalia had been fighting ever since the British gave part of Somalia land and its people to Ethiopia during the colonial era. The western and eastern blocs take advantage of this rift by supporting either side against one another. The leaders of Africa should know better, the west produce ammunitions therefore any war are lucrative to them despite reasons for the war.

Somalia engaged in warfare from 1969-2006, a span of thirty –seven years. This protracted wars brought famine to Somalia that was very severe and pictures of Somalia people shown across the globe was pathetic and sorrowful.

Barre succeeded Daar. Despite Barre initial good intentions of spreading education by way of reducing illiteracy and creating alphabets for official Somalia language Somali he became a dictator. Farrah Aidid took power in 1991 and his administration was not better than his predecessor Barre. Aidid even fought UN forces who delivered humanitarian aids to the Somali people due to intense famine. Somalia became fragmented into many independent entities each assuming autonomy. Some Somalia forces killed many UN-forces during this period including Americans. The UN–forces withdrew and peace eluded Somalia for a while.

Various warlords ruled the fragmented Somalia from 1991–2000. The Somalia constituted Parliament elected Abdullah Yusuf Ahmed president in 2004, and he governed from nearby Kenya. In 2006 violent broke out among the various warlords and Ethiopia intervened and launched airstrikes on Somalia.

In 2007, United States also launched air strike on Somalia believing it was harboring some members of al –Qaeda. The parliament had disagreements with Yusuf Ahmed because he was unable to broker peace among the various fragmeted Somalia people.

The economy of Somalia was dependent on banana, fishing, cattle rearing, and money from Somalia people in Diaspora. The ancient trade of aromatic woods, frankincense, and myrrh is still vibrant to the Somali economy. Somalia has large deposits of uranium, and petroleum exploration and natural gas are possibilities.

Somalia should realize that there is nothing to gain in war. People are killed, resources wasted and atmosphere of instability reigns the air. Countries that engage in long warfare have a lot to lose. Great citizens of tomorrow's progress are killed in warfare. Dialogue and diplomacy resolves issues not war.

Wars scars are never forgotten, they remain fresh forever. Somalia leaders and people should find lasting problem to the current quagmire.

Djibouti

The original inhabitants of Djibouti were nomadic people who traded in skins and hides for the perfumes and spices of ancient Egypt, India, and China. They had close contacts with Arabs over thousands of years. The people are the Issas and Afars. They were the first in Africa to accept Islamic religion.

The French came to the area in 1862 and anchored at Obock. The French eventually colonized the area and called it French Somaliland. The area was renamed French Territory of the Afars and Issas in 1967.
Djibouti became independent in 1977 with Hassan Gouled Aptidon as president.

The Issas had been in control of governance since independent and this has not sat well with the Afar people. Civil war erupted in 1991 between the government and the Afar party FRUD (Front for the Restoration of Unity and Democracy. A peace treaty was signed in 2000.

In 2001, Djiboutian government leased Camp Lemonier to the United States for fighting terrorism in the region. France shares Camp Lemonier with United States.
The economy of Djibouti depends on services connected with its strategic location on busy shipping route between Mediterranean Sea and the Indian Ocean. It provides services as a transit port and international transshipment and refueling center.
Djibouti has large salt deposit at Lake Asal. The majority of business activities in Djibouti are in the hands of foreigners particularly, Americans, Indians, Saudi Arabians, Icelanders, Turks and many more. What about the Issas and Afars people, are they not capable of being in control of their economy?

These foreign companies should invest in the occupation of the indigenous people to improve on their vocation that is predominantly nomadic and agriculture. The government should invest in education and train the Issa and Afars people to be full participant in the economy. The government in collaboration with all the foreigners could make life better for the Issas and Afars.

Kenya

Cushitic speaking from North Africa were the earliest inhabitants of the area now Kenya. Arab traders traded on the coastal towns in the 1st century due to proximity to Arabian Peninsula. The Bantu speaking people migrated from central Africa to the area in the 8th century. The Bantu had mastered the art of ironwork, farming, hunting, and fishing before they moved into the area.

In the 8th century, the people on the coastal areas of Kenya were known for their ship building industry, maritime trade, and fishing. They traded with the Arabs and Persians in the 9th century in ivory, slaves, and spices. Swahili was the lingua franca at that period. A group of people called Nilots lived along the western part of Kenya engaged in agriculture and cattle rearing. These people migrated from Kush area of Southern Egypt and comprise of the following ethnicity: Luo, Maasai, Turkana and Kalenjin.

The Portuguese explorer Vasco da Gama and his group reached Kenya in 1498. They controlled the trade in East Africa through India from Mombasa in the 15th century. The British, Dutch, and Omani Arabs joined the Portuguese in the 17th century and reduced Portuguese dominance of the trade. Eventually Britain and Germany took control of the area in 1880 and Africans who resisted their influence were placed on reservations. The British brought Indians to work in the construction of Kenya-Uganda railway lines.

After the World War I in 1914, Britons began to settle in Kenya. The settlers became very wealthy farmers growing tea and coffee, while the natives lived in poverty and deprivation of basic amenities.

144

Princess Elizabeth was visiting Kenya in 1952, when her father King George VI died and she immediately became Queen Elizabeth II while in Kenya. She left Kenya to England immediately.

There was uprising of the peasants against the continuous rule by the British in 1952 that continued to 1959. In 1952, the Kenya nationalist began demanding for freedom under KANU (Kenya African National Union) organization. It was a trying period of great sacrifice by the nationalist because many of them were killed, jailed and suffered humiliation on various times, they were over powered by British's logistics and military might.

However, in 1964, Kenya became independent and the first President was Jomo Kenyatta. Kenyatta died in 1978 and Daniel Arap Moi succeeded him. Arap Moi was in power from 1978- 2002. His reign was absolute and he suppressed opposition so that they could not be threat to him. Arap Moi was barred from contesting election in 2002 by parliament. Mwai Kibaki was elected president in 2002. The election of 2007 brought political turmoil due to closeness of the election results between Raila Odinga and Mwai Kibaki and dispute over the real winner. A coalition government was formed in order for peace to return to Kenya.

An oil exploration deal between Kenya and China was signed in 2006. China is everywhere in Africa just like the Europeans in the 15th centuries. When will the leaders of Africa leaned from the mistake of their ancestors. When it becomes the turn of Africa to industrialize what resources is Africa going to use. The resources being mined now are deplete able and not replenish able.

The leaders of Kenya should have the people's future in their plans and agenda. African development should be centered on developing the resources for the good of all and not for a few elites and politicians. African leaders continue to succumb to foreign people forgetting the struggle of slave trade. The effect of slavery held Africa back from progress, and the same game our ancestors played is what the leaders of Africa are still playing with the exception that our leaders negotiate away our economic independent and freedom to choose.

The Maasai people of Kenya are synonymous with the name Kenya and the government should assist them to improve on the way they raise cattle. They lose a large number of cattle stock each year due to drought. What happens to irrigation of graze land? The government of Kenya should develop iirrigation system for the Maasai people so that they can grow grass and produce hay for their cattle. Cattle ranches are in the western world and the governments subsidize the farmers. The government of Kenya could do the same for the Maasai nomads, and this would boost cattle production and possibly beef processing. The economy of Argentina and Australia depend on cattle and sheep rearing.

The Kenya people are determined and resilient, have contributed a lot to the world through sports, athletics, and literature to name a few. What is lacking is government who make people their main manifesto.

Ethiopia
Ethiopia is believed to be the oldest country in Africa and the origin of humans. Some of the peoples of Ethiopia are the descendants of King Solomon and Queen Sheba in the Book of Genesis in the Bible. The D'mt empire was in northern part of Ethiopia in the 5th century BC. and the Aksumite empire rose in the same place in 8th century BC. The Oromo, Amhara,Tigray, Samali, Sidama, Gurage, Wolayta, Afar, Hadiya, Gamu,Kefficho made up the people that inhabited Ethiopia empires. Ethiopia was at a point in time called Abyssinia. Greek missionaries introduced Christianity to Ethiopia in the 4th century. The first Muslims who fled from

146

Mecca in Saudi Arabia from persecution in the 9th century introduced Islam into Ethiopia.

The Italians tried to take over Ethiopia in the 1896 but lost to the powerful Ethiopian army led by Emperor Menelik II. Benito Mussolini of Italy brutally occupied Ethiopia in1936 and the occupation ended in 1941 with the help of the British. Haile Selassie became Emperor in 1930 after being a Regent of the throne. He was a powerful emperor and Ethiopian achieved great recognition in the international community during his reign.

Mengistu Haile Mariam troops over thrown Haile Selassie in a military coup in 1975. Mengistu adopted socialism form of government and got support from the then Soviet Union. He tortured and killed many opposition and members from Selassie family. Somalia attacked Ethiopia in 1977 and war broke out between the two neighbors. Ethiopian Red Force decisively drove back the Somali army.

In 1990, severe drought led to famine that resulted in civil disobedience and Mengistu fled the country and sought asylum in Zimbabwe in 1991. The TPLF (Tigrayan Peoples Liberation Front) and EPRDF(Ethiopian Peoples Revolutionary Democratic Front) emerged amid the chaos and took charge of governing in 1991. Eritrea broke away in 1993 and became independent and autonomous from Ethiopia.

Meles Zanawi became prime minister in 1994 from the EPRDF party. Eritrea attacked Ethiopia in 1998 and the war lasted two years. UN forces were dispatched to maintain peace. Ethiopia stationed troops along Somali border to deter Islamic extremists from crossing over to Ethiopia in 2008.

The economy of Ethiopia depends on on coffee exports, hides and skins, pulses, oilseed, and sugar. Ethiopia produces gold and petroleum exploration is in progress. The country has witnessed significant growth in recent times. Despite, the growth in the economy of Urban Ethiopia, life in the rural areas are still below the UN poverty standard. The living conditions of peasants are deplorable. Their lands are over used, drought has damaged grazing lands, and food production is on decline.

The peasants lack adequate education and as a result have not been able to partake in modern developments. The government should pay attention to human development instead of investing heavily in military wares. The west gains when Africans are killing themselves because the west produces the weapons. Wars in Africa are deadly and unproductive to the people, but it benefits the factories in the western countries on the hand, as demand for ammunitions increase.

Eritrea

Eritrea was part of the Ethiopia Empire until the fall of the Empire in 8th century. It was part of the Kingdom of D'mt in the 5th century and Aksumite Empire in the 8th century. They were part of the civilization of the Nile Valley; thus Egypt and Nubia. They minted their own coin in the 3rd century BC. The Greeks introduced Christianity into Eritrea in the 4th century, and Islam by the Beja people in the 7th century. It was an area of great civilization comparable to China, Persia, and Rome in the 7th century. Arabian invasion weakened the empire and it disintegrated into smaller kingdoms.

Italians invaded the coastal area part of Ethiopian Empire in 1885 and named it Eritrea. The Italians ruled the area from 1936 until World War II when the British seized it in 1941 from the Italians. The British administered Eritrea and in 1952 federated with Ethiopia. Ethiopia made Eritrea a province in 1962. Eritrea nationalist fought for secession and erupted into the Eritrea –Ethiopia war. Eritrea finally broke away from Ethiopia due to disarray in Ethiopian government caused by civil disobedience and famine.

Eritrea became independent in 1993. Frequent border clashes with Ethiopia since 1998 have cost the government lots of money and human resources. The conflict has been on for over forty years and had depleted resources and human lives. The conflicts resulted in many refugees who lived in neighboring countries. The government embarked on national service for reconstruction, defense, teaching, and all facets of work.

The government declared that all Eritrean living abroad be taxed 2% on their income to help develop the country. Over 80%, of Eritrea population are subsistence and livestock farmers. Eritrea has high level of illiteracy and the government has not put its resources to developing the people. The wars in Eritrea and most African countries benefit the leaders and elites. African leaders should know that governance is about people and not egoism and nepotism. The people of Eritrea are hard- working people but the government had not done its part to let people achieve their dreams.

Sudan

The history of Sudan is similar to that of Egypt due to proximity and movement of people during ancient times. The present day Sudan was Kush in the 8th century. Sudan's civilization has been over 60,000 years old. The Byzantine Empire established Christianity in about the 6th century. The indigenous people were Nubians, and Arabs from the Arabian Peninsula moved in and traded with the people. Islam was spread through inter marriages between the Nubians and Arab merchants who came to the area to trade. Other people that moved into area from the south were the Funj in 1500.

Egypt conquered the northern part of Kush in 1820 and ruled the area until 1885. The Mahdist controlled Sudan from 1883 to 1898 and their tenor was brutal to the indigenous Sudan people. The Mahdist entered Ethiopia in 1887 and were defeated when they moved into Egypt. The British

149

overwhelmed Mahdist force and colonized Sudan but the nationalist resented colonization.

Sudan fought in the Second World War in the East African Campaign against Italian troops. Sudan gained independence in 1956 from Britain and Ismail al Azhari was the first Prime Minister. No sooner did Sudan gained independence than civil war broke out between the Muslim Arab North and the Christian South. Gaafar Nimeiry became Head of State through a coup in 1969. An agreement in 1987 to separate Sudan into North Sudan and South Sudan did not work out. Sudan had been fighting among themselves for over twenty years after independence.

Omar Bashir came to power through a coup in 1989. The SPLA (Sudan People's Liberation Army) was formed in the South to resist imposition of Islamic laws on the Christian South. The war that broke out had debilitating effect on the people. Many people died, famine was everywhere and wide spread of diseases. The civil war was fought with weapons from America, Europe, and Soviet Union. None of the weapons were made in Sudan. The meager resources of The country were used to import weapons to kill one another. The economy was destroyed and thousands of refugees created particularly in Southern Sudan.

Crashes among nomads erupted in the region of Dafur in early 1970 and the Black-Arab militia called the Janjaweed, turned the clashes into a war of attrition against the black population. Over two million black people in Dafur died during the conflict and the international community called it genocide. The war in Dafur was the worst humanitarian crisis in recent times.

A comprehensive peace agreement was reached between the opposing parties in 2005 allowing sharing of resources between northern and southern Sudan. The co-vice President John Garang died in a helicopter crash three weeks after the signing of the agreement and this caused another round of riots and civil disobedience in the South. In 2006, a peace agreement was signed between the government and SLM (Sudanese Liberation Movement). The Janjaweed did not honor the agreement and continue to kill people and children became malnourished. The Janjaweed blocked all access to aids from the UN

Sudan is ranked the 17th fastest growing economy in the world and yet millions of the live in poverty and ignorance. Sudan exports crude oil and has large deposits of the following mineral: gold, silver, chrome, asbestos, manganese, lead, uranium, copper, kaolin, cobalt, granite, and tin. Instead, for the government to use the resources to improve the lives of all its citizens it engages in war. The government uses the resources to import ammunitions to kill its citizens. What is wrong with Africa leaders?

Most of Sudanese are subsistence farmers and livestock herders. The River Nile runs through Sudan and yet the government had not provided adequate irrigation systems to aid the farmers. The government or entrepreneurs should establish cattle ranches so that the nomads would stop roaming in search of graze for their herds. Perennial drought is a menace to the Sudanese farmers who contribute close to 40% to the Gross Domestic Product. The leaders should build irrigation dams to assist farmers. The African leaders only want power and do not know the art of governance.

Uganda
The following empires: Buganda, Kitara, Bunyoro-Kitara and Ankole existed in the present day Uganda. Bantu speaking people moved into the area from the central Africa about 2500 years ago. The Bantus brought along iron working skills and lived in social and political organizations. The Nilotic, thus the Luo and Ateker entered Uganda from the north around the same time the Bantus moved into Uganda. Arab traders came to the area around the 1800s.

151

The British explorers in search of the source of River Nile reached the area in 1860 The Protestants and Catholic missionaries arrived in the area in 1877 and 1879 respectively. The British integrated the various kingdoms and named the area Uganda in 1914. Sleeping sickness epidemic ravaged the area and killed over 250,000 people between 1900 and1920.

Agitation for independence from Britain led to the formation of political parties in 1960s. The two main parties were Uganda People's Congress and Kabaka Yekka Party. Uganda became independent in 1963 and Edward Mufeesa II King of Buganda was president and William Wilberforce Nadiope, Chief of Busoga the Vice- President.

Milton Obote overthrew the traditional leaders and became the president in 1966. Series of coups followed Milton Obote coup of 1966 and Idi Amin became head of State in 1971. Amin's rule was brutal and devastating to the progress of Uganda. Amin detested foreign control of Uganda's economy and he seized properties and deported most foreigners from Uganda. Amin's reign ended when Uganda exiles invaded Uganda and that led to Uganda –Tanzania War in 1979.

Milton Obote returned to power once again in 1979 and was ousted by Tito Okello in 1985. The National Resistance Army overthrew Tito Okello after only six months as Head of State of Uganda. The leader of the National Resistance Army, Yoweri Museveni became President in 1986. The Lord's Resistance Army is a movement in Uganda that has been opposing the government of Uganda since 1987. The Lord's Resistance Army created by Alice Lakwena as a spiritual and military movement was to oppose the government of Uganda. The main purpose of the movement is not clear since they had been involved in series of atrocities against the Ugandan people.

Due to instability and governmental policies, Uganda rank among the poorest countries in the world. Uganda has excellent natural resources. These are fertile soils, regular rainfall, mineral deposits of copper and cobalt. Uganda has reserves of crude oil and natural gas. Over 80% of Ugandans are engaged in agriculture. Coffee is the main cash crop.

The basis of governance is the well-being, security, employment, and progress of citizens. Unfortunately, African leaders do not have the above plan for their citizens hence poverty and misery amid plentiful natural resources. The people who got into power in Uganda do so for selfish reasons. They do not have plans to move the people and country forward. The governments of Uganda could learn governance from the developed worlds. Countries exist for the development and well- being of the people. Unfortunately, this simple principle has been eluding African leaders and the situation in Uganda is getting from bad to worse.

What African leaders need to do is to form associations with business leaders from the Western and Eastern countries; sign agreements whereby they would contribute in developing the areas they buy raw material instead siphoning the resources to their respective countries. This would help development of Africa and the politician would not have the abilty to divert the resources to thier personal use. People can develop better when they have basic amenities and they would love their country more. There is no place like home, Africans move abroad become their governments have not created an enviroment where the individual can develop natural talents to improve their lives or actualize their dreams.

Rwanda
The earliest inhabitants of Rwanda were the Twa, who are short stature around 3000 BC. The Bantu people called Hutu

moved into the area and co-existed with the Twa. The Hutu people were agriculturalist who lived in family settlements. The Hutus made iron implements and potteries. The Tutsi who lived a pastoral life came into the area later. The three groups of people organized themselves into small states. The states extended as far as Lake Kivu in the 1900s due to migration of people.

The Tutsi established a monarchial system whereby they held control over the earlier inhabitants of the area. The Mwami, King was very powerful. The Mwami had complex administrative structure where division of labor application was used. The kingdom was relatively peaceful except occasional raids across the neighboring kingdoms. The kingdom instituted a judicial system called Gacaca.

The coming of the Europeans into the kingdom in 1893 destabilized a hitherto organized and corporative existence. The Europeans adopted the divide and rule method that they employed to control most Africa people. The European aligned with the minority to control the majority and this yielded the result of confusion and commotion. In Rwanda, the different physique of the people was the method adopted to alienate the people among themselves. This method created constant conflict between the Tutsi and Hutus who hither to the coming of the Europeans lived peacefully. Since the Tutsi have features close to the Europeans, they concluded that they are superior to the Hutus. The Tutsi were therefore, trained to hold administrative, military and police positions to the detriment of the Hutus.

The Catholic mission that came to the area adopted the same stereo type posture and this ignited clashes between the Tutsi and Hutus. The clashes between the Tutsi and Hutus became so uncontrollable such that the Europeans created two states of Rwanda and Burundi. The decision to create the two states took place in Brussels without any input from the indigenous people in 1890.
Belgium exchanged Rwanda and Burundi for Helgoland in the North Sea with Germany. The Hutus rebelled against

154

Tutsi domination and in 1911 war broke out and many people killed on both sides. The League of Nation entrusted Rwanda and Burundi to Belgium after the defeat of Germany in World War I.

The Belgians forced the people particularly the Hutus to grow large acres of coffee and the Tutsi were in charge of the quota system. Definitely, this arrangement brewed resentment between the Hutus and Tutsis. The Belgians ruled harshly and with draconian tactics. Many people fled Rwanda and migrated to Uganda ruled by the British. The preference accorded the Tutsis by the Belgians deepened the animosity between Tutsi and the Hutus. The ill feelings resulted in several clashes.

The wave of Pan-Africanism swept through Rwanda in early 1960 and a Hutu George Kiyibanda formed the PARMEHUTU IN 1953, while a Tutsi Dominique Mbonyumutwa also created the UNAR in 1959. These parties were militarized and clashes resulted in thousands of deaths. Despite attaining independence in 1960, the two groups of people the Hutus and Tutsi detested one another. The deaths of the presidents of Burundi and Rwanda who were Hutus in a plane clash was blamed on Tutsis by Hutus.

 Tutsi professional were immediately purged from governmental jobs and they fled to Uganda. The Uganda government assimilated them and some joined Uganda Army and rose in ranks. Paul Kagame the current president of Rwanda was trained in Uganda and he formed the Rwanda Patriotic Front.   The RPF invaded Rwanda in 1990 from Uganda and the Hutus launched and unprecedented attack on the Tutsis and thousands of people killed. The international community branded the atrocity genocide.

 Why should people who have lived for thousands of years together decide to kill one another? Who is fanning the fire of hatred between the people of Rwanda? People have different physiques and everybody contribute in their own way to build the world into what it is today. No single group of people can claim credit for the transformation of the world. The people of Rwanda should take advantage of their differences and build a peaceful society with respect for one another. The root cause of the conflict run deep, but the past differences should be buried, so that future generations do not repeat history.

The country of Rwanda has fertile and beautiful landscapes, and rich mineral resources. The government should concentrate on rebuilding and providing for all people of Rwanda to move the country forward. The president and all elites of Rwanda should ask themselves this question, who was the winner of all these conflicts? The winners of the conflicts are the countries that supply arms to Rwanda. These countries live on wars and the citizens of warring countries suffer. The citizens of Rwanda became defenseless and those countries that sold ammunitions gained from all the sorrows.

It is time leaders of Rwanda realize that all the people of Rwanda can live together in peace without outside intervention if each group of people respect one another. Everybody in Rwanda complements one another and war only benefit outsiders. A united Rwanda should be the focus of the new leaders and every citizen should feel important and be proud of being Rwandan and nothing else.

Burundi
The history of Burundi is inter-twined with that of Rwanda. The same group of people migrated to Burundi and Rwanda around the same time. These are the Twa, Hutus, and Tutsis. Burundi was a kingdom of the Tutsi for over two hundred years. Burundi and Rwanda were combined into Ruanda-Urundi under Germany and Belgium occupiers in the early part of the twentieth century. The Germans and Belgians who ruled over the Tutsis and Hutus created ethnic problem that is still alive today. The Europeans preferred the Tutsi to the Hutus because they had features that looked

Caucasian. This perception affected the development of the people because they were in constant clashes with one another. Ruanda-Urundi separated into Rwanda and Burundi after independence from Belgium in 1960 and 1962 respective fully.

The Hutus due to their number had been winning elections after election since independence and the Tutsi being the educated elites find it impossible to accept the Hutus as their leaders and this continue to create conflict that caused death to millions of people. The idea of people being superior to one another was the Europeans way of asserting their influence on people who do not look like them. This philosophy of superiority has eaten deep into people's consciousness such that millions of people had been killed from its impact on the psyche.

Every human being is important; no group of human being is superior to the other. All human beings complement one another. Some are better at other things than others but each human being contributes their quota to make the world better. If those who are good at technology conceive ideas and there are no resources to bring their thought and ideas to life, there would not be development for all.

The leaders who assume position of authority in Burundi instead of extinguishing the fire of discord continue to fan it and let it burn for their selfish ends of being in power, and control of resources of all. The people of Burundi deserve a leader who would look for means to develop the people of Burundi. The leaders use the revenue from the nature given resources to buy arms from the West and East and kill the people of Burundi is no way to move forward. No, human society is perfect but the West and East are more concerned in developing their people and environment. Burundi leadership should be concerned in human development and not ethnicity.

The resources of Burundi are uranium, nickel, cobalt, copper, and platinum needed in the West for production of items in the factories, but the leaders of Burundi exchange these vital resources for guns and ammunition to fight and kill their own people. The people of Burundi are hard-working people who want to live a peaceful and fulfilled lives but the leaders want power above everything else hence incessant killings and wasting of resources on guns and ammunitions.

The people that produce the following items- coffee, cotton, tea, maize, sorghum, sweet potatoes, banana, tapioca, beef, milk, and hides should never go hungry and poor. Alas, Burundi is one of the poorest countries on earth where children are malnourished. It should not be but it is. The leaders forget that the purpose of governance is to make living productive and comfortable.
The current president of Burundi Pierre Nkurunzia who came to power in 2008 should make history by sustaining peace in Burundi and lifting the people of Burundi from the horrors and scourge of poverty.

Tanzania
The earliest inhabitants of Tanzania were the Khoisan. The Bantus migrated into the area from central Africa. The Bantus were agricultural settlers. The Nilotic people came into the area later and were nomads who move around in search of pastures for their flocks and herds. Arab Traders moved into the area to trade in goods and slaves. Zanzibar was the centre of Arab Slave trade. The Portuguese arrived in the area in 1500. The European explorers and missionaries also were in the area in the 1900. It was a German colony from 1880 to 1919. After the World War I it came under the administration of the British.

The United Republic of Tanzania is the union of former Tanganyika and Zanzibar in 1964. The Zanzibar Revolution overthrew the Arab regime and merged with Tanganyika to form Tanzania. Tanganyika became independent in 1961 from the colonists through the struggle of the nationalist party (TANU) Tanganyika African National Union. Julius Nyerere was the first Prime Minister of Tanganyika. Nyerere adopted socialist ideology that was the trend in most newly independent African states in the 1960s.

Tanzania had a downturn in the economy immediately after independence so it had to rely on aids from the Soviet Union and China. The aids from China had a condition attached that Chinese labor would be used to complete projects meaning that people of Tanzania could not be employed and therefore could not benefit economically.

Tanzania economy depends on agriculture and mineral resources. The natural resources of Tanzania are gold, natural gas, diamonds, iron ore, tin, platinum, coltan, niobium, nickel; chrome and gemstones. It is one of the largest gold producing countries in Africa. South Africa is the largest followed by Ghana.

The Great Rift Valley runs through mainland of Tanzania and this attracts large number of tourist from all over the world every year.The Great Rift Valley has the largest concentration of wildlife and it is a great asset to Tanzania. In view of the tourists attractions Tanzania is faring better than countries around them. The government of Tanzania is doing better in relation to education but more needs to be done in creating jobs so that graduates can get jobs. Tthe traditional businesses like agriculture should be improve to attract young people and college graduates. The essence of governance is the safety and well- being people. Tanzania should be renowned by the development of its vast and diverse human resources, and encouragement of people to actualize their dreams.

Zimbabwe
The Bantu speakers settled in the area between the 9th and 13th centuries. They established kingdoms and used

sharpened stones instruments for farming and hunting. The following kingdoms thrived in the area before the arrival of the Europeans- Zimbabwe, Mapungubwe, Mutapu, and Rozwi. They built large stone houses and towers. The early Bantus traded with Arabs along the coast of East Africa in gold, ivory, glass, and cloth.

The Portuguese wandered into the area in the 16th century, followed by other European explorers, missionaries, ivory hunters and traders. Cecil Rhodes and his trading company moved to Zimbabwe in the 1880s. Members of Rhodes trading company named the area Southern Rhodesia after Rhodes after wrestling the control from the Bantu Kings. Cecil Rhodes organized colonization of the whole area of East Africa. The Shona and Ndebele a branch of the Bantus refused the annexation of their lands and foreign domination. The British were able to take the lands due to advancement in warfare and use of guns. Southern Rhodesia became a self- governing entity in 1923.

Southern Rhodesia governed by Ian Smith declared independence from Britain in 1965 and became a republic in 1970. The international community with the exception of South Africa imposed an economic sanction on the government of Ian Smith after the Unilateral Declaration of Independence.

Abel Muzorewa won the election of 1978 that made him the first black Prime Minister of Zimbabwe. Robert Mugabe became President in 1980, an ethnicity problems almost brought the country to a stand -still. Mugabe election caused ethnic tension and many people killed in clashes. There were many uprising in Zimbabwe from 1981-1990. The main political parties ZANU (Zimbabwe African National Union) led by Mugabe and ZAPU (Zimbabwe Africa People Union) led by Joshua Nkomo united and formed ZANU-PF to bring peace.

The electorate became dissatisfied with Mugabe's reign and riots broke out everywhere in 1990 when he won the presidency again. The stringent measures imposed on the people coupled with the economy not doing well, and salaries not paid to workers intensified the civil disobedience between1991-1996. On top of the mirage of problems the people were experiencing HIV/AIDS appeared in Zimbabwe around that difficult period.

Mugabe government began distribution of land to the people in 2000 due to the disproportionate land mass the whites own and their 1% population to 70% ownership in land. The white population cried out on this reform. The reform affected the economy and inflation grew to uncontrollable level, and life became a living hell for the ordinary person. The initiative to change the slums into healthy living environment would have been very successful if the government had put humanitarian effort into it. The government could have settled the people affected in temporary accommodation before implementing the plan.

The election of 2008 had a hitch but it was amicably resolved when the opposition leader Morgan Tsvangirai became Prime Minister and Mugabe retained the Presidency.
Zimbabwe economy depends on Mineral resources, tourism, and agriculture. Zimbabwe has the world's largest reserve of platinum mined by an Anglo – American company. The agricultural crops are tobacco, maize, soya, and indigenous staple foods. The main tourist attraction is Lake Victoria and Victoria Falls.

It is hard to explain why hard working people should be poor. The people that produce the aforementioned cash crops should not live in poverty. If the government of Zimbabwe focuses on the development of people, poverty could be eradicated with all hands on deck working towards the same goal and vision.

The main cause of frequent conflicts in Africa is that the governments have not made efforts to unite the different group of people that make the country. Unfortunately, different people were grouped together under the colonial administration to serve their purpose of divide and rule.

African governments should take advantage of this diversity by creating common purpose for all people within their country. The government should stop nepotism so that every Zimbabwe has a say and purpose in Zimbabwe. Freedom brings the best in human. The leaders should stop power tussle and let human development be their priority. The leaders would be amazed what freedom can do when people are given opportunity to bring out their best freely without coercion.

Zambia
The Khoisan and Bantu people inhabited Zambia for thousands of years before the arrival of the Europeans explorers who came to the area in the 1800s. David Livingstone was the explorer who located the fall on River Zambezi that runs through Zambia and he named it Victoria Falls after Queen Victoria of England. The people of Zambia called the Fall "Mosi-oa-Tunga". Livingstone accounts of the area made European explorers, missionaries and traders flood the area in the 1800s.
Cecil Rhodes a British Merchant claimed the area and named Zambia Northern Rhodesia. The Federation of Rhodesia and Nyasaland formed by Cecil Rhodes in 1953 did not go down well with the people, and led to various riots, clashes, and vehement agitation for independence. The people did not like the influx of the Europeans and there were several revolts and agitations.

In the 1960s, Henry Nkunbula and Kenneth Kaunda formed the following political parties, the African National Congress and National Independence Party respectively. Kenneth Kaunda won the president at independent in 1964.

In view of European colonization of Africa, most newly independent states adopted the Soviet form of socialist government. China aided Zambia on the condition that labor on projects would be Chinese, this affected the Zambian labor force because they were not trained to manage or repair the infrastructure built by China. This process continued to make Zambia dependent on Chinese technical support on the new infrastructures for a long time.

Over 68% of Zambian people currently live below poverty line estimated to be about $1 a day. The economy of Zambia is dependent on copper mining operated by An Anglo-American Company. The vagaries of the copper market had had devastating effect on economic plans and lives of people The government is promoting agriculture to reduce reliance on copper.

The people of Zambia were self -sufficient before the arrival of the Europeans. The leaders should look into the past society, study what sustained the people at that time, and improve upon them. The reliance on foreign investment would not improve the economy unless Zambians are actively involved in the building of a better society. The government should have manifestoes that evolves and revolves around the Zambia people. Any investor is there to make profit and maximize their wealth. If the governments and elites of Zambia are poised to make life better for Zambians, it can be achieved through involving the people in the developmental process.

Better quality of live for all people is the cornerstone of good governance. Zambia has the resources to make Zambia people achieve the dreams of most people namely: good homes, portable drinking water, lights, good roads, and excellent and functional education system.
Levy Mwanawasa was elected President by the election of 2001. He brought changes on the management of national resources. He died after a protracted illness in 2008, and

succeeded by the Vice President Rupiah Banda. Banda has
continued on the foundation laid by Mwanawasa.

Malawi

The Bantu speaking people settled in Malawi in the10th
century. These early settlers lived in kingdoms under kings.
They toiled the land with iron implements they made and
lived in stone houses. The Portuguese traders came to the
area in 1600s, and disrupted the activities in the area and
imposed Portuguese way of life. The people rejected the
Portuguese. The English explorer David Livingstone got to
Lake Nyasa in 1859 on his search for the source of the River
Nile. The report of Livingstone about the prosperity of the
area led to influx of English traders, missionaries, and
treasure hunters.

Cecil Rhodes an English trader colonized the area and later
merged Nyasaland (former name of Malawi) with Northern
and Southern Rhodesia to form Central African Federation in
1953. This amalgamation was rejected by the people
because the various group of people brought together have
differences in cultures, customs and speak different
languages.

The following uprising led to agitation for independence
from Britain. Hastings Banda formed a political party, (MPC)
Malawi Peoples' Congress that campaign vigorously for
independence. Malawi became independent in 1964 and
Hastings Banda, the first Prime Minister. Banda ruled from
1964-1994. Although Banda implemented socialist
ideologies, he uplifted the life of people and improved
agriculture, and industries.

Multi-political parties were formed in 1994 and Bakili Muluzi
won the presidency in the election. Muluzi was president for
a decade. Bingu Mutharika the current President won the
election in 2004. Malawi has maintained good relationship

with the international communities and as such received aids to sustain the economy when the prices of its major export commodities fell in the world market. Malawi has maintained relative peace by resolving differences through negotiation and compromise. Some Africa leaders can borrow a leaf from Malawi on internal conflict management.

The Great Rift Valley runs through Malawi, North to South, to the East is Lake Malawi (Lake Nyasa).The economy depends on mineral resources and agriculture. Malawi mineral resources are – limestone, uranium, coal, phosphate, graphite, granite, limestone, bauxite, vermiculite, aquamarine, tourmaline, rubies, sapphires, and rare earth. Agriculture products are- tobacco, sugar, cotton, coffee, sorghum, rice, and peanuts. Malawi also produces ethanol to supplement petroleum imports for domestic consumption.

HIVAIDS spread to Malawi in 1992. Almost 14% of the 14 million population of Malawi are infected with HIV/AIDS. High rate of HIV/AIDS is having a toll on the adult population. About 250 people die each day from this deadly affliction. . Thousands of children are orphans due to deaths of their parents from HIV/AIDS.
The following institution from United States are assisting the government of Malawi in the fight on HIV/AIDS -The Peace Corps, Center for Disease Control and Prevention, Department of Health and Human Services and the Agency for International Development.

A country can only develop from the involvement of the people. The government of Malawi should involve the people of Malawi in all aspects of development. Malawi relies on external help and this would not bring the best in Malawian. Malawian should be involved in every aspect of the development of their country.
Education is the vehicle that helps- to bring new ideas and appreciation of old ideas where people can develop and change their views and improve on what they have.

Education should be compulsory and affordable if not free. Education enables people to appreciate themselves and respect others. Education is not necessary learning the culture of other people but improving the existing culture and passing it on to future generation.

Common resources of a country need to be employed towards the development of the people and not for fancy projects that do not better the lives of the indigenous people.

Lesotho

The Khoisan were the earliest settlers in Lesotho. The Bantus moved into the area during the Bantu migration from central Africa. The Sotho-Tswana people lived in the area around the 3rd to 11th century. Lesotho was Basutoland under King Moshoeshoe I in 1822. The kingdom fought many wars with the Zulu of South Africa under Shaka Zulu between 1818 and 1828.
The Kingdom also engaged in several wars with the British and Dutch South African settlers. The British occupied the area in 1854 after winning a battle fought between 1851 and 1852. A large portion of Lesotho land was lost to the Dutch Boers in 1958. Lesotho became a British Protectorate in 1869. King Moshoeshoe I died in 1871 and the British colonized Lesotho.

Lesotho gained independence in 1966 and became a kingdom once again. In the 1970s, conflicts arose between the people and the monarch over administration because the people wanted more involvement in the polity of their country. Lesotho currently practices Constitutional Monarchy, where the King performs ceremonial functions. Members of Lesotho parliament are elected through democratic election.

Lesotho's economy relies on diamond exports, water sold to South Africa, agriculture, manufacturing, and livestock. It also exports wool, mohair, clothes, and footwear. Levis jean manufacturing and Russell Athletics maintain manufacturing factories in Lesotho. Despite, the wealth of Lesotho, majority of the people depends on subsistence farming and migrant laborer to South Africa for livelihood. Lesotho has adequate supply of electricity generated from Lesotho Highland Water Project. Secondary and higher education in Lesotho is funded by the state, and majority of children have access. The government is in the process of providing free primary education.

The adult population of Lesotho suffers from high epidemic of HIV/AIDS, and over 20% carry the disease. The King and parliament should not relent in finding lasting solution to HIV/AIDS epidemic. Poverty and low standard of living aids the spread of the disease. The leaders should be involved in improving life for their citizens instead of pleasing foreign investors at the detriment of their citizens. Countries can create wealth for their countries if all hands are on deck and every citizens work towards the same goal.

Botswana
The early inhabitants of Botswana were the Tswana people and later the Ndebele people moved to the area from the Kalahari Desert. The European settlers in South Africa attempted several times to dominate the area and the leader Kharma III, sought the help of the British in 1885. Botswana became a British Protectorate in 1885 under the name Bechuanaland. South Africa annexed Southern Botswana in 1910 to form the Union of South Africa.

The British granted Botswana Self –Governance in1964 after decades of resistance from the people. The head quarters of Botswana moved from Mofikeng in South Africa to Gaborone in 1965. The election of 1966 produced Seretse Kharma, leader in the independent movement, the president of Botswana. The next president was Quett Masire. Masire retired in 1998 and the Vice President Festus Mogae assumed power. Ian Karma won the presidential election of 2008. He was the leader of the Botswana Defense Force and son of the first President of Botswana.

Botswana is the least corrupt country in Africa and has a higher per capita income. Botswana is growing faster economically. The economy is dependent on diamond mining. The government owns 50% of the Mining Company Debswana, while foreign investors own the remaining 50%. Preparation to mine other minerals, gold, uranium, copper is in high gear.

The wealth of Botswana has not spread to majority of the people. Almost 25% of Botswana adult population is HIV positive. In 2006, life expectancy fell from 65 to 35 years. What an irony, wherever there are diamond mines, there are HIV/AIDS. The government is doing the best they can to control the spread of this horrible affliction on people but an endemic like HIV/AIDS whose source had not been traced cannot be easily controlled.

The government has made great strides in education, but more need to done to spread education to all children. The education system in place has not done much to improve the African culture. The primary education is the foundation of future leaders and should be strong and functional to prepare the next generation to live an improved life. The indigenous people should be well educated in order to be able to lead in their own communities. Botswana with all its wealth should invest heavily in education so that improvement can spread to all people in the society. Education breeds independent individuals, understanding between peoples, and awareness of surroundings. Educated people live a better live and can make improvement in their settings.   A functional education system creates jobs that people can do to live a worthwhile life.

African governments favor foreigners to their own people.   It is surprising that foreigners still manage and control most businesses in Botswana.

The people of Botswana are fortunate to have a land bleeding with diamonds and this richness should reflect on the people and not foreigners.

South Africa
South Africa has been in existence over three million years ago. The original inhabitants of this region were the Khoisan and Zulu people. The Bantus migrated to the area from central Africa in the 4th century. The Bantu were excellent in iron works for agriculture and some were herdsmen. The use of iron works by the Bantu people enabled them to engage in migration over long distances.

The Portuguese explorer Bartolommeo Dias reached the tip of South Africa in 1487, and named the area Cape of Storms. The Portuguese changed the name to Cape of Good Hope due to abundant rich resources they took from the area to develop Portugal. The Dutch, under the Dutch East India Company got to South Africa in 1652, and made the place their home and killed most of the indigenous population, particularly the Khoisans. Britain with its superior military power took over the area from the Dutch in 1795. The Dutch trekked inland and made fresh settlement encroaching on the land of the indigenous people. The indigenous people engaged these foreigners in many wars for freedom on their own land.

The discovery of abundant diamond and gold in 1867 and 1884 brought influx of Europeans to South Africa. The British and the Dutch engaged in wars for supremacy over South Africa and its resources from 1880 to 1902. Britain won and later the Europeans formed the Union of South Africa in 1910. Due to the diversity of different European people that came to South Africa, they picked whites to refer to themselves and called the natives blacks.

Apartheid was instituted under the National Party in South Africa in 1948. Apartheid was an institution based on assumed superiority of the whites over blacks and subjected the blacks to inhumane treatment. The whites took over most fertile lands and blacks were relocated on lands that were not productive, and only go to work for the whites under draconian laws and harsh treatment. Despite lack of resources, the blacks put up resistant for decades. The blacks paid huge supreme sacrifices, and prominent sons like Nelson Mandela and many other jailed.

South Africa became a Republic in 1961 and left the Commonwealth of Nations. The South African government operated under apartheid whereby the black people were oppressed, suppressed, and repressed. The international community isolated South Africa through trade sanctions and divestment. The African National Congress (ANC) was the leading anti-apartheid movement among many others, fighting to claim their dignity on their soil.

The South African government softened its stance on apartheid and called for a democratic election in 1994. ANC party won the election and Nelson Mandela became the first black president of South Africa in 1994. Mandela before becoming president spent for twenty- seven years in jail for demanding equal rights for black South Africans.

  The journey had not been easy for black South Africans despite the fact that they are in majority in government. Subjugation of many decades can change the character and psychic of people. It should not be surprising that black people of South Africa are going through to many changes. With time, the people of South Africa would heal from the wrong of the past and be able to accept what is happening now as reality and not a dream.

Unemployment is very high among black South Africans. The actions of apartheid of decades cannot be turn around within ten years, however, things are turning around in South Africa. Quality education that had been the privilege of the whites, now include blacks, and middle class is rising in the black community. The government has a big task of training the able body unemployed blacks due to lack of skills for the job market. These men deserve assistance from the government instead of labeling them as criminals. The long years of apartheid had deprived them of necessary education and help is what they need not acrimony Leaders of South Africa have a lot to do to bridge the vast economic gap between blacks and whites.

The end of apartheid brought another misery to South Africa HIV/AIDS. The spread of this disease is alarming. In 2005 according to United Nations report, 31% of pregnant blacks had AIDS, while 20% of adults carry HIV. The government of South Africa allowed the disease to spread deeper before rendering assistance. South Africa has lost and still losing a large number of its labor force to HIV/AIDS. Over five million blacks are infected with this heinous disease.
South Africa's economic is among the best in the world. The economic backbones of South Africa are as follows: diamond, gold, uranium, other minerals, wool, corn, fruits, and sugar. South African can be ranked as an industrial nation.

Swaziland
The earliest inhabitants of Swaziland were the Khoisans. The Bantu speaking people migrated into the area from the Great Lakes in the 4th century. The Swazis are part of Bantu people. The Swazis established iron working and community farming in the area in the 4th century. They established a kingdom ruled by Nkosi. Swaziland became a British protectorate in the 1800s. The European settlers in the area engaged them in many wars, especially, the Boers. Swaziland became independent in 1968 and established constitutional monarchy style of government. The head of state is the king, and the one on the throne in 2009 is Mswati III.

The economy of Swaziland depends on agriculture, forestry, and mining. Swaziland has a manufacturing sector that produces textiles, and sugar processing. Majority of the people of Swaziland are subsistence farmers.

There are two sets of agriculture land use in Swaziland. These are Title Deed Land, that is very fertile and highly mechanized where sugarcane, forestry, and citrus fruits are cultivated, and the other is the Swazi Nation Land where people work as subsistence farmers.

There is great disparity among the people of Swaziland. The king and the elites enjoy a high standard of living while many people are infected with HIV/AIDS.
The United States and European Union invest heavily in Swaziland and this has produced significant wealth for the country. This wealth is not reflected on the larger population.

The Monarch and his advisors control the wealth of Swaziland at the expense of the people. The government in Swaziland is inefficient and does not care about the plight of the people. The people live in deplorable condition while the Monarch lives in opulence. The western investors in Swaziland look away because all they are in Swaziland for is to maximize their investments. African leaders have not learnt anything from the past.   Africans leaders continue to make the same mistake their ancestors made in terms of entertaining foreigners at the expense of their own people.

Democratic Republic of the Congo
The central location of Democratic Republic of the Congo attracted many immigrants from the four corners of Africa. The Bantu speakers dominated the area around 2000BC to 500AD. The Bantus outnumbered the indigenous people the Europeans called Pigmies. These indigenous people are the Twa. The Bantus settled in the area practicing agrarian way of life with their developed iron implements.
 The European explorer Henry Stanley under the sponsorship of Leopold II of Belgium reached Congo in

1877. Many Europeans came to the area when the news spread about the rich mineral resources of Congo.

The King of Belgium, Leopold II claimed the area as his personal colony, and the Belgians dealt ruthlessly with the people and plundered the resources of the area to develop Belgium. He subjected indigenous people to inhuman conditions to produce rubber for Belgium. Quota production was introduced, and natives who could not cope had their limbs cut off. The rubber was processed into tires in Belgium for the growing auto industry in Europe and America. The colonization of Congo changed Belgium the King became very rich and built many buildings and monuments for Belgium.

Over 10 million natives died from over worked, exploitation and diseases between 1885 and 1908. The international community protested the killings, maiming and policies of the Belgian administration. Members of Berlin Conference transferred the administration of Congo from King Leopold to Belgium parliament in 1908

The wind of self- rule was blowing over Africa in the 1960s and Congo was part of it. Patrice Lumumba led the *'Mouvement National Congolais'* for agitation for independence from Belgium. Lumumba was elected Prime Minister and Joseph Kasavubu of the *Alliance des Bakongo* was elected President in 1960. Many political parties came alive in Congo in the 1960s. Crisis brewed among the various political parties shortly after independence.

The prime Minister and the president had rift and the head of the army Joseph Mobutu with financial support from the United States and Belgium committed a mutiny. The West fearing that the resources of Congo might be diverted to the Soviets supported Mobutu financially, militarily, and logistically. The West did all they could to hold their grip on Congo's abundant mineral resources and huge rubber plantation. The support from the West enabled the army to kidnap the Prime Minister Lumumba and they assassinated him amid the chaos in January of 1961.

Chaos and confusion overwhelmed the country and the military took advantage of the situation, and a coup led by Joseph Mobutu over threw the government in less than five years after independence. The West gained easy access to the mineral resources of the country without regard to the abuse of power by Joseph Mobutu. The west preach democracy but when it comes to what they need democracy becomes irrelevant. Mobutu amassed wealth from the patronage of the west from the diamonds, copper, zinc, coltan, and tin of Congo and they cared less about the plight of the people.

In 1966, Mobutu changed the names of cities and towns to their indigenous African names. Mobutu changed his country's name from Republic of the Congo to Zaire in 1971. Mobutu's power was boundless and he did anything he could think of. He even declared himself a Field Marshall. He was vey corrupt, brutal and had no care for the people he governed. He killed his opponents and critics but he was the most loved of all African leaders of his time by the west.

It was an unwritten agreement between the west and Mobutu's government that as long as our industries have access to your country's resources the doctrines of human rights does not apply. He visited the United States of America presidents in the 1970s and 1980s many times and travelled around the world in chattered French Concorde planes. Eventually, the wealthy conutry Zaire had to depend on aids from the west to survive.

In 1996, the ethnic wars in Rwanda spilled over to Zaire due to presence of Tutsi people in Zaire. Rwanda, Uganda, and some Zairian forces invaded Zaire, Mobutu's government was overthrown in 1997 and he fled with his family to Morocco where he lived and died.

Laurent Kabila became the president after the successful coup of 1997. Rebel forces assassinated Laurent Kabila in 2001, and his son Joseph succeeded him. Kabila changed the country's name to Democratic Republic of Congo. The forces from Uganda refused to leave and militias from Angola and Zimbabwe forces joined in and this developed into a huge battleground were over five million lives were lost. The United Nations deployed peace- keeping force to the area in 2001.The fighting continued into 2006.

Joseph Kabila won the election of 2006. The country became unstable again and the president reached a power sharing agreement with the militia leaders. The war in Rwanda had contributed to the instability in the Congo and more lives were lost in the wars than the Second World War. This war was dabbed African World War because all western countries sent troops to side opposing parties. This is Africans killing one another with ammunitions made in the West and East.

The Democratic Republic of Congo has not had any tranquility since independence in 1960 so how can they assess their surroundings and make progress for the future. The politicians and the military leaders behave like thieves, they take resources and exchange them at whatever price for ammunitions to kill and destabilize their citizens. They do not have plan for the progress of their country and people so it does not matter what money the resources are worth as long as they get something to satisfy their greed. The leaders should stop the power tussle and think of the progress of their country and the development of the people. People of a country are the reflection the leader.

Democratic Republic of Congo is the world's largest producer of cobalt ore, copper, and industrial diamonds. Democratic Republic of Congo produces tantalum use in components in computers and mobile phones. Tin is also mined commercially on a smaller scale. Why should a country with such a vast important resources be poor? The leaders of these militia groups should realize that they are destroying their own country with foreign made ammunitions.

There is diversity in every country but most countries use the diversity to their own advantage. Wars have never solved any problem. War creates suspicion and mistrust. Wars divert resources from life improvement projects. The Democratic Republic of Congo can never estimate how much resources it had wasted on power tussle wars. These monies could have gone into building schools, infrastructures, markets, water resources, houses and many more amenities, and improving the way the people live. The people who gained from the war are the manufactures of all the weapons used. It is time the leaders of Democratic Republic of Congo stand up for improvement of lives of their people and make the country a comfortable place to live.
 The Democratic Republic of the Congo had been known at different times as Congo Free State, Belgian –Congo, Congo Leopoldville, Congo-Kinshasa, and Zaire.

Republic of the Congo
The Mbuti people often referred to as Pigmies were the earliest inhabitants of the Congo area. They lived in the thick tropical forest and moved from area to area in search of food and proper accommodations. The Bantus migrated from   central Africa and settled in the area establishing kingdoms and farm settlements. The notable kingdoms of the Bantus were Kongo, Loanga, and Teke.

The Portuguese explorers reached the Congo River Delta Basin in the 15th century. They established trading post and traded in goods and slaves captured from wars within the kingdoms. The slave trading was heavy in the Republic of Congo. Eventually, the power of the kings came to and end when Britain abolished slave trading in the 19th century.

French occupied the area in the 1880s. France created a form of federation for the French African territories in 1908, under the name French Equatorial Africa and Congo Brazzaville was the capital. The countries under the federation were Equatorial Guinea, Democratic Republic of the Congo, Gabon, Chad, and Central African Republic. France extracted mineral resources from the territories and shipped them to the developing industries in France. The French extracted the minerals through forced labor and human abuse. France and the French became rich and wealthy while the African territories became poorer and ignorant.

The French administered the territories through divide and conquer, whereby they prefered some natives to other and this created tensions among the people and caused unending hatred between the people. The Republic of Congo became independent in 1960 and Fulbert Youlou, a catholic priest, became president. Youlou faced serious ethnic unrest shortly after becoming president so he had to flee the country. The military took over and established a one party socialist state under the Mouvement National de la Revolution led by Alphonsa Massamba- Debat.

The Soviet Union and Cuba supported the division within the new republic. Debat was overthrown in a coup in 1968. Ngoabi became president and he renamed the country Republic of the Congo in 1970. Debat also faced ethnic division and chaos in the country and was assassinated in 1977 by a militia group. General Yhombi Opango took over the mantle of power and the military controlled the state. Sassou-Nguesso overthrew Opango in 1979 and named himself president. Nguesso got support from the Soviet Union and was able to suppress all oppositions. The support from the Eastern bloc continued until the dismantle of the Soviet Union in the 1990s.

Political pressure was mounted by the ethnic leaders for democracy and Nguesso caved in and allowed multi-political parties. Pascal Lissouba won the election in 1992. As usual in this part of the world, ethnic tension grew again

177

and various militia groups sprang up. The former president Sassou- Nguesso formed the Cobra, others militia groups formed the Coyotes, and Ninjas to counter one another. The clashes that resulted in 1994 claimed many lives. The Republic of the Congo has continued to be plagued with power tussle and ethnic politics since independent in 1960.

The French got involved in 1997 supporting the government of Sassou- Nguesso their crony. The power tussle cumulated into a civil war in 1997, and close to a million people died. Sassou- Nguesso came to power again with the help of the French.

The west can never leave Africa alone because their economic development depends on the resources from Africa. The resources from Africa grease the western economy. The politicians and their western and eastern allies do not care about the lives of African people. The same west turn around and look down on African people as undeveloped.

Whose fault is it? The under development of people of African is the fault of greedy leaders who continue to breed ignorant citizens and reap them of their legitimate resources. The main concerns of the foreign friends of these African politicians are to take African resources to improve the lives of their own people and then turn around to send aids to Africa.

Due to the long political battle, the governments had neglected the people and poverty and diseases had taken hold on the people. Mortality from AIDS has drastically reduced the population of Republic of Congo. The current population of merely four million is small in comparison to other African countries. Water borne diseases are prevalent due to lack of portable water in rural areas. Malaria and sleeping sickness have taken a heavy toll on the people.

Unfortunately, education that aids people in understanding the world and uplift lives has not been the priority of the

178

government of the Republic of Congo. The percentage of Gross Domestic Product that goes into education is meager in comparison to military.

The government of the Republic of Congo should realize that the world assesses the people's progress and not the ill-gotten wealth of the leaders. The people of the world would respect Africans if the leaders use the vast resources to develop their citizens.

The economy of The Republic of Congo depends largely on petroleum products and mineral resources like gold, diamond, phosphate, iron ore, copper, and zinc. The mineral sector is in the hands of a Portuguese Company Escom and Canadian Company AfriOre. The following foreign companies Italian-Agip, Chevron, Exxon, and French-Elf are in-charge of the petroleum sector of the Republic of the Congo.

The majority of the people depend on farming. They produce cocoa, coffee, peanuts, rice, corn, sugar and tapioca. Forestry is also a sector that produces timber logs for export. The government of Sassou-Nguesso had mortgaged the resources of his country to the foreigners. This is the main reason they make sure he stays in power despite terrible human abuse and dictatorial regime. The west preaches democracy but they throw it to the wind when resources for their factories are at stake. The population of Congo is decreasing at an alarming rate. The killings in this region through unnecessary war should stop. The government is killing the people and giving the lands to farmers from another country to farm. This is a great injustice to the inhabitants of Congo.

The people of the Republic of Congo should never go hungry or live in poverty if the vast resources were employed for the good of the larger society. The people are hard-working people who want the best life for their families. The leaders of The Republic of Congo should make the development of the people the cornerstone of whatever they do. If African people are not respected, so do the   leaders, irrespective of their illicit wealth.

Mauritania
The Bafours were the earliest inhabitants of Mauritania. The Berbers migrated to the area around the fifth and seventh centuries. The Bafours were settled group that engaged in agriculture for livelihood. Islamic warriors, the Al Murabitun attacked and took over the area and settled in the area. Soon many Arab looking people moved into the area and dominated trade that had flourished in the kingdoms for thousands of years. Some of the notable empires in the area were Ghana and Mali.

The people resisted and fought Berbers and the Arabs between 1644-1674. Since the Berbers and Arabs were warriors they were able to dominate the people. They enslaved the indigenous people and took control of the empire. The Berbers assimilated with the Arabs and accepted the Islamic religion.

The French came in and subdued the Moors and Berbers. The descendants of Bafour known as Sonnikes moved back to area when the French took control. The area was under French administration until independence in 1960. The first president was Moktar Ould Daddah. He ruled under one party state iron handedly.   The first president Daddah, was ousted in a military coup in 1978. The country was devastated by two groups of militia the Polisario Front and the Sahrawi. These fought over political power and left the economy in shamble after their operations. Mauritania had not been stable since independence due to incessant coups.

Three groups of people populate Mauritania, The dark skin people, black Arabs and the mixed Arab and Black called the Moors. Slavery had been a part of Mauritania for ages and it is still vibrant. International communities have delved in to stop the practice but to no avail. In view of this, there has always been tension among the people of Mauritania. The conflicts resulted into a civil war in 1989 in which many of the black people were expelled from Mauritania and many killed.

The economy depends on agriculture, animal rearing, fisheries, and exports of iron ore, copper and gold. Petroleum was discovered in 2001 and production commenced immediately. Mauritania has very large illiterate population. The government spends less than 3% of Gross Domestic product on education while close to 6% is on military expenditure. Mauritania is a diverse country and in order to bridge the gap of poverty among the various groups the government has to invest in the development of the people. The leaders of Mauritania have been taking advantage of the ignorance of the people. The few elites fight among themselves in order to control the resources of the country. The majority of the people are poor and the less privilege live as slaves in their own country.

The leaders of Mauritania should be ashamed and embarrassed by the situation of citizens in their own country. How do the leaders of Mauritania face the world when majority of their citizens live as slaves. The government should let people be free and be able to have access to jobs and be paid reasonable wages to live a decent life.

Morocco
Morocco is currently not part of the African Union. Morocco prefers the Arab identity to Berbers however, the Berbers are proud of their African heritage. The Berbers have been inhabitants of the area Morocco for over 5000 years before the Arabs invasion in 670AD. Morocco was once part of the Roman Empire. Morocco was once under the control of the Vandals from Europe. The Greeks also ruled over Morocco briefly. The genetic pool of Morocco comprised of many different people who once occupied Morocco. The dark skinned people of Morocco called Haratian or Gnawea. The Haratin or Gnawea comprise about 40% of Morocco population. They are part of the original inhabitants of the

area. The Gnawea are renowned for their transcendental music.

The spread of Islam reached Morocco in 640AD. The Arabs who spread Islam also introduced their cultures and way of life into the Berbers culture. The Arabs after spreading Islam and their culture took over control of the area and created their own kingdoms and dynasty in the 11th century. Later in the 11th century, the Berbers created several Berber dynasties and the Arab Dynasties lost political control. The following dynasties: Almoravid, Almohads, Marinid and Saadi tossed political power among themselves and ruled Morocco. The reign of these dynasties extended to the Southern Spain and part of Portugal.

The Arabs took control again after the Moors or Berbers were driven away during the Reconquista in the Iberian Peninsula in Europe. Ismail ibn Sharif (1672-1727) organized the kingdom during his reign and was able to suppress opposition from the Berbers.

Morocco was the first country to recognize United States of America as a sovereign country in 1787 and signed the Moroccan-American treaty of Friendship to protect American ships in the area from piracy. Morocco had enormous wealth in the early 1700. Morocco was the envy of European nations who on several occasions tried to take control of the area in 1800. Eventually, Morocco became a protectorate of France and Spain. Germany was not happy with the arrangement and crisis ensued among France, Spain, and Germany over Morocco. France and Spain took control and Morocco became a France protectorate in 1912. Morocco became independent from France in 1956. Morocco operates a constitutional monarchy form of governance. The King on the throne in 2009 is Mohammed VI.

The economy of Morocco depends on tourism, agriculture, mining, and manufacturing. Fishery is an important component of the economy. Morocco is world's third largest producer of phosphorous. The dark skin people known as the Haratin or Gnawea comprise about 40% of Morocco population. They are part of the original inhabitants of the area. The Gnawea are renowned for their transcendental music.

Algeria

Berbers had inhabited Algeria for over 10,000 years. Algeria has a long history with the Roman Empire and southern Europe. The area was part of the East Roman Empire in 200BC. The Arabs came to the area in the early 8th century to spread Islam. The Arabs conquered the Area from the Berber rulers. The Berber dynasties were the Almoravids and the Almohads .

In the 16th century, Spain attacked Algerian coastal towns, killed many people and took control of the area. In 1512, The King of Algiers, Samis El Felipe had to submit to the authority of the King of Spain after the conquest. The King of Algiers sought the help of Ottoman Emperor for military assistant against Spain. In 1516, the Turkish army liberated Algiers from the Spanish rule and Oruc Reis the leader of the Turkish army became the ruler of Algeria. Algeria became part of the Ottoman Empire.

Algeria became a great military might in the region and attached all vessels that moved in the Mediterranean Sea and Atlantic Ocean in the 1600-1815. The men captured in the raids were sold into slavery. Oruc Reis and his men attacked Southern Europe and sold the captives into slaves.
After many years of torment by the Barbary pirates, the French finally invaded in 1830. This battle took a decade and thousands of lives were lost due to resistance from the Algerians The war weakened the Algerians and a heavy toll on the population. The people in Southern Algeria were the Tuaregs and they fought gallantly to resist French occupation. They lost to French superior military might.

The following Europeans, Italy, France, Spain, and Marta moved to Algeria and took over large acres of land and farmed. The Algerians suffered a set back in development. The French controlled Algerians for over three centuries. The Algerians began to fight for independence from France in 1952 and achieved independence in 1962 after decade of bloody war of resistance. The National Liberation Front (FLN) spearheaded the fight for independence. The first president of Algeria was Ahmed Ben Bella. He was over thrown in 1965 after only three years in office. FLN dominated Algerian politics till 1991 when a multi- party election was held. The Islamic Salvation Front won the election but the military cancelled the result because they did not want an Islamic State. The event culminated into the Algerian Civil War. Thousands of lives were lost in the Civil War. The war lasted a decade from 1992-2002.

French and Arabic have been the official language of Algeria but the Berbers are pushing for their language Amazigh to be part of the languages spoken officially in Algeria. Amazigh is currently part of the official language in Algeria.

Economy- Algerian economy relies heavily on petroleum exports. The vagaries in the petroleum markets has significantly affected the Algerian economy. Algeria has large petroleum and natural gas reserves. A quarter of the population engages in agriculture. Algeria has fertile soil that supports the following crops: cotton, olives, palms, and tobacco. Grains such as wheat, barley, and oats are also cultivated. Algeria produces a sizable portion of fruits for exports. Algeria possess what if takes to be a great nation in Africa and make life better for the people.

Algeria invests heavily in military hardware that benefit the supplying nations. The government should invest in the development of the people by improving education and creating jobs. The Algerian people are hard- working people and the vocation of the people should be improved by investing in modern technologies to improve productivity.

Government exists to improve lives and not to destroy lives. Algeria has inadequate number of physicians to the teeming population because the government has not been investing enough in education. The government should be investing more in improving the lives of the people instead of ammunitions.

Tunisia

Tunisia was an important area in Ancient times. The city of Carthage in Tunisia was part of the Roman Empire. The region of present day Tunisia was invaded by the Vandals then occupied by the Byzantines and the Arabs in the 5th, 6th 8th centuries respectively. The Berbers were the original inhabitants of Tunisia. The Phoenicians settled on the coast in the 10 century BC and founded the City of Carthage. The Carthaginians invaded Italy under Hannibal, later the Romans re-conquered and the area became part of the Roman Empire in 2nd BC.

The Islamic Arabs spread Islam in the region in the 8th century and took over the reign of power from the Berber dynasty. The Berbers resisted Arab occupation for many years. Later along the line, the Berbers took over from the Arabs and ruled from 1230- 1574 when the Ottoman Empire invaded the whole North Africa and Southern Europe. The Barbary pirates flourished along the coast of North Africa in the 16th century. Tunisia was a French protectorate from 1881 until independence in 1956. The Berbers live mostly in the South Eastern part of the country and on the Island of Jerba. The majority of the population is Berber-Arab with mixtures of European blood that occupied the region in the past.

Tunisia was the site of the first major part of the Second World War from 1942-1943. The last Berber ruler was deposed in 1957 and Habib Bourguiba became the president. In 1987, Bourguiba was declared by his physicians to be unfit to rule so Zine el Albidine Ben Ali succeeded him. Ben Ali has been a dictator and suppressed all forms of opposition. Tunisia was where the Arab mass protest began in 2011 for citizens' participation in the political processes.

The Tunisia economy depends on tourism, agriculture, mining, manufacturing, and petroleum products. Tunisia has the highest per capita income on the continent of Africa. Despite the wealth, most college youths are unemployed. However, education takes a major priority. Close to 6% of gross national product is spent on education. The government relies so much on external labor force to run the country. In view of this, it attracts international companies that invest in the country.

Libya

The Berbers were the original inhabitants of present day Libya many millenniums ago before invasion and occupation first by the Carthaginians, the Greeks, the Persians, the Romans, the Vandals, the Turks and the Arabs. The Arabs occupied Libya in the 7th century during the spread of Islam. It became part of the Ottoman Empire in the 16th century. Italy invaded the region and occupied it from 1911-1951. The Italians killed many of the indigenous people of Libya during their occupation. In 1951, two major towns of Libya Tripoli and Cyrenaica came under the administration of Britain and Fezzan under French after the defeat of Italy in the Second World War.

Libya also became independent in 1951 under King Idris. The discovery of petroleum reserves in 1959 and income from petroleum made Libya a wealthy nation. The military led by Muammar Gaddafi over threw King Idris in 1969 and Libya became a republic. Libya operates a dictator ship form of government called the Third Theory since 1969. Individual freedom is limited in Libya and human abuse is common. Citizens have to abide by the rules set by the government without opposition.

The relationship between Libya and the West became strained for a long time due to differences in ideology. It is presumed that the invasion of Iraq in 2003 by the United States of America and the subsequent execution of Sadaam Husein softened Gaddafi. Libya established relation once again with the West signing treaties with Italy and United States to amend the wrongs of the past on both sides. The revolution that started in Tunisia down to Egypt in 2011 spread to Libya. Gaddafi refused to read the writings on the wall that his time was up, and should vacate and adhere to the voices of his people.   He was stubborn and was killed by the Libyan National Army in October 2011.

The economy of Libya depends on revenue from petroleum. Due to low population and wealth from oil reserves, the government has been able to raise the living standard of the people. The government provides a high level of social security by way of housing and education. Education is free and compulsory up to secondary level. Libya has the highest human development in Africa. The level of poverty is very low in comparison to many Africa countries.   Libya is gradually moving towards privatization and foreign countries are investing.   However, the government has to allow the people to make political choices and express themselves.

Egypt
The land Egypt has long and deep ancient history. The Merimde culture flourished in Lower Egypt in the 4th millennium BC.   Egypt has over six thousand years of recorded history. The earliest inhabitants of the area were the Nubians, the Abazas, Beja, the Berber and Neolithic speakers. Egypt on various times in its past had been invaded by different people from Asia, and Europe. The invaders usurped power from the native rulers and also became pharaohs and ruled over Egypt. The earliest people to invade Egypt were the Assyrians, the Kushites, the Greeks, the Romans, and the Arabs.

The current population of Egypt is therefore a mixture of Sub Saharan Africans and Eurasia. Two new religions Christianity and Islam replaced the worship of many gods by the Egyptians and the later had a lasting impact on the people. The language and culture changed to that of the last invaders, the Arabs.

The area in the ancient times had successful agriculture systems where the surrounding nations from Europe and Asia depended on. Egypt also developed a sophisticated writing system during the time of the pharaohs. Architecture and advanced construction techniques also developed that enabled the building of pyramids, sphinx, and obelisks. Glass technology and mathematics developed in Egypt. It was not surprising therefore, that many nations dominated and claimed Egypt. In view of constant occupations of Egypt by different nations, the identity of original inhabitants has melted into the identity of the occupiers.

Some may ask why is it that Egypt is no longer advancing as it did in ancient times? Probably, because most of the indigenous people were killed during the years of invasion/occupation and foreign blood had been mixed with the surviving people. The Ottoman Empire invaded Egypt in 1517. The Crusaders invaded in the 16th century and the Asian Mongols also occupied Egypt in later part of the 16th century. Egypt also suffered a devastating death of over 40% of its population from Black Death that plagued Europe around this time that spread to North Africa. Egypt economy suffered due to the death of many people and the Portuguese became an important force in trade in the region.

The French invaded Egypt in 1798 and the Ottoman Empire regained control of Egypt in 1801. The leader of the Ottoman regiment was Mohammad Ali an Albanian and became a Sultan of Egypt. He established his own dynasty and ruled Egypt until the Egyptian Revolution in 1952. He focused on expansion of his territory. He annexed Northern Sudan from 1820-1924, Syria and parts of Arabia in 1833.

The European powers fearing his ambition clipped his wings by waging wars against him.   Mohammad Ali, changed the face of Egypt from ancient civilization to modern, based on Western industrialization.

Cultivation of cotton was introduced into Egypt and the economy shifted from food production to cotton, a cash crop. Cotton price rose in the 18th century due to American civil war and there was influx of foreigners once again into Egypt. The Suez Canal was built by a joint venture of France and Egypt in 1869 during the reign of Ismail. The heavy cost of the Suez Canal bankrupt Egypt. Egypt had to sell its share of the Suez Canal to Britain in 1875. The creditors France and Britain took control of administration of Egypt in order to collect their debt. The people became dissatisfied with the arrangement that imposed heavy taxation on the people.

In 1879, a nationalist movement was formed by Egyptians who were dissatisfied with British domination of the affairs of their country.   France, and Britain bombed Alexandria an important city in Egypt and defeated the Egyptian army in 1822. In 1914 Egypt became a British protectorate. There were many riots to resist British control and administration was almost impossible so Britain declared the Kingdom of Egypt independent in 1922. The Monarch Farouk was ousted in a coup in 1952 and his son Fuad became king. Egypt was declared a republic in 1953 and Muhammad Naguib became the first President. Naguib was forced to resign in 1954 by Gamel Abdel Nasser a prominent member of the revolution that. Gamel Abdel Nasser assumed the presidency in 1956. He nationalized the Suez Canal immediately after assuming the presidency and this caused the Suez Canal Crisis that involved Britain and France.

Israel invaded the Sinai in 1967. Nasser died shortly after and Anwar Sadat became the president. Anwar Sadat on the contrary became close to the West instead of the Soviet that his predecessor relied upon. President Anwar Sadat was assassinated in 1981 while inspecting a military parade.

Hosni Mubarak filled the presidency immediately in 1981 and has held the post since. Mubarak is currently under arrest to answer for the atrocities that accurred during the recent peoples revolution in Egypt.

The economy of Egypt counts on agriculture, mining, manufacturing, petroleum products, tourism, and receipts from traffic on the Suez Canal. Egypt has been receiving substantial aid from the United States of America since 1979. Egypt has a large deposit of coal in the Sinai Peninsula. Egypt has a booming and vibrant stock market. Egypt has enormous wealth but this has not trickle down to the masses. Inflation is high and it affects the purchasing power of the average person. However, the government of Egypt invests heavily on education. Education is free from elementary to University level.

Chad
Human existence has been in the present area of Chad since the 7th Millennium BC. The earliest inhabitants engaged in agriculture and livestock herding. The area was a crossroad of ancient civilization where Trans- Saharan trade with the East and Africa flourished. The strong kingdoms in the area were the Sao and Kanem. Islam spread to the northern part in 1085 AD. Arab slave traders raided people and sold them into slavery. The kingdoms were conquered and united by Raba el Zubayr and he ruled from 1883-1893. The French captured Zubayr; executed him and took over the area in 1900. France used the people to grow cotton to feed the burgeoning French textile industry. Over 15,000 Chadian fought for France in the Second World War. The people were not satisfied with the way the French administered them and riots and resistance were very common.

After many years of struggle under French rule, it became independence in 1960 and Tombalbaye a revolutionary leader became the president. His regime was autocratic and was ousted from government and killed in a military coup in

1975. The young nation was thrown into a state of chaos after Tombalbaye death, Libya moved in to support the rebel in the north and the French who were not ready to let the country go to Libya also moved in to defend the South. A civil war ensued and the people of Chad suffered the most. The international community mediated and a transitional government held the helms of affairs. Hissene Habre took over power in 1980. The rebel forces in the north continued their aggression and Hissene Habre with international help was able to suppress them Over 40,000 people were killed under Habre.

Idriss Derby over threw Habre's government in a military coup in 1990. Derby allowed multi- political parties to form. He has been winning presidential election since then. The administration of Derby on the people of Chad has not been better than his predecessors did. African leaders for reasons hard to find govern without regard to the well-being of their people. They rule absolutely. The main purposes of government are better life and security for the people; however, African leaders neglect these vital components of democracy. The democratic system in Africa operates like monarchy. The African leaders perpetuate themselves on the seat of power and protected by foreign leaders who depend on the resources of the country.

The influx of refugees from Sudan and Central Africa into Chad has increased the problem of this landlocked country. It is also plagued with internal tension among the numerous ethnic groups. Despite the aforementioned problems, corruption is also endemic in Chad. The larger population is poor and depends on subsistence farming and rearing. Petroleum mining began in 2003, and the ruling elites mismanaged the revenue derived. Cotton also contributes to revenue of the nation. Chad receives aids from the United Nations for the running of the country due to long years of war and the increase in refugee numbers from Sudan and Central Africa.

The elites live in opulence while majority of the people live in object poverty. The leaders do not have any sustainable plan for the development of the people of Chad. Chadians are hard -working people and the government should assist in providing basic amenities to all corners of Chad to reduce over crowing in the metropolis like N'djamena. Chad is very poor in terms of human development. One wonders how the leaders of Chad react to the faces of their people shown on the internet looking poor and miserable. The various people of Chad deserve a better life than what the government makes possible. These people wake up every morning to struggle for daily existence. The government should direct people towards a better and an enlightened future. The leadership emphasis should be the people and not political power.

Niger
Niger was the center of the ancient civilization of Songhai empire that flourished in the 14th century. Before then human existence had been in the area for more than 10 thousand years. The Tuaregs migrated from the borders of the Sahara Desert to northern part of Niger in the 1200s. The Fula people, a pastoral people became influential in the area in the 1700. The Hausa states also flourished in the southern part of Niger.

European explorers Mungo Park and Heinrich Barth explored the area looking for the source of the River Niger in early 1900s. The French established their posts in the Niger in 1896. The people rebel against their presence and the French subdued the people with their power arms. The continuous riots of the people made administration impossible for the French, therefore in 1922 the French handed the administration to the leaders of the area.

Niger formally became independent from France in 1960. The first president was Hamani Doiri. He run Niger on one party state and the economy flourished during his tenor as a result of demand for uranium on the international market. By the way, Niger is among the countries that have large deposit of uranium. The country experienced long drought from 1968-1975 and this affected agriculture outputs that resulted in famine.

Diori was ousted in 1974 in a military coup led by Seyni Kountche. Kountche organized a multi-party election in 1976 in which he was elected president of Niger. Kountche managed to win all subsequent presidential elections until 1993 when Ousmane Mahamane won. Mahamane was deposed in another military coup led by Ibrahim Bane Mainassara in 1996. Mainassara became the Niger's president. Mainassara while conducting inspection of his guard was assassinated by a member of the guard in 1999. Tandja Mamadou was elected president the same day of Mainassara's assassination.

Niger's economy relies on donations from both Western and Eastern countries. Niger sits on one of the world's large deposits of uranium. Uranium is an important commodity needed in the industrialized countries for the production of nuclear bombs, electricity, chips for computers, and many electronics products. Uranium commodity is scare but has high demand. Yet the country with large deposits of uranium has become a beggar nation. It cannot provide adequate electricity, portable water, and basic amenities for its populace. Poverty is vivid everywhere.

Niger also has large petroleum reserves, gold deposits, coal, iron, phosphates, iron, limestone, and gypsum. Unfortunately, foreign nationals are in control of the above resources. The two Uranium mines are owned by SOMJR and OMINAK . The gold mines are owned by SML, a joint venture between a Moroccan and Canadian companies. These companies own 80% while the Niger government own 20%. The coal is operated and owned by SONICHAR company. The petroleum exploration permit was granted to China National Petroleum Company and ExxonMobil-Petronas. ,

Despite scanty rainfall and desert in the northern part there is substantial agriculture activities that produce the following crops: pearl millet, sorghum, cassava, rice, peas, onions, garlic, peppers, potatoes, wheat dates. In the Sahel animal rearing is the main occupation of the people. The Sahel is grassland that sustains cattle, goats, camel, and sheep. The government needs to improve the way these farmers raise animals in other to improve production and improve the quality of life of the people. There should be changes in the way animals are raised to meet the challenges of the modern world.

The educated elites should put their knowledge to use by educating the farmers on how to reap the most from their herds. The following people: the Hausa, the Tuareg, the Zaram-Songhai, Gourmatche, Fualni, Kanuri and Toubou and many more are hard working people who want the best for themselves and their family but the leaders of Niger have not created opportunities for these people to aspire to be the best that that they could be.

The African elites do not care about the people they rule. They only care for political power at the expense of the citizens. There is no reason why Niger should be poor with all the resources and the diversity of its people. The leaders do not have vision and this affects their processes. In order for any nation to move forward in this modern world the development of the different peoples in the country should be the focus. African leaders have not made their people the center of development. The Niger people like most Africans are people who want progress for their families but they cannot handle this issue alone unless the government creates parameters that make human developments possible.

The First African Nationalists

The first African Nationalists were well educated Africans who were trained in the West and were prepared to change Africa for the better. They knew what governance was. The first presidents of most African countries were overthrown one after the other in the 1970s after less than a decade of independence from the colonists. These coups were the beginning of woes for the African people. The coups created chaos, corruption, ineptitude, mistrust, mischief, and disappointments in the way these military leaders governed. These military leaders depleted all the reserves of their various countries and African people became refugees and hunger stricken people across the globe. The former colonists who said Africans could not govern themselves were proved right by the chaos and poverty the military left African countries they governed. Africa people are living in the worst situation and condition ever.

The vision of the Nationalists who fought for freedom and independence from colonial domination were not what the soldiers or the military leaders that took power immediately after our political independence had. These groups of military head of states had no plans. The only thing that was obvious was the fact that they wanted power, money, control, recognition, and status. The nationalists fought for independence for the progress of Africa but unfortunately, Africans have not seen the expected progress after independence due coups and political dishonesty.

These periods of coups in Africa coincided with the United States and the dissolved USSR trying to gain supremacy in the world community. The USA practiced democracy and capitalism while the USSR practiced communism blend with socialism. This was also the period after the two world wars when these major nations tried to re build their various countries and there were economic depression and instability particularly in the United States.

195

The raw materials to rebuild like petroleum, minerals, crops-coffee and cocoa were in African countries. The West believed that the new Independent Africa States were flirting with USSR and the best way the West thought fit was to stop the flirtation before African countries adopted communism. These Nationalist leaders like Patrice Lumber of Congo and Dr. Kwame Nkrumah of Ghana became casualties.

The black people in USA were fighting for the abrogation of the various segregation laws, and demanding more recognition as people with equal freedom, and the right to live and move freely in their new country. The whole world was in transition in the 1960s.

The former colonial powers secretly are glad about what is going on in Africa today because the African leaders have even perfected the act of mistreating their own people. The West indirectly still controls the resources of the countries that clamored for independence from them. The leaders of Africa are a laughing stock in the world because they do not know how to govern and develop their resources to improve the lives of their people.

Diseases, poverty, and famine have become the circumstances of a people with resources the whole world industries depend upon for the progress and advancement of their people. Africa needs foresighted leaders that are committed to the progress of black people. The wants and aspiration of the black man is not different from other humans. Irrespective of location on the planet earth, every human wants happiness, protection and continuity of the next generations. The black skin color is for protection from the intensive heat of the sun. The hair texture is to hold moisture to protect the skull from the sun's heat. The black person aspires to enjoy the things in the world just like anyone else.

There was nowhere in Africa history where African live in communal communities. African people have always been independent and each group or clan specialize in vocations. The agrarian depended on the nomads for meat and the nomads depended on agrarians and vice versa. Capitalism is the way people have lived in most societies, it is the natural way of exchange among people. Capitalism has been in Africa since time immemorial in the sense that Africans traded their goods and wares long before the adventure of the Europeans. Peoples in Africa had various trades. There were artisans, masons, farmers, trades, weavers, doctors, priests, and many other trades depending on the people. Families specialized in these trades and passed them on from generation to generation.

The young independent African countries had no opportunity to establish their new countries before soldiers staged coups and took charge. The military intervention has given Africa a big set- back. It is over fifty years since Ghana the First black African country to get Independent aside Liberia. How many communist countries are there in Africa? There is none because Africans believe in individual endeavor and not communal. African people believe in individual freedom and communism cannot work among freedom loving people. No country in Africa practices communism because it is not their way of life. Africans believe in individual progress and the success of every one is the success for all.

African countries are independent states and their progress is in their hands but there are invisible hands that operate to make sure the black man does not become completely independent. It is common practice for other independent nations to meddle in the affairs of black nations as if they are incapable. Other nations interest override the interest of people in Africa in the eyes of African leaders. The leaders believe they have to sell their people short in other to be in the good books of the west or east. This perception had brought unimaginable toll on African people.

The soldiers who took over most of African countries have not been able to implement programs that aid human development. The new military leaders became dictators and turned their countries into one party states suppressing opposition and democracy. They nationalized most of the investments the West had in Africa. They became impossible to control by the West and were replaced by coup after coup. The West and the East were supporting fighting factions and African countries became a battle- ground where Africans were killing themselves with military assistance from the West and East. The more chaos there is in Africa the more ammunition and weapon merchants become richer.

Some African leaders particularly, those from the French colonist were left untouched after independence from France because they were still serving the French government instead of developing their people and their countries. A case in point is Cote d'Ivoire, where after independent from France in August 7, 1960 the first President Felix Houphy uett-Boigny ruled until he died on the presidency in 1993. That was a period of thirty-three years as president in a democracy. This pattern was common in former France colonies. The irony is that chaos takes over after the death of a sit tight leader due to his autocratic style of governance. The country could disintegrate if care is not taken .A similar situation happened in Czechoslovakia when Tito died.

Since Nigeria's independence in October 1960 as a Republic it has been governed by more military Head of Stated than elected governments.   The leaders become instant millions and friends around them become richer. They were not accountable to the people; the government coffers were like their personal wallet. They ruled with fiat. These leaders plunged Africa of its wealth. The only thing they strive for is amassing wealth for their families and cohorts.

There is no reason why Africa should be stagnant after over fifty years of independence from colonial rule. Are Africans telling the rest of the world that they cannot govern themselves or what? Democracy is not practice in Africa on democratic principles. Elections are usually not free or fair and the same leaders elected all the time despite their obvious incompetent in office. These leaders do nothing to improve on the people or the environment and they fool people by rigging election and claiming winners. These leaders in Africa behave like monarchs where absolute power.

Democracy is the government of the people by the people and for the people. The government of the people means the people elect the leaders and not an imposition. The citizens should elect democratic leaders and not through coercion, or manipulation of electoral results as it happens in most black African nations.

Africa is falling far behind in term of human development. Africans are not moving at all, let alone move forward in terms of development.

It is over three centuries after the last Trans- Atlantic slave trade but Africans particularly black Africa has not done much to improve the status of the people. Black people sit on the fence as if they are spectators in this world. The black person should be involved in this world instead of just going by the flow. The black person waits unconcerned and accept anything that comes his or her way. We do not question anything.

We use items produced for other people for their own benefits. You are great learners but you do not use what you learnt to improve your lives. The life of the average black person in this world is deteriorating day in day out. Any known disease created by the modern man finds their way among the black race. You just look while millions of you die each year. The disease HIV/AID did not start in Africa but it is now ravaging Africans and most black people all over the world. You just sit and watch while your population is decreasing through diseases.

Malaria is spread by mosquito parasite, and it has devastated Africa for centuries and nothing significant has been done to eradicate this disease. Mosquitoes breed in stagnant waters, lagoons, ponds, and lakes. Insecticides have been developed that can kill mosquitoes and their larvae but alas malaria is still one of the leading killers of Africans Why? African leaders do not care about the well-being of their people. Most Africans become politicians not because they want to make changes to people's life but to enrich themselves from the majority purse.

One thing these politicians do not realize is that they are not given due respect in the world community because they know the source of their wealth. These Africa leaders are praise by their foreign mentors in the eye of the public and the same mentors ridicule them in private. These African leaders are welcomed in the West and East because they need the raw materials of their respective countries to run the factories in the developed world. These foreign leaders know very well that what their friends are doing to their people is wrong but they always turn the blind eye.

Human beings are on this earth fighting one another for the resources provided by mother earth. How then can black people expect competitors for the finite earth resources assist them to move to a better level. There is a common saying; everyone for himself and God for us all. The development of black people should be their own responsibility. Africans or black people should have realized long ago that their advancement as human beings means less earth's resources for other people. You think about it, would a competitor advice you to beat him in a race of course not. The same thing with the resources on earth, on one is waiting for blacks to catch up in the race.

Africa has abundant resources and yet unable to use the resources to improve the lives of the people. Africa supplies most of the world's commodities but do not have any commodity market. What is wrong with Africa? Their leaders take Africa's money and save then in Swiss banks and the Swiss use the money to develop their economy and the people. What an irony. The world is in the twenty first century, do Africans still need someone to tell them they need lights, good drinking water, houses, and infrastructures?

Africa is the cradle of most black people all over the world and these people are waiting for Africans to make them proud of their heritage. When is this going to happen, Africans? Africa needs to develop so that Africans in Diaspora would have a place they would long to visit. African –Americans, Afro-Latinos, Afro-Cubans, Afro Brazilians long to visit Africa but we have not developed Africa to meet their expectations. They believe Africa is a jungle like is portrayed in Tarzan movies. Africa is portrayed in Western media as a continent of poverty and misery. African- Americans in America have come a long way despite their humble beginning from slavery. These people have contributed immensely to the development of America. If Africa opens up with leaders who love people, Africans in Diaspora particularly African Americans could be a source of investment funds for Africa.

If Africa leaders would sit down and think of the future of their children, and grandchildren they will stop all these wars going on in Somalia, Sudan, Uganda, and all squabbles all over Africa. We kill ourselves with ammunitions made in the West and East and they look at us as if you are some animals. It is time Africa nations stop fighting and see what they can do to enjoy this beautiful world. If you go round the world, all you see is black people working and the rest of people enjoying. We should be creating wealth instead of just working to make a living. Blacks work hard. We do all the menial jobs the other people would not do and yet they turn around and say blacks are lazy.

We study all the principles and writings of both the West and East hoping we can become somebody but we end up in frustration; we are told we do not belong in the profession we have chosen, and we end up doing menial and under employed career because life has to go on. We only and only us know the pain we go through in this world. We keep our sorrows and pains to ourselves. Our life expectancy is shorter than that of our ancestors. We carry most of the modern diseases for instance diabetes, hypertension, tuberculosis, and HIV/AIDS. This is due to stress, change of life style and environment.

Since the 14th century, we have been learning the way of others and have even forgotten how we were. We eat food that probably was not compatible with our body chemical composition. The first sign was we gained unnecessary weight and lost our shapes. The weight we gained seemed normal because beauty and attractiveness was unexpected of us anyway. Our new physique made it easier for our body to develop diabetes and hypertension. These two diseases are deadly. Most black people die through these deadly diseases particularly among black people in Diaspora.

African leaders send their children to study abroad and do not believe that they can create the good educational institutional in their own backyard. These African leaders do not have the vision to visualize that, what had been possible in the West and East is possible in Africa too. If there is commitment to make changes and focus on human development, great opportunities are possible in Africa as well. Even deserts in Arabia have turned into magnificent cities right in our own eyes. What are Africans waiting for?

Go back in history and see where the West and East were before the enslavement of African people. You would see the strides they made in the last six centuries.
Many Africans who had the opportunities to be trained do excellently in their professions but unfortunately the leaders who direct the countries do not appreciate their own people's intellect and talents. Africa has many doctors, nurses, engineers, professors and scientist who live and work in the

West and East. Why do these talented Africans leave Africa that needs them most? The reason being that there are not enough jobs to absorb them, the salary structure is so ridiculous that one may end up a poor person, there are few infrastructures to make commuting pleasant, and housing and health facilities are not adequate.

Africa leaders travel overseas for health care because they do not trust their own doctors and do not believe the facilities in their country is good enough for treatment. This is a shame and ridiculous. Are they saying the Western trained Africa doctors are incompetent? If the hospitals and health facilities are not well equipped, is it not part of their responsibility as leaders to offer their people the best. The educated Africans had over time looked down upon those who are not fortunate to be educated and do not assist these people to improve on their conditions.

African educational system is based on the cultures and ideas of the West, so by the time a child graduates from high school in Africa he longs for all the good things he learned in school that does not reflect in his environment. He/she dreams of seeing the things learnt in school. He longs to go overseas meaning to the West. He is an African but his mind is that of the West. The knowledge acquired being foreign does not relate to the immediate environment. The young man or woman dreams of going where things learnt are not abstract but practical, and felt on the environment and human existence.

Nothing is changing in Africa. The black African accumulates western knowledge that he has not been able to apply to his immediate environment and circumstance. The same knowledge and information changed the West and East. There is nothing wrong in acquiring knowledge but application of the knowledge is the most vital. The black Africans have not been able to apply the knowledge to improve their own environment and this is why poverty and hunger is still prevalent on the Continent. The birth of knowledge changed the Western World. The birth of knowledge that changed the west is call renaissance. Unfortunately, African governments are looking for miracles for transformation. There is no miracle anywhere, except concerted efforts on the part of leaders to improve the people and the environment. African leaders should make the people they govern the most important item on their agenda in order to bring development to their people.

Africa leaders struggle and kill for power not because they want to improve the lives of their citizens but to squander the wealth of their nations. Charles Taylor of Liberia, turned his country into a battleground, used the wealth of the country to buy ammunitions, and fought his own people for political power. Liberia is a country rich in Diamond and other important mineral resources. Should there be poverty in Liberia? No, but poverty is where we turn. Politics of personal aggrandizement should stop in Africa.

The politics in Africa in this new decade should be people centered. Western puppets have ruled Africa for too long and African people deserve a better life like other people on Planet Earth. Why did the African Nationalist fought for independence from the colonial masters? If it was rule through proxy, colonial administration should have continued. The new African leaders due to greed; perpetuate themselves in power and are propped by external collaborators.

Africans have been leaving Africa risking their lives in the hope of finding greener pastures abroad. The leaders do not see the drain on the labor force of their respective countries as a concern. The meager resources these governments allocate to education trained most of these emigrants and the governments do not care to find out why these people are migrating. As long as the majority of Africans live in poverty, the few elites do not command any respect in the eyes of the rest of the world.

Nobody will develop Africa for Africans. If Africans do not get their acts right, the continent can be taken over again. The partition of Africa that took place when Europe invaded Africa and the various European languages imposed are still in place. Africans still speak English, Portuguese, and French. Countries in East Africa, Zanzibar, Kenya, and Zimbabwe tried having a lingua franca Swahili but did not achieve its intention. The black race should wake up from its slumber, the world is moving fast and Africa is sleeping.

We might soon became an endangered human species at the rate diseases are taking our lives. The most deadly being HIV/AIDS, Malaria, diabetes, high blood pressure, heart attacks, and even cancer. Our skin is becoming light and we lose melanin the natural protection from ultra violet rays. Why are we so susceptible to diseases now than in the past? Is it our immunology, poverty, or the changes to our way of living in recent history? We should take our destiny into our own hands. We should stop looking up to others for salvation. Our salvation lies in our own hands. We should be active participants in what goes on in the world. The world belongs to everyone on the earth planet.

We wait and catch anything other people throw at us. Do we wonder why other people treat us the way they do? You have not taken charge of your own life. You wait just like children to be told what is and what is not. You believe and accept anything without questioning or making your own input. The population of black people is dwindling from diseases and poverty. You do not even eat the food that sustained your ancestors for millions of years. Black people are so busy working to acquire unnecessary material acquisition that most do not have time to even cook to feed anymore.

Black people have become workers like the worker bee in the bee-hive. The worker bee works for the queen bee and dies. We eat canned or already cooked food. We eat anything, from Chinese, Mexican, English, Indian, Italian, and to American. What happened to African dishes? What happened to our green vegetables and beans?   Just like everything else, we are not represented anywhere.   We exist but do not exist.   Africans have healthy dishes, which do not produce obese in people, but it is not promoted. Who should do this?   Food business is an area an interest should exist between Africans on the continent and Africans in Diaspora.

The educated Africans on the continent can compile recipes, promote, and market them so that the world would know that Africans have healthy foods. Food industry is a huge market and a great contributor to revenue in the world where different countries sell their food and dishes.   Food industry is an area, African leaders and entrepreneurs should look into to create jobs for Africa. There is a huge potential market for African foods in Diaspora.

 Every human sect has food that they thrive on and it varies among different group of people. Nature provides food that nurtures and sustains people in their immediate environment. Can you imagine changing the diet of a lion from flesh eating to grass? Or require herbivores to be carnivores. The movement of black people from their original home to different parts of the world has brought many changes to their physique and the way they look due to different diet that may not necessary be suitable for their body chemical composition.

 It is time the black man learns to stand on his own feet to get credibility from the rest of the human race. We have become so dependent on others progress as if we cannot create our needs anymore. We are the ones copying other people. No body copy from us, they take from us and make it their own.

The only story of Africans and Africans in Diaspora you read about is people doing negative things.   Positive and negative activities are part of human existence. The western media takes delight in reporting the negative activities happenings elsewhere while covering up same incidents in their locality. What is civilization? Is it killing others to claim what they own; or the divide and rule strategy that permeates the world now? The West want to have the upper hands in the world affairs as if other beings do not have the capacity to do what is right.

The current World has created more diseases through their unchecked curiosity into nature. The world has done havoc to the earth through their desire to take charge of the world they did not create. The new civilization has polluted the atmosphere so much that the world finds it difficult to admit it errors. The world digs fossils from the belly of the earth and oceans to extract petroleum and other petrol-chemicals that have large components and residues of carbon. These carbons are now in the air causing all sorts of distortion in the atmosphere, affecting climate and the weather. Instead of facing reality and curbing this development, the world keeps denying the cause of global warming.

Humans have continued to deface the surface of the earth. A lion or tiger will kill a prey because it wants to feed on it, on the other hand, humans kill to destroy. Since the beginning of modern civilization or renaissance, humans have killed and maimed millions of its kind. Animals get more protection than human due to of lack of respect for one another and hypocrisy under the disguise of protecting animals.

Laws are in place to protect animals; this is laudable provided the thought behind the law is not to ridicule some people who do not have the power to take part in the law process. Some people will rather save animals than protect a fellow being. This civilization is premise on material acquisition and little care about people who through no faults of theirs are less privileged. Greed and selfishness have become the norm. People no longer know when to stop and think about the fact that resources are finite, and a large percentage of humanity have not had the opportunity to have even the basics, for example portable water.

African continent is the worst when it comes to amenities. Where does the fund for development go in Africa? According to the World Bank, millions of funds had been lent to African countries for development but Africa has not changed much. These funds for Africa development end up in Swiss Bank accounts of these African leaders but the World Bank and International Monetary Fund turn blind eyes to the dubious activities of these African leaders.

The people of Africa should demand accountability from their leaders as is done in the western world. African leaders have mortgaged the future of African children by owing the World Bank with nothing to show for it in terms of amenities. Most countries that have huge debts have projects and infrastructure to show where the funds went. There is nothing to pinpoint in Africa for the huge amount of debt African countries owe. The people of Africa should stand up and say enough is enough to these greedy leaders.

Africa has to develop and move from the state of misery and helplessness to prosperity, respect, and opportunities for Africans and Africans in Diaspora and friends of black people. If Africa has opportunities for people to achieve their aspirations most educated Africans would not emigrate from Africa. We are highly educated in the western culture but are not using our knowledge to our advantage. Africans should begin to apply all the knowledge acquired to develop Africa. The same knowledge learnt and applied are what made the west and east developed, prosperous and beautiful that everyone throng to. We can make Africa prosperous if African leaders stop using public resources for their own benefit and have the interest of the people they rule at heart.

Some African government spent huge sums of money training university graduates without opening up opportunities for work creation and encouraging individual contribution to create jobs. African university professors spend many productive hours on researches that wind up on shelves. There are no entrepreneurs who want to invest in ventures or take risks. The professors themselves are not aggressive enough to bring awareness to their projects.

We are hardworking and resourceful people but have not been aggressive to change our ways and improve our environment and people to meet up with the world we live in. We do everything for others that make them great but have not applied same knowledge and eagerness to improve ourselves. We produce most of the raw material that goes into manufactured products but have not bargained fairly for our products. We are not assertive and competitive enough to claim our share in the world market.

The elites or the educated Africans have neglected the uneducated and the Africans who still hold strongly to their ancestral culture. These latter group of Africans, control the market, they are into retailing, that is selling the products imported from abroad manufactured by the west and east. These Africans are the farmers, using local and crude implements to farm, they are the nomads, rearing cattle, sheep, and goats, they are the artisans making pottery, carving, black, and gold smiths, and they are the carpenters, masons, bricklayers, and painters. They are versed in African tradition and legends. They are the custodian of what is left of African culture. Despite slavery and all the impact of Europe on Africa, these Africans still hold dearly to the way their ancestors lived. These people are the faces of Africa the world knows.

The various governments in African countries should visit the plights of these Africans by making it possible for them to improve on what they do and enjoy modern amenities. These Africans are not beggars and do not want free stuff, they have the resources to pay for any service provided if the government give them recognition and let what they do matter.   Provision of modern amenities and assistance with modern techniques to improve what they already do would increase efficiency and productivity.   Doing things faster would obviously increase productivity.   Doing things with modern techniques would lure young people into the old vocation and the young would create new ideas.

 Africa has work for people to do except that the procedure for performing the work has not improved to attract the western influenced young Africans. The problem is that the way the traditional work is performed is not attractive to the young man or woman who spent most of his/her youth learning the way of the west and east in the area of agriculture, commerce, culture, attitude and way of life.   The difference between a western world farmer and the office worker in terms of quality of life is none in respect to availability of basic amenities.

 However, there is a world of difference between the African farmer and the African office worker. The African farmer depends on his ability to farm and produce what his efforts will allow. The African farmer has no agriculture specialist advising him on how to improve his crops or herds. The African farmer does not have basic amenities like portable water and yet he produces to feed the nation and produces cash crops for export.

Chapter Four

Being forgotten

This is the twenty first century, approximately six centuries after black African first encounter with the western world. Africans have not been able to come out of the terrible humiliation they went through during slavery and European domination. Europeans were able to enslave Africans due European possession of gun power that was new to Africa. Africans witnessed Europeans shot people dead with the gun and decided to surrender than face the same fate. All the same, there were great resistance from Africans but the weapons of Africans was no match to gun power. Europeans took millions of Africans across the Atlantic and used them to develop North and South America.

The attitude and actions towards black people speaks louder than words. The achievement of the current world would not have been possible if not for the free labor of the black man. The perception of other people who are not black is that a black person is good only if he serves and not a master. There are people some consider to be of lower status in every human setting but to categorize a whole group of people whose color is darker than yours as inferior is a wrong that happened six centuries ago but persists today in the 21st century. Despite the long relationship between black and other people; the attitude of most other people towards the black person is that of condescend.

In most countries in the world, the black person performs the services other people reject. The black person who is a citizen of a country cannot enjoy the same privileges as other people. On records, he or she is a citizen quite all right but when it comes to reality, other people feel he is not capable to do certain things. There is no basis for other people to feel they are superior to blacks because of the color of the skin. There are variations in color of people just as there are in most things in nature. The notion of superiority of some people over others is a fallacy; unfortunately, the incidence of slavery makes others believe it to be true. Slavery was not by the consent of the people enslaved but by brutal force. Therefore, where lies the superiority, the master was afraid of the slave just like the slave was afraid of his master because of his gun power. All kinds of pseudo scientist have come up with their interpretation why they think other people are superior. The black community has been silent for too long on the erroneous notion of superiority of one group of people over another.

Hardly is there any human endeavor that the black person does not contribute in one way or the order. No single group of people could lay claim on all the achievements of the human race today. Whatever the world is today is a contribution from everybody that occupies this earth. Everybody has been directly and indirectly involved in the processes of the world. Resources and ideas are from all people all over the world to make the world what it is today.

The black man's contributions to the western world had been glossed over due to the unfortunate incident of slavery. The world should not forget the contribution of the following people of color:

United States of America.
Elijah McCoy-: 1843-1929-Invented an oil dripping cups for trains.

Lewis Latimer -: 1848-1929 -Invented the carbon filament for the light bulb. He worked for Edison and Alexander Graham Bell.

Jan Ernst Matzeliger-: 1852-1889 - Invented a shoe-making machine that increased production speed by 900%.

Granville T Woods-: 1856-1910 - Invented the train to station communication system.

George Washington Carver-: 1860-1943 -Invented the peanut butter and four hundred other plant products.

Madam C. J Walker-: 1817-1919- Invented a hair growing lotion. She was the first African –American female millionaire.

Garnet Morgan-: 1877-1963- Invented the gas mask.

Otis Boykin-: 1920-1982-mInvented the electronic control devices for guided missiles, IBM computer, and the pacemaker.

Dr. Patricia E Bath-: 1949- Invented a method of eye surgery that has helped baling people to see.

Lonnie G Johnson-: 1949- Invented the famous Water-sun, super-soaker.

George Edward Alcorn-: invented a method of fabricating an imaging x-ray spectrometer

Phil Brooks –Invented the disposable syringe.

Benjamin Carson-:1951- A pioneering surgeon at the John Hopkins Hospital. The principal surgeon in the twenty-two hour separation of the Binder Siamese twins from Germany.

John Christian-: Invented new lubricating used in highflying aircraft and NASA space mission.

David Crosthwaite-: 1891-1976- invented the heating systems, vacuum pumps, refrigeration methods and processes and temperature regulating devices.

Charles Drew-: 1904-1950- He discovered blood preservation –by separating the liquid red blood cells from the near solid plasma and freezing the two separately-the Blood Bank.

Philip Emeagwali- Nigerian born won the Gordon Bell Prize in 1989 for supercomputers-programmed the connection machine to compute a world record 3.1 million calculation per second using 65,536 processors to stimulate oil reservoirs. This also helped stored the largest weather forecasting equation with 128 million points in 1990. He invented the hyper-ball computer networks.

Meredith Gourdine-: 1929-1998- pioneered the research of electro-gas-dynamics (EGD)
He successfully converted natural gas to electricity. He was blind.

Lloyd A Hall-: 1894-1977- Developed curing salts for the processing and preservation of meats.

Emmett Chappell -: He pioneered the development of the ingredients ubiquitous in all cellular material. He created the technique for detecting bacteria in urine, blood, spinal fluids drinking water, and foods.

John Christian-: invented new lubricant used in high-flying aircraft and NASA space missions.

Donald Crosthwaite-: 1891-1976 Outreach Heating Systems, vacuum pumps, refrigerator methods, and processes and temperate regulating devices.

Mark Dean and Dennis Moeller:- created a microcomputer syste4m with bus control means peripheral processing devices.

Thomas Elkins-: An improved refrigerator to chill corpses was patented in New York.

George Grant-: Dentist designed a prosthetic device for treatment of the cleft palate.

Lloyd A Hall-: 1894-1977 Developed curing salts for the processing and preservation of meats. Developed a technique of sterilization with ethylene oxide,
 Still used by medical professional today.

George Edward Alcorn-: invented a method of fabrication and imaging x-ray spectrometer.

Henry Blair- Invented the seed planter.

George Caruthers -:1939- He developed the first based space observatory, an ultraviolet camera that was carried to the moon by Apollo- He invented image convector for detecting electro-magnetic radiation in short wave length.

Frederick Jones-: 1893-1961 He invented automatic refrigeration system for long haul trucks and railroads cars, also developed self-starting gas engine and series of devices for movie projectors.

Dr. Percy Julian-: synthesized *physotignone* for the treatment of glaucoma and cortisone for the treatment of rheumatic arthritis. He produced aero-foam that suffocated gasoline and oil fires in the World War II.

Dr. Edward Just: His researches made advancement in the field areas of egg fertilization, hydration, cells division effects of ultraviolet rays in the increasing chromosomes numbers in animals.

Joseph Wee: He invented improvement to the dough kneading machine.

Ruth J Miro: He invented a personalized paper rings binder.

Cordell Reed:- Improvement to the methods of producing nuclear electron power.

Louis W Roberts: He invented a gaseous discharge device-microwaves, optical techniques, plasma, researched solid state compact.

Henry Sampson: He invented the gamma-electrical cells, binder system for propellers, explosives, and care bonding system for cast composite propellants.

Richard Spikes -: invented automatic car washer (1913) beer keg tap (1910), multiple gun barrel machine (1940). He died in 1962.

Ruth J Miro-:She invented a personalized paper ring binder.

Velerie Thomas: She invented an illusion transmitter.

John Thompson -: Lingo programming used in macromedia director and shock wave.

James West-: His research in early 1960 led to the development of foil electric transducers for sound recording and voice communication.

Dr. Frank Crossly: He was a pioneer in the field of titanium metallurgy.

Michael Moldier- Originally from Haiti –research associate at the office of Imaging Research Development with Kodak Eastman.

Mary Dixon Kites-: developed the process of weaving straw with silk. (1809)

Sarah Mather-: invention submarine telescope and lamp. (1945).

Mather J. Colton-: patented her late husband idea of pyrotechnic flare.

Ann Moore: He developed a baby carrier; called snuggle and patented in 1969.

It is just amazing how these black people despite abuse and relegation were able to contribute to society that almost deprived them of their dignity as human. The resiliency of a black person is immense. Black people have contributed to the progress of these earth but they get the least enjoyment due to greed from those who have redefined the life most people live. People who are not of color for reasons better known to them feel they are better people than colored person. It is an unwritten principle but that is the perception. Whether colored or without color all people go through the same processes- birth, growth, sickness and death. Death is the ultimate equalizer of all people.

Africa has been the world's puppet and pet; everybody claim to be helping Africa and one wonders where the help goes. Africa is getting worse and worse. Diseases are increasing in number and complexity and poverty is rendering people useless. Africans are not lazy people. Africans are hard-working but their productivity is not reflecting on their standard of living. The African environment is the most neglected in the whole world. Africa has beautiful climate and landscapes but the leaders of Africa have not been able to use these to their advantage.

Africa's climate does not go through many changes during the year. Most crops and plants grow all year round without much tendering. Yet Africa cannot take advantage of the excellent climatic condition and have enough food for the people. Africans have taken these givens for granted and are not making any effort to preserve or improve the environment than the way nature left it. We have left our environment for nature to nurture them for us. All we do is to depend on nature for everything. Everywhere around is changing and Africans need to change their environment and take control of it.

Africa has large virgin places that the air is clean and clearer. The African environment has not seen much pollution from recent industrialization, but some scrupulous industrialized countries have been dumping toxic waste at the coastlines of African countries. In recent times, African skies are usually dusty during the day from dusts and pollution from used cars imported from the west and east. Africa produces petroleum and has large deposits of granites and limestone but has not thought it fit to use these products to tame the dust from unpaved roads and paths

The world has moved away from waiting on nature to take care of things. Africa has ample resources to change the environment for Africans to live a better life. Africans have not done justice to their environment. The people exploit the environment for mineral resources; the gains from the resources are not invested in the environment to make it beautiful and even safe for the people. The money make from African resources are used to import things from the west and east thereby none of the money is invested in Africa.

Africans should realize by this time that their children are behind in terms of development and enjoyment in what the current world offers. The time has come for us to start planning for our future and that of our children because we are way behind in terms of human development. Our attitude of not being curious and adventurous has made our children to be the least developed technologically among the people of the world. We do not have to go to the moon but can make our world healthy and beautiful for our children. All we need to do is be concerned and caring for our own people. We should realize that we deserve to enjoy this world just like anybody else.

We do not need any one to tell us that living in a clean environment is healthy. We spend a great proportion of our income on clothes, shoes, jewelries, cars, and accessories others manufacture while our environment is filthy and dirty. We should be able to take care of our environment. Our ancestors lived in clean environment, they swept and used herbs to keep smell away; they were healthy and strong people. We should go back to the way they were. Cleanliness was the key to their pride. We can do this. If we make cleanliness one of our top priority we would be able to eliminate most of the diseases that plague our people particularly malaria and dysentery. Even without light and portable water, absolute cleanliness can change the look of Africa. We have many children who have the best of western education but unfortunately, they have not been able to apply what they have learnt to their environment.

Surprisingly, we do the things we cannot do for ourselves for other people. Many of us leave Africa and go to Europe and America to sweep their streets and work in their sewage but cannot do the same for Africa. We sit on the fence and criticize Africa but what are we doing to make it better. We keep on having children without planning for a better future for them. Do we want our children to continue to be associated with poverty and diseases? It is about time we, as black people change our ways and make the next generation proud of whom their ancestors were. We should wake up from day dreaming and help Africa to be associated with wealth and prosperity for all citizens rather than diseases and poverty.

Man created wealth and we should believe Africa could create its own wealth. Africa has all it takes to be a great continent and restore the dignity of black people, instead of a place that is full of misery and the people live in object poverty and seeking international aids and grants. Africa is not poor and miserable it needs to take charge of its resources and affairs. The rest of the world look at Africa as if Africans are hapless and helpless people who cannot help themselves and always needing help from other people . Do we blame them for having this view? No, we should not because we have not been able to show that we are capable of improving ourselves without expecting aid or grant from the rest of the world.

We should be able to use our education to help elevate our people. In order for us to get respect from the rest of the world communities, we should be ready to improve the lives of our people. Black people will continue to trail the rest of the world in terms of environmental improvement unless the educated Africans make a concerted effort to contribute to their own society instead of jeering the backwardness of their people. The educated African feels he/she is not part of the rest of Africa so it does not matter. Please listen and you will hear. The way the development of Africa is does not portray we have well educated people. The birth of knowledge changed both western and eastern worlds. The essence of education is to improve one's life and the world around. If truly, there are educated Africans then Africa should not be the way it is. Africa should not be the way it is under any circumstance.

Europeans developed Europe, Americans developed America therefore it is the responsibility of Africans to develop Africa. Nobody will have the interest of Africa at heart except Africans and people with African heritage. After the two World Worlds, people of Europe and people of European heritage developed Europe and restore its glory. The two world Wars affected Africa but no visible development or help came to Africa. We are not doing enough to help develop Africa.

We are in the 21st century and there is not much difference between now and 1492. We do not need charity as our political leaders think to move Africa forward. The Jews have limited lands but they have been able to make the best of it. Our politicians do not have the progress of their citizens at heart. These African politicians care only for their families, associates, and cohorts. They do not know what governance is all about. They still behave like the African Kings and Queens of old who ruled absolutely. The essence of government is to find ways of making life better for the governed.

In the modern world the cornerstone of good government are: security, full employment, education, orderliness, health facilities, clean environment, stability of currency and freedom of choice, speech and protection of citizens and the last but not the least the ability of the people to freely vote for whom they want to lead them. If African government had been following these principles, Africans would have moved forward. The people of African believe in the dignity of labor but the leaders are not doing their required part. Africa needs patriotic leaders who care about the progress of their citizens. African leaders should learn that good leaders serve the people and not the other way round. Good leadership derives respect from the people and they are willing to sacrifice themselves for the good things that come with good governance.

Africa can change if the leaders begin to see the significance of making life better for their citizens. All hands must be on deck to lift Africa up. Africa should be a continent that has its destiny in its own hands and not a puppet or pet before the turn of this century. A quarter of the world population can trace their ancestry to Africa and they are not proud of the present condition of Africans they see on their media and books. Africans should develop Africa instead of looking for already developed countries to migrate. Africa does not belong to the rulers but to the hard working people of Africa.

Africa is the last to develop and it would be the best among the continents. Black people wherever you are come together to lift Africa to its rightful place. The leaders can change Africa by just providing the basics like clean environment and the rest would fall into places naturally.

Most Africans build their houses from scratch with no loans or financial help from the government or creditors so if they get little pushes from their government they would make tremendous changes. A healthy people are a wealthy people. Africans are not poor but they need to set priority to develop themselves instead of running to already developed areas of the world. Black people should stop being carbon copy of other people, they should use their initiate and given talents. Cleanliness of the environment should be a top priority to move Africa closer to the rest of the world. Keeping the African environment clean and healthy could be accomplished from volunteers and donations from the wealthy Africans. The monies kept in Switzerland banks alone by corrupt politicians could help Africa solve most of its problems. Africa has been blessed with good climatic conditions, resources, and, people and yet it remains the poorest continent. All we need is to harness our resources and people and Africa would be a continent among continents. This is our time to leap forward as people.

It is about time Africans began to think of making Africa a better place to stay instead of running to places all over the world for greener pastures. We can create greener pastures in Africa too. Europe and America sprung through dedicated leadership that had concerned for the people. There are so many opportunities in Africa. What Africa is lacking are leaders who are dedicated to improve the lives of all not a few. Africans do not have to build modern conveniences from the scratch. The basic technologies and techniques to provide electricity, portable water, roads, and other infrastructures are already available in the world. Plans and strategy to provide amenities for rural Africa should be the way forward for any government in Africa. Every African should have access to portable water, electricity and roads and other infrastructures. Embarking on these projects would create jobs for people and the consequences would be a better environment and healthy people who are engaged in improved and better vocations.

There is the erroneous notion that some Africans object to modern amenities. This is a fallacy there is no human in this era who would not want to live in a lighted environment. There is always resistant to changes but if people see the benefits of the changes, they accept the changes eventually. Some African leaders for reasons best known to them have segregated their own people. The governments in Africa have not given attention to the following group of people in Africa: the Maasai in East Africa, the Fulani in West Africa, the Tuaregs in the Sahara, Xhosa in South Africa, and the Twa people in Congo. These people would appreciate electricity and portable drinking water.

The Maasai and the Fulani are both nomad nations. They move about with their herds looking for pastures for their herds. It is about time these people are given lands to develop ranches and have settled life. If these people live on ranches, the animals they raise would be healthier, the people would be healthier, and there would be healthy and nutritious meat for the populace. The citizens of most Africa communities depend upon the Maasai and Fulani other nomads for supply of meat. If the Maasai and Fulani, and other people who are nomads in Africa live on ranches, there would not be clashes between nomads and crop farmers. Most communal clashes in Africa are consequences of the nomads herding their herds to feed on farms of farmers. These perennial clashes between nomads and farmers could be stopped if African governments settle the nomads on ranches as is done in the developed worlds.

Some of you contributed to the invention of the modern world technologies but have not taken advantage of the technologies to improve our way of life. We prefer to be dependent instead of independent. We jump at helping others but hesitate to help ourselves. The attitude of making our needs secondary to others, make us different from the rest of the world. Most people believe in helping themselves first and that was why it had not been difficult to enslave others, to go to war and in some instances to eliminate an entire group of people to get what they wanted. Our attitude of complacency and not being aggressive to develop and grab resources is really helping other people because they continue to use our resources to develop their people while our people continue to live in object poverty.

African resources greased the industrialized world; Europe and America in the fourteen centuries and now China is using our resources to develop China. The population of China is over 1.3 billion and that of Africa as a whole is 905.9 million including the settled Arabs in North Africa so can you imagine what will happen if China continues depending on Africa for resources. Could you envisage what would happen to Africa resources by the turn of the century? Africa's population is only 14.2% of the whole world and, unfortunately, it is the poorest in terms of human advancement but rich in resources that other people take to develop their own people.

Could you envision a way out for Africa's predicament? It is the African environment that defines black people, despite the dispersion of Africans all over the world through slavery and later immigration Africans still possess the same unique characteristics of being considerate and accommodating to other people. We have warm hearts and love all humanity. Every person of color should be involved in building Africa because it is our ancestral home. Africa is where Nature landed colored people. Colored people should therefore redeem Africa from neglect and extortion by other people. All Africans and black people have a stake in the African continent, and should be involved in lifting Africa up.

 The next item that requires awareness after clean and healthy environment is our food. Do you know we are fond of other people's food We eat varieties of food, but our food is not on the world's menu. Italians have been able to perfect their pasta and pizza and these have created billions of dollar industry for Italians and their economy. Chinese food is eating everywhere in the world. We talk about not having employment for our teeming population. The food industry is one way we can create international market for our food and earn foreign exchange instead of looking for aids and grants from the United Nations and those who get rich from our resources.

Where is the market for our food? People of African descendants are all over the world and they are craving for authentic African delicacy. Start with our black eye peas; consumed all over black Africa. Cassava is a common product and stable food in Africa. Where else is cassava eaten as stable food? Cassava is like potato except it contains more starch than potato. We know the different types of dishes we can make from cassava. We can develop easy recipes, demonstrate, cook, package, and market our food, and there would be employment for many of our people.

This is just an example of few things Africans can do to entice the rest of the world. We have universities everywhere in Africa and yet researches are not done to see how we can improve our food from the way our fore mothers and fathers prepared and consumed them. Yes, we started making some inroads into developing *fufu* in Ghana and *iyan* in Nigeria. What happened? We do not promote ourselves, other people are not better than us, they appear better because they promote themselves and we have been convinced that they are better. That is the power of marketing. Marketing is not new to us, but it has developed into a higher level that we get mesmerized with the current marketing gimmicks. Now you know what to do. Rebrand yourself and market what you have. You now know the power of marketing and the importance of rebranding and marketing yourself

Corporations expend billions of dollars to actors and sports men and women to market their products. If you invented or created an item and you did not create awareness or market its existence the item will not be known to those who might need it. Marketing is a very powerful tool, people accept what is marketed to them and do not bother about its truthfulness.   Africans should begin to be involved in this world and stop expecting someone to solve their problems. Let us do something for ourselves and stop behaving like a child who needs to be taking care of.   No one will tell us what to do unless we realize what to do ourselves.

We know there is only one earth and all people are competing to have as much of it as possible.   You see why we should stop sitting on the fence, and get involve in things around us and make our part of the world better for our children yet unborn.   Many generations before us and our generation have suffered enough. Some of us were enslaved, colonized, and we fought for our freedom. We took our continent back and got our independence from our colonial masters but we never received economic freedom. Can you not see what is happening to our people?

Yes, we need economic freedom. We do not have economic freedom. We are still dependent on our former colonial masters for everything. We have not figured out how to be economically independent therefore nothing has changed. The way to be thoroughly free is to have economic freedom. If we have economic freedom we would decide what we need and be able to produce them. We forced the colonists from our continent, yet we travel to them and request help for our progress. We are so naïve that we believe they would help us to progress like them. We can only be like them, through
our collective efforts.

We are competitors for the resources of the earth and help from them for us to have the upper hand would never happen. The lower we are on the spectrum of economics the better they feel. That is the human nature and the nature of competition.   It is over fifty years since they left your continent, what have we done to make life better for our people. Not much, we keep on imitating the life style of the people we drove away and we seem not to have a culture or history. People without a past and culture cannot progress forward. Africans need to trace their steps back if they want to improve on their present predicament.

Black people have some rich and affluent people but they are not the yardstick to measure Africa's progress. Africa in the eyes of the world is poverty and suffering. There is poverty and misery everywhere but other people ignore the poverty right around them and see the poverty far away. There is hardly any nation without poor people. In fact, poverty is relative. We need to improve on the next generation of Africans so that they can be proud of themselves in this world. This world belongs to all therefore every person has a right to live a better life. We have the capacity to improve ourselves since we have equal opportunity in the world. What is stopping us?

We need to develop our environment and start caring for our people. Every person on earth is fighting for the preservation of its people. What are we doing? It was diseases and now HIV/AIDS destroying lives. This new ailment HIVDS is destroying a very high percentage of our youth. What are we doing to curb this fatal disease? Cancer has not killed many people as HIV/AIDS but millions of dollars are into researches to find cure for cancer. What are black people doing about HIVAIDS? All deadly ailments find their way into our blood stream. We are humans but have relied on others to solve our problems for us. It is about time we start doing some researches into diseases that afflict us most? It is time we talk on preservation of ourselves or we become like the dinosaur that walked the surface of the earth but now extinct.

We have to start talking about self- preservation. Our color is disappearing. By nature, we are not aggressive. We trust others more than we trust ourselves. We need to be involved more in activities on earth in order to be able to improve our people and preserve our future. The environment is the key. If the environment is clean and made conducive to aid human development then imagination and creativity would set in and development would spur without much effort. We need to harness our people so that efforts are directed towards improving life. Every person is important and each individual contributes to the good of the society through the vocation one engages. If individuals work to improve their families, it would in turn impacts the larger community.

Do you know we are the only people who speak other people's mother tongue? This fact brought about the making Swahili a lingua franca in Tanzania and parts of East Africa. Nigeria tried with Wazobia, but did not materialize. Africans versed in the rudiments of their trade dominate the economic activities in African countries. These people do not have formal education but have been trading from generation to generation. They have capital, but their perception of environment and health is different from the current view. These are the people the various government should form alliance with in the process of improving the environment.

In most instances, these people do not derive benefits from government and continue to live in slums despite their wealth. Individuals by themselves cannot provide portable drinking water, electricity, roads, functional schools, recreational area without joint effort of the government and entrepreneurs. These African entrepreneurs are not dependent on government but they need to be carried along in order to give Africa a face lift. There are two sets of people within African nations: The African elites who have political power and the illiterate or partially educated Africans who control the market and capital. The latter people need to be involved in any comprehensive plans for Africa. Their economic activities are vital but the governments have not provided them with the necessary assistance they need to improve. We need to work hand in hand with these people if we want to move Africa forward.

The essence of education is to bring about improvement and make living better for the majority. Alas it is not so in Africa. The educated segregate themselves from the less educated people but they consume the food these people produce. The uneducated follow the traditions of their ancestors to do things whereas the educated use the western way. We live in two worlds. In order for black people and Africa as a continent to move forward the western educated few and the majority traditional Africans have to interact and find solutions to African myriad problems. The black race all over the world is looking to Africa to be organized and be on a direction to improve lives of the majority of the people instead of the educated few. We are least among the human population on earth and yet we are involved in ethnic cleansing than any other race. Each ethnicity in Africa should complement one another. There is a reason we have differences in culture and language and yet so close. That is a mystery of nature that no human can resolve.

Slavery took away a large percentage of black Africans and instead of unity to strengthen Africans, ethnic cleansing has become the new face of Africa. It started in the Nigeria civil war in the 1970s, then, moved to Central Africa, Uganda, Rwanda, and now Sudan. The Darfur people of Sudan are being killed by their neighbors, the Janjaweed. They are neighbors because they have coexisted for a long time. The Janjaweed are nomads while the black Africans are farmers who own the land.

Clashes between nomads and farmers are problems all over Africa and government after government have not found peaceful solution to these quagmires. Farming and herding are two main occupations in Africa prior to colonization and independence. African leaders should have settled this problem by creating ranches for the nomads so that they do not have to move their herds around to trample and eat farm crops. Animal rearing and farming are the occupations for most people in the world before the advent of industrialization and technologies. The way of rearing animals have changed all over the world with the exception of Africa.

The Janjaweed should be educated on how to raise animals on ranches the way of the industrialized countries. The government of Sudan should invest the money they spend on ammunition to purchase land and build ranches for the Janjaweed and or encourage them to build ranches and raise their animals. There would be peace and the people of Darfur and Janjaweed can coexist peacefully. Human beings need to learn from one another. Resolving conflict by removing the causes is the way to bring peace. The United Nations should have intervened and settled the conflict by educating the Janjaweed to purchase grazing land and raise their cattle just like the Australians, Europeans, Argentinians and American farmers raise their animals.

The millions of lives wasted in Darfur would not have happened if the government had been proactive instead of reactionary. Governments in Africa should learn to resolve issues through solutions to problems instead of force. Power brokers turn blind-eyes to problems because war creates money for those who make weapons and the brokers get their share of the profit from the sale of weapons. There are so many conflicts of interests such that it has become difficult for people to show genuine interest in other people's problems.

People of the world are all competing against one another for the same resources so it is almost impossible for a set group of people like the blacks to think the rest of the world will look for solutions for their problems. The world watches while the governments who are supposed to protect citizens massacre thousands upon thousands. Could you tell me what the massacre in Uganda, Liberia, Sierra Leone, Uganda, and Rwanda brought to Africa? These massacres were a sizable reduction in black African population. The system of governance that is practiced in Africa is not

231

intended to improve the life of the masses but to create more problems for future generations.   These governments place too much emphasis on ethnicity for political gain instead of uniting the people.   Every country in black Africa has similar problems of bad infrastructures, unorganized economy, inadequate amenities, poor sanitation systems, uncontrolled drainage systems and no maintenance culture.

It is quite amazing that African politicians do not use the hospitals in their countries when sick but rush to hospitals in Europe. Most of these politicians die while undergoing treatment abroad. It is time for Africa leaders to invest in good health delivery system so that they and the people could have access to quality case like the one they go to in Europe.   African universities train medical doctors who work in hospitals in Europe, America and many countries around the world.
These politicians could not entrust their lives to the African doctors who are accepted and work in hospitals they go to overseas. We fought for our independence from the colonial masters but we can entrust them with our lives. There are many highly trained African physicians but our hospitals are not properly equipped to enable them practice what they have learnt.   African physicians are over the world working for other hospitals while our hospitals are dearth of doctors. The money spent on treatments overseas could equip our hospitals and make them efficient.

The next generation of Africans should love Africa and not run away from it to go overseas and do jobs they would not do in Africa.   The west was developed by people and I believe Africa could equally be developed.   Africa leaders think of your grandchildren yet unborn and invest in Africa instead of Switzerland and other foreign countries.   Africa would be the best place on earth if the children of Africa take care of Africa the way children of other places take care of their land.   Africa has a lot to offer so we should take care of Africa to see its beauty and actualize her worth.   A chunk of Africa's wealth was taken away to develop Europe now

232

China is seriously eyeing Africa to take away our resources to make China reach its dream.

Children of Africa that are scattered all over the world help Africa develop so that we can also lay in the sun on the beaches that African has been endowed with.   We have waited so long, suffered so long but it is time we realize we have the capacity and ability to enjoy life fully.   Our destiny is right in our own hands , let us make use of it or else we might lose it again.

Chapter Five

Moving Up

When it comes to achievements, black people have come a long way. We have famous sons and daughters across the world doing fantastic contributions to make the world a better place but alas not much to be proud of about Africa's progress. Some of your children have made notably contribution to help Africa develop but it is not showing because the problems of Africa are myriad. In order for Africa to claim its rightful place among the communities of the world it has to be able provide basic amenities to its youthful population. It has to be able to develop its agriculture system to feed its population. It must improve its culture instead of continuously copying cultures of other lands. Each land's culture is a continuum of a long history and changes according to the demand of each era.

The system of the West is for the people of the West and is a continuation and improvement of what their ancestors did and recorded. The culture of the west brought to Africa has created more problems than solutions. It has created two distinctive groups of people the western educated and the traditional African. The traditional African follows the African laws; though unwritten has passed from generations to generations.

Africa has to organize its cultures and economy so that it can have reliable statistics for all cultural and economic activities. The western educated Africans should document what the traditional Africans do in order for the African cultures to be part of curriculum in schools, and the next generation can improve upon as it is in most developed cultures. Africa can boast of millions of highly western educated sons and daughters but they have not been able to apply the knowledge to develop their continent. The African system served our ancestors so it should be able to serve us if you study and improve upon it.

Our education system should be centered on our cultures and improve upon them to be par with modern cultures. Most cultures of the world take the good part from the people they encounter and augment it with their own where relevant. The western educated Africa is abandoning the cultures of their ancestors and assimilating the culture of the west to the detriment of the future generation. The events of yesterdays should be recalled, what history do we intend to leave our children?

The West we copy did similar things they took the best from various cultures improve it and made it their own. That is the reason they have been able to move forward and ahead of most people in terms of standard of living, decent and efficient environment. The West has developed to such extend that even the poorest enjoy basic amenities provided the means to pay is available. The West has been able to conquer the environment to their advantage; cold and snow that used to be a hindrance had been developed into exciting winter sports. The Sahara and Kalahari deserts in Africa has been expanding and turning arable lands into deserts but people move away instead of trying to conquer the situation. Droughts are serious problem over Africa but people have not devise means to store water when it rains or create irrigation from the water level underground. There is water underground everywhere if you dig deep enough. Africans should use their initiative because that is the only way to create prosperity and better life. Manna does not fall from the skies any more. Man has to be imaginative and creative to get manna these days.

We do not deserve to deprive ourselves of things the rest of the world take for granted. Black people work all the time and hardly think about comfort and convenience. It is about time we raised our heads up and observe what is happening around us. We began to slow down almost six centuries ago and kept on retrogressing instead of progressing. Blacks are hit the most whenever there is economic downturn anywhere. Most black people are poor despite the hard work.

The world is in the twenty-first century and we are still in the medieval age. Most of the world is lighted up but a large portion of Africa is in darkness the moment the sun goes down. We get the sunshine more than twelve hours each day but have not been able to capture the sun to provide lights at night. Africans are very lucky, the west has developed solar energy technology, and all we need to do is to invest in this technology to provide lights for our people. The black African is an independent individual and it abhors begging so if the governments provide electricity to the citizens they would pay for its use.

The problem with Africa is leadership not the people. For the sake of future generations African leaders should be concerned in making life better for their citizens. We have what it takes in terms of brilliant sons and daughters. Let us go back to the drawing table and review what is wrong with us that our sons and daughters are always among the poorest wherever they are on the planet earth. Even in the west, with advancement and available opportunities, most black people are always the poorest. We can change this perception if we harness our resources and make conscious effort to make the life of people the essence of existence and change the status quo.

Africa is not a poor continent it is just that it has been taking advantage of by its own people and people from other continents. Most riches of the world were taken from Africa during the triangular trade period. Until black people develop a viable economic system where they can trade on one and on one basis with the rest of the world we would continue to be poor and relegated to the background in world affairs.

Our sons and daughters are attracted to the developed world due to the opportunity of decent environments. Most of these people have western education and can only live and function like a westerner. These people are black only by the color of their skin but their view and perception is of the west.

Blacks have been in the west for over four hundred years and yet are perceived in some quarters of the West as if they arrived from Africa yesterday. Slavery was abolished over two hundred years ago but its ghost is well alive. You smell it everywhere. Do you blame anyone for this? We as people have allowed ourselves to be treated so.

After we secured geographical and political independence, we forgot economic independence. We stopped developing our resources. Initially, we were producing cash crops to feed the industries and factories in Europe and suddenly oil wells were discovered all over Africa and the continent stopped still. Africans put their eggs in one basket by depending on natural resources like, petroleum, diamonds, copper, tin, cobalt, and rare gems. When the economy of the importer of our product has economic down turn, it affects us too. Is this not an irony?

Some petroleum exporting countries in Africa do not even have enough refineries to refine the petroleum they consume. We sell crude petroleum cheaply and buy refined petroleum at exorbitant price. Africa has large supply of raw material sold to the west but Africa cannot boast of even one commodity market. All commodity markets are based in the west. Africa needs to develop commodity markets for the raw material they export in order to take control of its resources instead of others controlling what the Africans produce. African leaders should begin to look ahead and plan for their people. Africans should be involved and be part of shaping the world economy since it supply most of the raw material for production of most items the world depends on. Majority of what the world uses in the technological theatre comes from Africa and yet Africa is the poorest and least developed. African leaders are satisfied with the way things are because they enjoy the little benefits that trickle down to Africa. Do you now that being black not much has changed?

In order for black Africa to improve on the predicament of the continent and have a lead way in this world, it has to take responsibility for its economic development. India is doing it and it is moving ahead to be a member of the industrialized world. China is moving ahead and it is importing resources from Africa to do so. Nobody cares about development for African people except where African forest can be used to correct the global warming the industrialized countries created. United Nations have decided to use Africa's forest to correct global warming and air pollution by growing trees that absorbs large quantity of carbon dioxide and large amount of water? The United Nations is advising African farmers to plant trees to absorb the carbon in the atmosphere instead of increasing food production and animal rearing that is deficient.

The United Nations has not settled these farmers on a ranch or provided them with modern amenities to make their own livelihood better. It looks as if Africans are there to serve other people's needs. Africans are always sacrificing for the rest of humanities. Where are the black leaders? When are African leaders going to fight for their people's right and well-being? African countries are the only place on earth where external factors control what happens internally. It has been the same process since the first Portuguese came to Africa and the system continues and nothing had changed. Which of the African leaders is ready to take Africa to a better situation from the doldrums of poverty and diseases in the 21st century?

The leaders should encourage development of talents of the youth in other to capture and nurture their talents. Africans have not taken charge of their environment for development.

This attitude is one of the main reasons for under development of the people and the continent as a whole. In the West everyone is their brother's keeper and that is the reason the rich uses their resources to create jobs and philanthropic organization abound to fill areas the government cannot be. In the West, volunteers are everywhere helping people and improving the environment. Businesses and entrepreneurs are funding researches to improve lives of the people. What are the rich black people doing to lift their own kind? Despite the fact that capitalism is the economic mode of the western world they still assist the less privilege in their societies. Everyone in the west has access to basics of life such as lights, water and shelter, though not free but it is available to any able body and people with physical challenges as well.

The talented Africans leave Africa and go abroad where their efforts and talents are developed and appreciated. The African leaders enjoy portraying Africans as poor because they get the grants from the advanced countries and use them mostly to their own advantage. These leaders are only in denial of their atrocities to the people they lead; the people are unable to raise their voices due to persecution and other unforeseen consequences. There is no African countries where there has been talents search in order to nurture and develop them. What is wrong with African leaders?

Blacks should reevaluate themselves and reassess their position in this world. Blacks should be involved in things around them and take charge to improve life for the generation yet unborn. Having educated population without providing where they would be productive with the knowledge acquired is like using a basket to fetch water. It will never be full.

Africa is still a dark continent just like the first Portuguese explorer found it. Despite all our laurels and personal wealth, we still do not evoke respect because we have not put our money where our mouth is. We labor harder than most because we must perform twice as much to be recognized. Should it be that way? No! When will this stop? It will stop when we realize who we are and be ourselves instead of copycats. We have done so much for others so let us work to improve our environments and ourselves and claim back our glory.

Have you pondered over why black people have to labor harder for their achievement and livelihood? We have the ability and resiliency to move mountains and yet have not used our strength and ability to claim our rightful place in the world. We do things to please others instead of being who we are. We are selfless. We are kind, sentimental, thoughtful, compassionate, caring, and just, but unfortunately most people do not act the way we do. The world is more aggressive and competitive now than ever. Our virtues are our weaknesses.

Despite all the advancement in technology, there is still a great deal of ignorance or insecurity among human beings or else after six centuries of coexistence it should have become known that our color is for protection from the sun. If we were different then we would not procreate with other people not of our color. Despite the obvious that humanity is of the same stock with the exception of the environment some still carry the old sentiment of ignorance and arrogance.

Necessity due to the difficult terrain and cold climate made the West search for solution to conquer the adverse environment and they stumbled upon our continent where the sun shines and we had nothing to worry as far as the environment was concerned. The necessity to overcome their difficulties made them innovators and creators. They gain trust of others and learnt about their weakness of other people through trading and introduction of their religion. The West was able to convince us that everything we had and did was bad and we became a perpetual adherence and believer in anything West. In view of that, we had not developed our culture and it is at a standstill at the level it was when we encountered the West.

We are to be blamed for the way others see us and treat us. We have not made improvement to our environment. The generations of the people that came and took us away over six hundred years ago have not changed their ambition and their perception of us. They still go all over the world making discoveries and finding new things to make life even better for their generation yet unborn. They still teach us how to live. They dictate the way the world goes. What are we as people waiting for to improve ourselves and enjoy the benefits of this world?

The perception, they hold about us have not changed. We have acquired the same education that brought tremendous changes to their culture and improvement in their lives and health but we have not been able to use the acquired knowledge to make like better for us as it did them. Most things that make life comfortable have been made and we have not been able to take advantage of them. We were able to free ourselves from their domination, but have not been able to use the freedom to improve the lives of our people. We control most of our resources, but we do not know how to sell them to our advantage. The importers of our resources control our economy because the decision of how much our product worth lies with them and this has effect on our internal development. Our financial and economic control is not in our hands so what freedom do we have?

Remember, they first came to us to trade. They trained us to like what they produce and we have slowly become addicted to their goods instead of improving what our fore fathers left behind. Take a close look around us and name things made in Africa. The education we have been acquiring has not helped us to improve upon ourselves and culture but to create a massive consumer market for the goods manufactured in Europe and elsewhere. If this was our intention, why did we fight for independence?

We are creating another set of intelligent educated people who cannot find jobs in their own country, but go overseas to work on menial jobs with university degrees. Graduates become cab drivers, street cleaners, house cleaners, cashiers, and nurse aids. Europe and other countries derive the benefit of educated Africans who go abroad and do menial jobs with university degrees in the name of earning a living. The countries of their birth did not prepare them for their work life, and do not have the basic necessaries of life even if they look to be creative and innovative.

Once, a Nigerian president came to America and met with some professional Nigerians and he said they should be grateful to the American government for providing them employment. Such a statement could only come from an African president to his citizens who are sojourning abroad due to lack of work and bleak future for them and their families in home countries. This president should have been ashamed of himself and buried his face in the sand. It is the responsibility of any democratic government that his people have employment. A good government should make the environment conducive so that people are ready to invest in the economy and resources are available to make people innovative to create jobs.

All governments seek full employment for its people. It does not seem that the governments in Africa even think it is their responsibility to ensure that every citizen has a sustainable livelihood. The African people are hardworking people and have been doing the best they can with the meager resources and inadequate infrastructure available to keep on struggling unabated. The present conditions and situation in Africa lies at the feet of the leaders. The essence of a leader is to provide direction and have strategies to move the people and nation towards self-reliance, development, security, and dignity. The beauty of leaders is to be ready to serve the people and vice versa. The leaders of Africa despite their western education and taste for everything west have not been able to emulate the western system of governance.

The West practices democracy for governance and capitalism for the economy and social tendency where human compassion is required. In short, the West practices a mixed government. African leaders practice democracy only at the ballot box that is if the election is not rigged. Look at the whole picture and you will see that African leaders have been deceiving themselves at practicing democracy.

Democracy stands for the government of the people, by the people, of the people and for the people. The only part of the democratic ideology practiced in Africa is of the people because Africans now rule Africans. In most instances, these leaders are puppets of some external forces. The world is in a period where leaders in most countries are competing to make life as convenient as possible for the citizens. Africa leaders are doing nothing to improve the lives of the average citizens. The few that are making efforts are totalitarians they listen to no one but themselves. This dictatorial tendency makes it difficult for freedom loving people to express themselves in the way they are governed.

African leaders are embroiled in fighting for political power instead of teaming together to look for avenue to improve the lives of average African who struggles day in and day out just to survive. There will always be a loser in politics and African leaders should be aware of this. The best politic is the politic that have the people at its center. African politicians do not see people in this light. Their politics is for themselves, families, and cohorts. If African politicians care for the people they govern, significant progress would have emerged on the continent of Africa.

Africa has enough western educated sons and daughters at home and in Diaspora who could transform Africa if the leaders of Africa are ready to welcome new ideas for moving the continent forward. Africa is lacking in everything humanly possible for the people and no one is talking about improving the continent. There is plenty of talk on preserving the exotic animals in Africa and not the people. The continent of Africa connotes nothing in the West but exotic animals and people who do not know their right from their left.

The Africans who live in the deep forest of Africa are not seeing any light of the modern way. They have survived that life for centuries but their population is decreasing due to pollution and contamination from using modern things without education on how to use them. They come to African cities on occasions to buy powdered milk to feed their children but do not know much about the hygiene of preserving the left over milk. The milk is contaminated and fed to the kids and results in deaths of the young infants. What actions are various African governments taking to educate these people on consuming imported milk and other canned products? This sounds basic, but that is the level of Africa's development if Africans would be honest with themselves. Consumer education is constant in the developed world despite their advancement.

Africa has produced a son for the United Nations and many in world organizations and yet developing Africa was never part of their agenda. Whenever someone talks about black people, they refer to all of us and not only the poor. Europe was once where Africa is now. The newly found intelligentsia in early 1600 century realized that the way the monarchs were ruling Europe was not the best, these people fought for the creation of republics to serve and improve the commoners. These people changed Europe for the better and they have never looked back. Some nations in Europe kept their monarchs but their political power was limited and others eliminated monarchs altogether and lived under republics.

The descendants of Africa wherever you may be, come to the aid of Africa. Africa has fallen behind in terms of human development and there is nothing in sight to show that this trend would change sooner. Africans usually do not admit that their continent is behind in terms of environmental and human development. There are no genuine plans or strategies to move Africa forward. The African people have not taken charge of their continent. Leaders who only care about themselves are in charge of situations in Africa. They sell lands and allocate resources anyhow, and any way they desire without any accountability to anyone. The political power they wage is not to provide electricity to villages and towns, not on how the nomads can have a settled life and educate their children.

The world is currently in electronic and nuclear age and Africa still lives in medieval times. Do you believe we contributed to this current age by way of resources and labor?
Africa has the free sunlight from nature but have not taken advantage of this abundant light and heat to create solar energy. We get twelve to thirteen hours of sunshine each day and yet most Africans sleep in complete darkness at night. Those in industrialized nations who do not have enough sunlight have been able to tap the little sun light they have to produce solar energy to provide heat and lights to their homes and factories. We are so lucky, most things we need are there and given and all we need is to make the effort to improve our lives. We behave like a spoiled child, who wants provision without lifting a figure. The world is changing and countries are taking care of their own instead of others. Our leaders should be living for the people instead of behaving like monarchs in the medieval times.

Have you noticed how susceptible we are to diseases now? There is nowhere in our past before 1400 that we had epidemic like the black death in Europe. We have abundant of greens, herbs, roots, tubers, grains, cattle, sheep, and goats, chicken and fish to live on. We produced our medication and had specialist in administering them. We had division of labor and specialization in all facets of human endeavor. Different people specialized in different trades and passed on the trades to their successors. Even now, in some places in Africa some families still bear names of the occupation their ancestors were doing before encounter with Europeans.

What are we doing now? We have created slums all over Africa that was not existence years gone by. Majority of our people live in slums while the few educated live in sprawling mansions and western styled houses. Do you know some quarters in the western world believe we live in the jungle and feed from the jungle like it is depicted in the movie Tarzan?

Let us take a cursory look at the Jews. They have gone through many sufferings in the hands of other people just like us, but they have been able to develop themselves wherever they were and never forgot who they were. The Jews were all over the world that it was at times difficult to locate where their origin was. They were able to trace their origin. Their land was small but they have been able to develop the land and people and have not lost their identity. East or West to the Jews Israel is still their home.

We have a whole continent and resources to ourselves and what are we making of it. The people and resources in Africa have become the property of the rest of the world. Africans leave their countries and work in other lands and remit funds home. This is ironic. Africa is rich with resources and people and yet our leaders go over the world asking for grants and loans. These leaders and the people worked hard to develop to the level they are and Africans could do the same if the leaders believe in the people they govern and make them part of the decision processes.

Moreover, the West and East depend on our vital resources to develop their environment. It is amusing anytime our leaders ask for transfer of technology form the West or East. How in the world could that be possible? The Japanese and China never asked anyone for transfer of technology; they developed on what they had in the past and copied from other people by studying and observing.

We should start doing something for ourselves instead of asking for aids and transfer of technology because it will never happen. The first thing that we need to do is to create an enabling conducive business and investing environment where people can have the basics of life like portable water and electricity.

We have moved up an inch in terms of education but even that needs improvement to make it meaningful, functional, and easy to apply in our peculiar situation. We are very resilient. Every human society has rich past but they built on it and incorporated modernity into the past to make it relevant to the present. Africa is for everyone, irrespective of social or political standing. Africa should be a place where people want to come to and live and not a place where sons and daughters are fleeing from to other countries that provide basic necessaries of life.

Do you know the rigors Africans go through to live in foreign lands? It is pathetic. It is better in America because our cousins are part of America so you feel at home because you meet people who look like you. Unfortunately, despite over six hundred years of co-existence some people have not overcome racial barrier due to the color of our skin. These people are ignorant of their own past so do not know the contributions of the blacks to their advancement. They have been brain washed to believe they are superior and this un-proved and untested theory keep being pass on from generations to generations.

Do you know anytime you excel in any academic endeavor the world marvels? The black race had been civilized before the encounter with the west. Europeans had always been a warring people so they developed advanced war implements than Africans. They had guns; Africa had bows and arrows, clubs, knives. The gun kills faster. Africans were afraid of the sight of guns when they saw how it killed in an instant. The European noticed how scary the African was of the sight of guns so they were able to run them up by just carrying the gun with them. Later some brave ones took the guns and nothing happened. Therefore, when the European put the gun beside the captives and left thinking the people would be there as usual when he got back; one of the captives took the gun and shot him. Africans began taking guns from the Europeans and fighting them. The Africans were able to copy the guns and made their own guns since they already had the iron technology. Africans were able to copy the gun technology then, why are the current crops of Africans unable to copy the technology of the west and provide water and electricity for themselves?

Our people have come a long way; and it is about time we moved up. We have brought so many changes to the world despite the brutality and the hard and tedious journey we have travelled. We are more humane than most, but only our mistakes catches attention. An example is that of Michael Vick a professional football player who was convicted of the crime of dog fighting and as a result had to go to jail.

The human race is interdependent and no group of people could claim credit for all the good things happening in the world. Ideas were brought alive due to others people's strength and faithfulness. The rich live on the poor and the poor on the rich. The rich know how they got rich, but the poor does not know how he became poor. Nature did not create poverty it was of human invention and greed.

Despite oppression under slavery and colonization, we came out strong. We started to excel the moment we were freed. We started our initial trade in sports and music by using the strength and talents nature gave us. We become land - owners and own our plantation. We built our own houses. We set up schools and universities to equip ourselves in the new country. Our access to education was restricted out of fear that we would succeed and that would make us competitive. The men were separated from their wives and husbands travelled far from home to earn money to keep their home. Wives and female children worked in the homes of our former masters as house cleaners and care- givers.

While blacks in America got their freedom, those in South Africa had to keep on fighting for a long time before gaining freedom in the 21st century. Blacks lived apart most of the time from whites yet are supposed to be citizens of the same country. While Africans in North America became free, the continent of Africa was partitioned by European countries among themselves for the resources needed for the factories and a new way of life that sprung up in Europe in the 17th century. The quest for Africa's resources was so vital that wars were frequent among the European countries. What else could equal the humiliation the black man suffered in the hands of western adventurers? Millions of Africans who resisted the occupation of westerners were killed in the most barbaric way by poisoning their source of drinking water and then starvation.

Despite all the dehumanizing treatment Africans have endured under the West, there has not been any change of behavior from Africans towards the West. You know just recently, a man fell on a train track in New York while a train was fast approaching a black man dropped himself on the fallen man to safe him from danger. Who else could do that? Only us could do that. We are compassionate and that is probably the reason the rest of humanity has been taking advantage due to this virtue. We are most humane. We cared and nurtured the children of our captives. We became their best friends and yet they despised us.

.

We produced a leader of the United Nations, the best golfer in the whole world, the richest single woman in the whole world, many athletes, the best soccer players in the world, the best brain surgeon and yet dabbed lazy and respected and not recognized. Do you know why? It is because we have not been able to develop our continent and most of us still live in the most deplorable places.

Everything needed to make Africa great is in place but we are doing nothing. The current development in Africa is the standard the rest of world use to measure black people. Whether a black person is an African or not he or she is profiled based on the progress in Africa. Therefore, sons and daughters of Africa become involved in the progress of Africa. We have what it takes to make Africa great again. Even our ancestors who could not read or write made great impact. Their contributions are visible in African towns and villages. Until we realize who we are and improve the life of the majority of the people, we would continue to be relegated to the background in world affairs. We do not deserve to be where we are now. We have contributed greatly to made the world what it is today. You will not be believed, but it is the truth. Without our free labor under slavery, most beautiful things in the world would not have been possible. All the wonders of the world were built mostly through free labor for example, the Suez Canal, the Panama Canal, Eiffel Tower, the White House, and other notable icons in the world today.

.

South Africa has diamonds and gold and a sizable percentage of the people are dying of Acquired Immune Deficiency Syndrome every day. Where is the benefit of riches when it does not bestow compassion on fellow human? What is splendor without a heart that cares? Some body created the virus that causes HIV whether it was deliberate or by accident. A ravaging war does not kill as many people as AIDS is doing to the people of Africa. The world will continue to give lukewarm attitude to Africa's problem unless we as people realize we have to preserve our stock as other people have taken it upon themselves to preserve their own generation.

Africans are not doing enough to care and preserve its people. We are fighting among ourselves. People who have lived thousands of years together are unable to tolerate one another anymore. People are no longer using dialogue to resolve concerns, everybody results to killings. Killings had never solved any human problem because it creates more animosity among the incoming generations. If you look closely enough, you would realize your neighbor is just like you. We are living on the same earth and breathing the same air and blood runs through our veins.

We should have learnt by now but alas, we have not learnt from the past. Whatever happened in the past can happen again in the future only it will come in a different shape and form but if we look closely enough we would see that it is the same wine in a different jar. We have not developed ourselves to fight but we can save our people by providing them the basic things of the modern world like clean environment, water and light and giving them opportunity to be productive enough to provide their own food and sustain themselves and the next generations.

The West has made all that are required to live a comfortable and healthy life. They come up with statistics to let us know we have not been able to take care of ourselves and we have the lowest life expectancy among humanities. What prove do we need to change our view on life and our current situation? We do not eat our natural foods any more. We live on food meant for other people. We develop diseases unheard of in the life of our ancestors. Our ancestors were very strong and healthy people. We have degenerated into unhealthy people on earth. We failed to improve on what our ancestors lived on. We eat food that is not required in our hot environment. We eat foods that generate body heat to keep the body warm in colder climate. People created to live in warm environment do not need body heat producing food.

You see, the Creator of the Universe that our ancestors strongly believe in gave each group of people what they required to exist. We abandoned our culture and way of life because we were convinced that what we have been eating since the creation of the world is no longer good enough. The results of our action are diseases and weaknesses in our strength.

We can improve on the way our ancestors made dishes but to abandon our stable food is a mistake. It is about time African brands of food could be located in groceries stores where millions of blacks who yearn for African delicacies live. What are the African entrepreneurs doing? In fact we are losing what is rightly ours and embracing what belong to others. Africa is rich with different types of food that are nourishing and nutritious. Africa has rich agricultural lands that can sustain any crop or plant introduced to it and yet we go hungry. People in Africa should not go hungry if we decide to harness her resources and make her fruitful and prosperous again.

We have turned ourselves into children who are always looking for help from outsiders. It is not by accident that we are so dependent on foreign foods. It was so designed by the West so that we will be perpetually dependent on them for our needs such that we work all our lives for their generation yet unborn. We have to keep the factories and industries of the West running while our people live in object poverty and branded the uncivilized. Can you not see what I am seeing?

We have to go back to the basics by producing food and have excess to export. We can introduce Africa's indigenous food to the West because they are ready to try different tastes. There are good things to learn from the West. They have established principles and standards for doing things and these have helped them and made life easy and convenient for their people. There is nothing wrong in coping what is good and beneficial from other places. There is a large market potential for Africa foods all over the world. The prevalent of high blood pressure and diabetic among black people could be due to the food they eat now. We eat too much heat producing food that might not be good for our systems. We live on excessive salt, sugar, and solid fat. We do not need excessive heat in our body because our natural environment produces enough heat. We are the only ones that can make positive changes to our people. There is a saying that goes," everyone for himself and God for us all". We have tried but it is not enough.

Nothing has changed. We still expend a large proportion of our hard earned money to import worthless goods into our countries instead of engaging our people in a productive manner so that they can be engaged and enjoy the good things that life can provide. We have become a consumer continent. We are still a dark continent, poverty stricken, and now a junk consuming continent a new added adjective. Africans import used cars, used clothes, used appliances that might not work, expired medication, prohibited items from other countries, expired can foods and any junk the rest of the would not allow their citizens to use. Is the existence of taking other people's unwanted item what we want? Please that is not the way to go Africans. Africans should sit up and re assess its progress since decolonization. The rest of black people in Diaspora look for improvement in African people.

We neglect ourselves and our children. Africans still engage their children in hard labor. Most children in Africa do not experience childhood as it is in industrialized world. Apart from the children of elites most African children start work as early as six years particularly those who do not have access

253

to formal education. We need to make our offspring enjoy the goodness in this world by allowing them to enjoy childhood and then prepare them for a prosperous adult life. Have we ever asked ourselves why we keep on having more children when we do not have plans for them to live in a clean environment and enjoy life? We keep on having children without plans for their future. Look at the recent earthquake disaster in Haiti some mothers had to give their children away because they do not have the resources to take care of them.

The world does not need many children to work on farms anymore so there is no reason why we should have children we cannot take care of and let them grow in misery and poverty. This happens mostly in our community. Children are the most precious thing on earth but if we do not plan for their future lives they suffer when disaster strikes, Nature did not create anyone poor we human beings created poverty due to greed of some people.

Education is very important because it allows you to explore the world beyond our immediate environment. Despite great strides in education, the African continent has not changed in terms of quality of life. It is time Africans research and look for solutions to their current situation and the way forward. The black race needs to define itself as a people instead of fighting each other for political power.

Does your heart not bleed about the killings in Uganda, Sierra Leone, Ivory Coast, the Congo, and in Sudan? People who had lived together for centuries are now killing one another on the streets in Nigeria. We kill ourselves with weapons made in the West. The manufacturing of weapons is job creation for their people and also generation of revenue that increase shareholders wealth. The West finds a way to support opposing parties whenever war breaks up in Africa. A war in Africa is a lucrative market for weapons factories in the West. What is wrong with the leaders in Africa?

There is no place in the world where volunteers provide humanitarian services than the western hemisphere. People in the west are always ready to help themselves because they know that if any part of the whole is not right the whole is not right. Africans should start thinking of the whole instead of the individual. We wait for disaster to happen before we render help; we help one another only in crisis. We tend to be proactive instead of reactive. Anytime there is catastrophe or crisis, be it natural or manmade the black community becomes helpless. This happens because we do not plan beyond the immediate needs. We live as if there is no tomorrow. We have to be concerned about the future and know that nothing is permanent or finite.

Every continent is progressing at an alarming rate and are not using their own natural resources so that they would not be depleted. They are patronizing Africa again for raw materials as if the source is infinite. The world has gone to the Moon and making preparation of going to Mars. There are satellites all over the sky and yet Africa cannot even feed itself let alone going anywhere. For how long would black people continue to depend on outside decisions in running their day to day existence?

We have sat on the fence for too long. Are we spectators in the world or part of the community? The West has not stopped exploration and expedition to improve and advance on life their citizens despite the great leaps they have made. It is true that all human enjoy all the benefit that comes along but it would be better if we participate and make contribution and have a voice to say no when certain events and outcome are nor favorable to us. The global warming is an example in the array of events where the world is looking for solution to come from the forest of Africa.

We have a rich history, let us rewrite our good past and develop them into movies and let the world see our past heroes and heroines. Show the world how they lived and

255

contributed to the society. Have you read or watched Harry Potter movies? It the past of the west brought back to life. This move portrays the past superstition of the West and the way things were that looked parallel to past African believes. Africans have rich folk stories but we have not turned them into books and movies. That is another big way for productivity for folks. India was colonized by the British but the Indians made use of what they had and retained their religion and culture and that is why India has made big leap into the world economy. India is moving to be part of the industrialized world.

The world is in the age of service and not products. The service industry is growing at a very fast pace, and blacks should not be left behind this time around. African countries can make revenue from developing their historical sites by improving on them and making them attractive for other people to come and see and learn. African leaders should look for ways of creating revenue internally instead of looking up to the West and East for funds. Remember they are human beings too and anything they have done we could do if we put our mind to it and care for our people. An adage that says, Rome was not built in a day implies that for anything to be realized it must commence from a humble beginning and can grow big if the will and dedication exist. We should believe that black people deserve to live a better life and the leaders should direct their actions towards a prosperous path and have concern for the dignity of the people they rule.

The problem of black people is being individualistic. Blacks are very individualistic, we do not trust one another and this gives other people the opportunity to set us up against one another. It is time we realize that we face the same problem in this world whether rich or poor. People improve when the few who have foresight and vision decide to change the majority for the betterment of all. We can read the history of any prosperous or advance nation; and you would see that the few changed everything for the wellbeing of the majority.

Black people need to move up to more prosperity and the possible way is if the enlightened impact their knowledge to the society to make it a better place for all. It is everybody's responsibility to create a better standard of living for the next generation and stop being second -class in the world. The Jews moved up despite despise by other people, and China and India are on the right path. What is Africa doing to be part of the great leap in the next decade?

Africans have musical and dancing talents but they need to polish it to meet the world standard. The world is a big market and there are many competitors and for Africa to survive it has to be competitive and aggressive. Africa has to rebrand itself. Africans have to believe that they are as good as anyone and could do better to improve on its current situation. The world has become a global village and what is acceptable in Africa is usually not acceptable on the world stage. The world prefers synchronizing performance to random that is typical of African dancing. Africa needs to move with the world and not behind.

We need not be at par with the rest of the world but we can make our people feel better by making food, water, and basic infrastructure accessible and wonders of the human mind would unfold itself. It is about time Africa moved forward in world affairs because it has lagged behind for too long. Africa has produced sons and daughters onto the world stage but they have not done much to impact their continent. They joined the status quo that black people cannot improve. Africa has a lot the world can learn from if African leaders would focus on making their own environment better instead of investing African resources in the West and East.

Contracts are giving to foreign companies ignoring national businesses. There should be partnership between African companies and foreign companies operating in Africa in other to create cooperation and mutual respect.

You see, in the west, the wealthy used their resources to create opportunities for the less fortunate among them. The wealthy by so doing increase their wealth by way of profits and the less privilege improved their lives living in clean environment and have access to the basics of the modern world. There are still pockets of poverty in the West but it is not as apparent as it is in Africa.

It was the wealthy in Europe who sponsored the exploration and expedition that brought the world under the feet of Europe. Those investments paid off. The people of Europe are in three continents permanently today, Europe, North, and South America and Australia. There may not be new frontiers to conquer but Africans can improve on the well - being of their people.

Let Africans love Africa. Let Africans be patriotic and want to live and enjoy Africa instead of running away and moving to the West. It is the same sky, the same moon, the same sun and the same earth except climate changes differently due the rotation and revolution of the earth. Children of African heritage should develop Africa to restore her pride and dignity once again. A tree does not make a forest. All sons and daughters of Africa should rise and work towards improving the continent of Africa and not a supply depot to the rest of the world. Please raise Africa up and put her in her rightful place.

Look at the Jews they were enslaved in Egypt longer than any enslavement in human history but they are one of the powerful people on earth today. The Jews are spread over the world. They sojourn in all six continents of the world doing very well but they continue to contribute to the development of Israel wherever they are. To the Jews Israel is still home despite their displacement from their home centuries ago.

Why are black people not doing the same thing? Why do black people do not have strong attachment to Africa?

Despite poverty and lack of modern amenities and other privileges other people enjoy Africans are hospital and humane and welcome all people. Majority of Africans are color blind in terms of people. They welcome every human irrespective of color of the skin. Other people should have the courage and reciprocate the gestures of black people. Developing the continent of Africa would give her pride and her children would settle home instead of going to places all over the world to labor under undignified conditions. Europeans enslaved and later colonized black Africans the Arabs settled among us and rule over us. Africans fought for their independence in the mid- fifties until towards the end of the twenties when apartheid South Africa elected the first black president, Nelson Mandela.

We made big strides but have not developed our gains into economic prosperity for majority of our people. Until the majority of African people have access to the basic necessaries of life, such as lights, portable water, and paved roads, our political independence is meaningless. African nations have been governing themselves for over fifty years now, not much have changed in the way of people's living conditions. Life in Africa is deteriorating instead of improving. We should stop looking up to outsiders to come and redeem Africa. We can only redeem ourselves. The elites and the rich in Africa have been taking advantage of their own people. Leaders are supposed to be stewards of the people not robbers like most Africa leaders are. They are not accountable to anyone and use the resources of the people in any way they deem fit. These leaders amass wealth by looting their countries treasuries.

Africa has many natural resources sold on the world markets each day. Where does the money go? There should not be poverty in Africa and yet Africa is the poorest continent in terms of human conditions and way of life. We have to go back to the drawing board and access ourselves and have plans that can move Africa and the people from the doldrums of poverty and wants.

Africa has the resources and wealth to change life for its people if only the politicians have the will to direct the resources towards improvement of the lives of their citizens. The world is in the twenty first century with lights everywhere and most part of Africa is still in darkness just like the middle ages.

Africa is a place where other continents still go and take what they want to continue developing their people while sons and daughters are in collaboration. We should remember that without African people taking the initiative to develop their place of the world nobody will. They come to Africa to take what they need since the fourteen century and nothing has changed. They still take what they want without hassle. In fact, it is easier to exploit Africans now that it was in the 14th century. The people then resisted until overpowered by firearms. We corporate and collaborate in depleting the resources for paper money. The money realized is use to buy manufactured goods made from resources taken away from us. This process has become a visual circle. Africans spend their money on clothing and things that do not create wealth for the continent. A huge proportion of money Africans made is use in buying imported consumables and not durable goods.

Africa is the ancestral home of black people and the development of Africa will have positive reflection on black people all over the world. The perception of African people around the world is very negative. Some people will never touch a black person let alone have anything meaningful to do with us. Black people have been in the West for over five hundred years, yet not fully assimilated and accepted as part of the western society. In most western countries, blacks live apart from their fellow citizens. It is amazing how this system has survived over the six centuries of encounter. Despite the large population of black people in the Americas, any discussion of Africa the ancestral home of these people is presented negatively. It is always stories of diseases, starving people, and the animals. Sometimes you wonder, are these the only happenings in Africa. The movies depict Africa in the worst of light yet, a significant percent of the West can trace their roots to Africa.

Do you know that anytime people in the West know you are an African, the first conversation they would have with you is about animals. You wonder whether they think you live in the jungle. Africans have been living in large communities before the events of the 13th century. We lived in homes built with dried or baked clay and bricks that was excellent for cooling in the hot environment. The fact that clay absorbs and retains moisture made the inside of the homes cooler. Instead for Africans to improve on these building material and make it strong they abandon it and build with cement though durable but not good for hot climatic condition. This is one instance, where the education the West left us is for creating market for their products. Africans spend billions of dollars every year to import cement to build residential homes. Even in the West cement is use to build only foundation of homes and not the structures. Physical slavery is over but economic and brain slavery is on the rise. No matter how many Africans get western education, it would be useful when Africans can use the knowledge acquired to improve on the people and their continent.

We have come a long way but we still need to take huge strides to make significant improvement within the black communities all over the world. Black predicament is the same where ever we are in the world. We only can change that. We deserve the good things in life too. We have served the world long enough and it is time we enjoy the good things too. We are benevolent, not greedy, unselfish, honest, and compassionate people.

Chapter Six

Waking Up

Why have we been sleeping for so long? The world is not waiting for us. Remember the world is dynamic not static. We have been static. Look around you, everybody is moving up economically and we are stacked in poverty. Africa has abundant resources, hardworking people endowed with great talents and, intelligence but we have not taken advantage of them. We watch while all these resources are taking away to develop other places and people. Frankly, we look stupid in the eyes of the world. The same resources taken away from us are processed, repackaged, and sold to us at exorbitant prices.

It is over six centuries since Europeans came to the shores of Africa and took some of us away to work on their plantations in North and South America but their conception and perception about us have not changed. We have freedom and individual choices. Freedom and choices in what they have provided. After the abolition of slave trade and decolonization of African countries, did the laws that operate during the horrible period in human history change? No. Even in most African countries, the laws are mostly what the colonial masters left.

Are you there? There is nothing wrong in keeping anything or coping what would be beneficial for the majority. Since the laws under slavery and colonization have not changed nothing has changed then. We are not slaves or subjects any more but we perpetually work for the industrialized countries. Successive leaders did not restructure African countries economies after the end of colonization and continued with the same system the colonial powers set in place

The only visible change in Africa is that Africans now operate on behalf of external forces and their former colonists. African leaders do not have confidence in their own people so they rely heavily on expatriates to run Africa. There are millions of educated Africans working in strategic and sensitive positions in industrialized countries and yet Africa leaders would not make use of the knowledge of these talented people to move the continent forward. These leaders know well that the Africa's intellectuals would not support the abuse of resources so they use these expatriates to siphon Africa's wealth overseas. The money are banked overseas and use to invest in that country's economy for the benefit of the people while Africa countries lack investment funds. When is Africa going to move forward in terms of development and be able to take control of its affairs and resources?

The world is changing fast but Africa seems to be retrogressing instead of progressing. The gains and progresses African countries made immediately after independence has evaporated. The nationalistic spirit in Africans is no more. Africans are so dissatisfied with the way things are in their various countries that educated Africans are fleeing Africa in large numbers every year. Unfortunately, the leaders in Africa see nothing wrong in the emigration of their people to other countries. Not even one country in Africa has the leader worried about people fleeing. They are happy that educated Africans are working underemployed overseas and then remit the money earned to Africa. Aside from Africa, there is no country that has the progress of its people at heart that would allow the well-educated to leave without thinking about the long term consequences of the labor flight on the country.

Why are educated Africans fleeing Africa to go to other countries and perform menial jobs with university education? What is wrong with black people? The black people are the only people on earth who look to other people to solve their internal developmental problems. Until black people realizes and have interest in the overall development of everyone in their various countries they would continue to lag behind as far as modern human advancement is concerned. The West and East have technological advancement because the leaders who made the leap included everybody and assisted one another.

What is spectacular about living abroad? The inadequacy of basic necessaries of life such as portable water, irregular electricity supplies, and infrastructures drive people away from Africa rather than employment. Everybody in Africa is engaged in one vocation or the other, but most of these are endeavors operate at the basic subsistence levels. The governments and entrepreneurs should invest in the local industries to expand or improve upon them. The local trades and vocations had sustained the Africa societies for centuries. Africans themselves do not take pride in what they have and admire the same things elsewhere. There are tremendous opportunities in Africa but the continent is dire of visionary leaders who have the continent and people at heart.

Human societal needs for existence are basic everywhere and they are: food, medication, housing, security, procreation, and recreation. It is the same yearnings for people everywhere on earth except that some societies have been able to improve these needs and advanced them through technologies. These advanced societies are protecting their citizens and would do anything to preserve the good things of life their predecessors established.

The expectation of the average African has changed but the leaders are not listening to their own people. African leaders have been importing different systems and ideologies to rule the people instead of looking into their peculiar situation and look for solutions and what works.

Human beings all over the world aspire for the same things. These basic things are protection for family, security, food, shelter, clean environment, infrastructure, spirituality, and the ability to actualize ones dreams. African leaders need to change the way it has been handling the affairs of the people. It is time African leaders make the people the reason to govern or lead.

We have foods that are nutritious and healthy, but we spend our hard- earned income on importing food items that are hazardous to our health. People in the West and East eat tropical fruits all year round. They import these foods from us but we do not have enough to eat. Produce is plenty during harvest period in Africa but most of them rot because there are no preservation and processing facilities. Food production, preservation, and processing are industries African countries could focus on to create employment and improve on the life and living condition of the African farmer and citizens to a large extend.

African countries should establish commodity markets where the crops are bought by commodity merchants from the farmers before harvest and all the farmer has to worry about is bounteous harvest and not worry about the logistics of marketing. The first industrial leap for any country is the ability to produce adequate food for the people. Africa had large population of nomads whose occupation had been the rearing of cattle, goats, sheep, and camel. The ancient long occupation had not changed despite changes on the continent. These people supply meat and milk products in the same traditional way. It is quite amazing that no African government or enterprise had stepped in to assist the nomads. There were nomads everywhere in the world but most countries have assisted them in providing them with land to raise their animals more profitably and providing sedentary life for the nomads and their families.

It breaks the heart to read about nomads in Africa losing herds of animals due to drought. There is water everywhere but year in year out the same problem persist. There is water underground, and on the surface of the earth and yet drought had become another problem for Africa. Irrigation started long ago in Africa along the Nile River. What is wrong with the leaders of the black people? The Maasai and Fulani are among the nomads in Africa and the governments have not be involved in improving upon the way they raise their animals. The various African governments should help the young generation of these people to improve upon the ancient trade by educating them on modern animal husbandry. These people produce milk and cottage cheese and no African entrepreneur had caught on the idea to invest in the business and make these foods available for all. African countries import milk and cheese from Holland instead of encouraging the production of milk and cheese in Africa.

Profit is the goal of every entrepreneur or trader; precaution or sentiments are not part of his /her goal. Every nation or country has its own standard for doing things but alas, African countries have not set their own standard of expectation for economic activities. Everything is acceptable in Africa. Why should it be so? Are we not capable of seeking what is good for ourselves? Are we not responsible for the wellbeing of our children and ourselves? Have we not learned anything from the past? Look, we are not trying to be antagonistic to other people but a time has come for us to take our rightful place in the human community.

There is none of the food we import, that cannot be grown and processed in Africa. Take rice for example, it is the staple food for most peoples of Africa. Luckily, there are many variation of rice suitable and grown on the continent and yet we abandon this and import over processed rice from other countries. The rice variation in Africa is rich in vitamin B a useful food nutrient component. The polished rice we import, eating of time without adding vitamins causes a skin disease called Beriberi. This disease is rampant among our less educated people. They used to eat the indigenous rice rich in vitamin B, but our leaders and our foreign entrepreneurs convinced them to believe that the polish rice is better. We collaborated with foreigners to deceive our people because of money and selfishness. The African merchants could invest in the local rice production and process them and these would create more income for the African rice farmer and create jobs in the food processing industry. The merchants can still make their billions of money if they invest in the African farmer to grow rice and establish the processing plant. Africa cannot continue to be dependent on other countries for food. The world population is increasing and each community would need to take care of its own as we move further into the future. This scenario happened in the 13th century and may repeat again. The implementation of growing and processing African rice would empower the rice farmers, create jobs and there would plenty of rice at affordable prices. It is time Africans begin to feed themselves instead of relying on handout from the industrialized world. Africans are industrious people; it is the leaders who do not have faith in the abilities of the people they govern.

Preservation and processing of food is what Africa can do to stop starvation of its peoples. During, harvest periods there are abundant food everywhere, and many of these rot away because there are no preservation or refrigeration system to preserve the excess. The hard working farmers seeing that their hard work and its fruit rot had to sell at rock bottom prices.   Hence, the decrease interest in farming by some farmers and children of farmers.   The few who continue farming continue to live in poverty because they have to sell their harvest at the cheapest price since there are so many harvests on the market at the same time. Food processing is one area Africa needs help. Africa should go into mechanized farming in order to be able to improve on food production.   Agriculture mechanization tried in most African countries immediately after independence did not produce the required results because of management by governments and did not involve investments from entrepreneurs or investors.

In most part of the world the governments, entrepreneurs, and farmers work hand in hand to make sure there are abundant food supply all year round. The entrepreneurs invest in the farmers to produce and they would buy harvest from the farmers while the government lend or grant money to the entrepreneurs. The government purchases the excess from the farmers and preserve or give them to poor countries in Africa. You see this way the farmer in the industrialized world is never poor. They live and enjoy life just like any other occupation.

There is also something called the commodity and future markets in the West. The entrepreneurs search for produce that are in demand in the market and enter into contract with farmers who would plant the crops. A commodity buyer seeks farmers who are specialized in the type of produce and enters into contractual agreement with the farmers that they would buy whatever quantity produced. Another is the future commodity market whereby the entrepreneurs pay for the crops the farmer is yet to plant in the future. Please, tell me how can the farmer in the West be poor? No, and never. Even in the deepest economic recession food consumption must continue.

This is the reason why Africa leaders, entrepreneurs, and governments should wake from slumber to feed their people. Africa should never be hungry or go hungry if the African entrepreneurs, the leaders, and government have the interest of the masses at heart instead of their pockets and their families. Most people in African should not be living in poverty if the educated, the professors, and the scientist would study the African way of life and see how they could use their vast knowledge to improve it instead of living on foreign land and continually blaming Africa for lack of progress.

Education is to improve the past, preserve the past, create new things for the future, initiate new ideas, and build for the betterment of ourselves and the rest of the community at large.   Any student of history knows that the West did not get to where they are now without sacrifice from the leaders and followers. They paid a high price for freedom they are enjoying today. They fought among themselves, they killed for it, they displaced other people for it, and they conquered lands for it. We also contributed a lot to the development of the West by way of free labor and ideas. Why not use all the strength and knowledge we have to develop Africa instead of waiting for the West to help us.

The West would never help Africa to develop, because, it is the place where they get cheap resources and the consuming market for their products. This is practical common sense, if Africa is able to provide for itself who would buy the surplus production from the West and East. Africa is also the playing ground to watch animals and people they tag the primitive. If Africa becomes industrialized, where would the cheap raw materials come from and who would consume all the unnecessary things they produce mainly for Africa? They have two sets of standards for things they manufacture in the West and East one standard for exports and the other for their own country. Due to caring nature of governments in the West and East for their citizens, standards are set for production of anything for the people. Companies producing items for the West and East have to go by the standards set by the governments.

What about Africa there are no standards sets for things coming to Africa because the governments do not care about their citizens. These African governments care about the cut they would get from the manufacturers and companies. All malfunctioning products manufactured in the Western and Eastern countries are exported to Africa through unscrupulous African entrepreneurs since no standards are required from the African governments for goods the people consume. When will this stop?

We cannot blame the West and East. We are competing for the same limited resources nature provided. They have found a way to own most of the resources on earth. They have been using the same strategy over six centuries and getting whatever they want all the time. The same divide and confuse tactics, and strategy the West used to take over Africa has not changed. It is time for leaders who care about the future of black people and Africa to stand up and be involved in making sure Africa produces food to feed it growing population has healthy drinking water, decent shelter and clean environment. Of the six continents in the world, Africa is the only one that is under developed and lack basic amenities like electricity and portable water for majority of the population. These amenities are taken for granted in developed countries.

All we need to do is to improve our environment, improve the quality of human life, have respect for ourselves, and look within for solutions to the myriad problems. All said and done, there are people in the West and East who genuinely would be eager to help Africa if Africans get ready to help themselves. The aristocrats in the West used to live the way African elites and rich are now living but the poor and peasants people revolted for their rights in living a better life. The rich in the West understood what that meant and started setting apparatus in place to create an environment where life would be pleasant and fair for both rich and poor. The rich improved upon the basic work the poor was performing and went through the industrialized revolution where many factories sprung up and able men and women could work and provide comfort for families.

Fortunately, the world is awash with different technologies now where the leaders of Africa can tap into to provide basic necessaries for the people they govern. Governance is not about leaders but about both the governed and the governor. African leaders, it is time to wake up and face reality of what the hard working people of Africa are going through. They cannot provide the necessity of the current world without your involvement. In Africa, the African work hard to build a house, he provides his own electricity by way of plants or generators else no electricity in the house; he provides his water or none and provides his own security.   The African is not asking free services from the government. The African works hard for everything so he knows he would have to pay for services when provided.   Providing these services would open avenues for innovation and creative ideas, imagination, and job opportunities would open.

This is the twenty-first century and Africans and black people all the over world should wake up to their responsibility as a vital part of the world community. We have attributes for survival under any circumstances and it makes us thrive under conditions that would not sustain many people. We are resilient and adaptable and accept any situation we find ourselves. Most people do not perceive life the way we see it, they want more like Oliver Twist in Charles Dickens novel. They have more and still want more and more. Remember they took lands all over the world and made them their own. There is a large Europeans resident in Africa. They live in Africa but do not live among Africans. They live away from us. They control the economy and own most productive resources. We are not complaining but they should treat us as part of the community after all it is our natural abode. We are not asking them to leave Africa because we are hospitable and compassionate people.

We need to start evaluating the way live. We crowd ourselves in tiny spaces while we have vast land sprawling around. The rich and governments in Africa live in sprawling estates while the majority of the people live in homes without lights or water. The streets leading to the estates of the rich and governments are tarred with asphalt, while the roads leading to the home of the majority of the people are not tarred and where the roads are tarred, they are riddled with potholes from neglect.

Sometimes, some benevolent African governments build low cost houses for the people but these homes are bought

271

by the rich who can afford them. You see the homes meant for the average masses end up in the hands of the rich. Greediness and selfishness are plagues among the affluent Africans. What else could explain the plight of the majority of Africans? The rich and the government of African use the resources of this continent as personal property. The African leaders have cohorts who enjoy benefits from the governments and the rich and they remain silent and turn blind eyes to all the atrocities happening in Africa.

The rich and the entrepreneurs could venture into housing in Africa where houses could be build based on specification of the various housing authorities. If individuals want to build their houses it should be allowed but have safety features. The environment is one aspect whereby entrepreneur could create several employment opportunities. There are very few recreational areas in most part of Africa. These are job opportunities for people in recreation if the opportunities are exploited. . The educated Africans only want to perform only white collar jobs or have career.   The government should encourage people who do the blue collar jobs by way of assistance or regulate the work they do for safety. The blue collar workers need governmental assistance in order to improve on the work and the work environments.

 A vast majority of African workers fall in the blue collar worker category but because there are no statistics to gauge what people do it is difficult to measure the output of these people. The blue collar workers are the artisans, masons, carpenters, welders, painters, plumbers, auto mechanics, cooks, and many jobs that do not require classroom education. These jobs are the foundations of human existence everywhere but they are seriously neglected by African governments. The concentration of African government in employment is in white collar workers.

Unfortunately, African does not have many white collar jobs and these Africans with only white collar job education become frustrated and want to leave Africa to the West where they believe they could get a white collar job but end up doing menial jobs they would never touch in Africa. There are thousands of graduate taxi drivers from Africa in the western hemisphere. They work for ages and never achieve the dream they came to look for and it becomes difficult going back to Africa without wealth or money. Some of these go back to college to get second and third university degrees with the hope of getting lucrative opportunities.

Improving on the professions the less educated do that has not been improved upon for centuries would open avenues for more jobs and increase the quality of life for these people. If these jobs are improved and the government set a standard of living for people the African environment can look like that of the West and Eastern countries. More people would be attracted to these jobs. The same kind of jobs are in the West and East but refined by government through regulations, standards and safety. African government should encourage the educated ones to learn the old trades of Africa and improve upon it. The system of education in Africa does not have relevance to the immediate environment and the knowledge gained get wasted without application. It is about time the educated Africans adapt the education into the immediate environment like it is done in China, Brazil and India.

The uneducated or semi educated is the largest concentration of the population in Africa. They control the commerce in Africa and have substantial wealth but due to lack of functional education they live the way they are used to. They do not care what water they drink or where they live. They do not care about hazards to their skin and bodies. They work on farms without protective body garments; fish without any protection; ride bicycle, and motor cycles without helmets. They climb trees and high altitudes without any body protection. They take many daredevil chances without thought to the consequences. The black man is a survival by nature but the world is changing towards comfort rather than raw survival tactics

There is limited recreational activity in the life of the average African.   There are games that are indigenous to African societies but most Africans due to outside influence have moved away from the old way of recreation. There are African games and plays, but have been overshadowed by western mentality that has taken over the African culture. Story- telling and riddles of African people should be in print so that other people can read about Africa instead of Africans learning about people and no one learns about Africa. Writing books on African games and play can earn money for Africans. It is time Africans start promoting who they are instead of letting others determine who they are. Computer developers and programmers should develop African games and plays into computer games that would be available everywhere in the world.

Most people are ignorant about Africa and its people and it is time Africans let the world know who Africans are by promoting Africa just like the West and East do through movies, books and plays. Marketing is the focus of the world where awareness of people and their culture are disseminate to the footsteps of other people. Africans should rebrand and market themselves and erase the wrong notions other people have about them.   Europe and America market themselves to the world and that is why people everywhere throng to Europe or America.

Everything African is good and all that remains is some polishing and publicity. Africans should realize that there is nothing new in the world, the same old ways have been polished and made better by the West and East.   Africans in Africa are gradually losing their identity and culture. No one promotes African cultures anymore. The new African politicians replaced the old African institutions with western culture that do not have relevance on the society. The new African leaders have abandoned the old African institutions and are practicing the old systems of the West.

Due to the high productivity and innovation from the East and West there are surplus products that are exported to Africa and sold to Africans to sell on Africa markets, and this deprives the local African industries from survival. The retailers in Africa make profits from selling products from abroad but the productivity of the products does not add value to the overall progress of Africa. The retailers sell all sorts of products imported from any country in the world but the economic benefit mostly go to the manufacturing country.

Products that are harmful to humans and animals are sold on Africa markets without any governmental control. This shows the level of concern African politician have about their own people. Prescription drugs sold openly over the counter. Talk about expired prescription drugs sold in the markets by people who do not have pharmaceutical knowledge. That is the plight of African people

Retailing imported products is easier than farming they say Some African farmers have abandoned farming and moved to big towns to live in slums and engage in retailing. The governments do not care about what happen to the people because if they do then laws would be in place to restrict and protect Africans on products imported into and on African markets.

Who should be able to effect positive change if not the educated African/black people? Instead, the educated live separate from their own people just like the Europeans did when they were in Africa. In order to move Africa forward the educated have to be part of the majority of their own people. There is lack of trust between the educated and uneducated because the educated Africans behave just like the Europeans who occupied Africa during the colonial period. This has to change in order to build trust. Trust amongst various people in an entity creates patriotism within the entity. There will be no nation building between the ruler and the ruled if there is no trust.

Africans lived together before colonization without serious ethnic problems. Although, there were some skirmishes over land for grazing and farming institutions were in place to address the issues. Africans who lived by one another inter married. Why have people who had lived together for centuries suddenly realized the differences among themselves in the 21st century? It is politics, it is power, and it is outside interference. The farmers and nomads need one another. That is the way it was and the way it should be. Everyone vocation is important and useful to society.

The educated who are in control of governance have neglected to make improvement in the area the uneducated live. In most cases the area the uneducated live lack modern convenience of life like portable water, lights, and good roads. The houses in these areas are very old and dilapidated. In order to raise the trust the educated should see to improve the way the less educated live. The sanitations in these areas are very poor and the people are usually susceptible to diarrhea, malaria, cholera and many other diseases that would not survive in clean environments. . The drainage systems in these areas are not good either and these places have become breeding ground for mosquitoes or many other insects like flies.

The politicians should pay more attention to these Africans because they have the largest population and they are the eyes of Africa. The world sees Africa through these people. These are the people the West portray on their television and prints as Africans. These groups of Africans have wealth but they lack modern education. These people have herds of cattle, goats, camels, and many domesticated animals and yet they are poor. These people own large farm -lands and yet they are poor.
The apparel the rich and educated Africans wear does not attract outside attention, rather the poor African child with sulky eyes and malnourished body does. If the educated Africans put resources together they can help in improving

the environment in their communities. There is no dust or mud on the streets in the western world because some visionary leaders saw the menace and use bricks to build the roads and covered the dust and mud. There is no stagnant water on the streets in the West because they built a drainage system that took care of street running water. All drainage systems in the West are covered. Streets in the West tarred with asphalt and coal tar even on farms..

There was mass-social education awareness campaign immediately after independent in African countries but they fizzled away when the military took over political power in the seventies all over Africa. The improvement of way of life awareness campaign should be in the language of the people. These people can contribute to the cost of the campaign if they develop trust and know the benefit that will come to them by adopting the changes. There should be co-operation between the people and the government for the campaign on the benefits of living in clean and healthy environments. Societal changes are not easily accepted but with time, the people would see the benefits and embrace the changes.

It is time the educated help improve the way majority of Africans live. What is the benefit of education if it does not benefit the majority of the people? Very few people started the renaissance in Europe but they spread it to all their people including the servants and serfs. Why have not the educated and politician Africans use their knowledge to improve the life of the majority of their people? Improving the way of life of the majority of Africans will erase some of the stereo type notion other people have about Africans and black people.

Entrepreneurs and governments should invest in amenities such water, electricity, roads, and drainage systems to improve life. The people would pay when the services are provided because Africans are used to paying for what they consume. There are millions of Africans and black people all over the world who would like to come back to Africa but the lack of basic amenities all over prevent them. I am are not suggesting that Africa should be like Europe or America but people everywhere can do with basic necessaries of life. The proposal is to African politicians the wealthy, and elite that Africans could live better and live longer if modern amenities are available to them. The average African is a hard working person and deserves a better living condition than what is available to him at the present.

 The politician should reason and let everybody enjoy some basic essential of modern life. It is only in Africa where one part of town will have bright light, potable water, and good infrastructure while the other half were the illiterate and poor live is in total darkness, lack of potable water and good roads. We all travel to the West and see how the people live. Why is it difficult for African government to provide the same life style for their people? Africa is asking for just the basics from his sons and her daughters.

It is the responsibility of governments to ensure that the people have employment and live a decent life. Employment is not necessary for the educated. The uneducated could work in areas where reading and writing is not required. They can work in construction, food processing, agriculture, mining, footwear, tanning, dyeing, and many more local industries. Most Africans are engaged in the aforementioned occupations except it is on subsistence scale. There is no government subsidy in Africa so people have to be engaged for day- to- day living. Most of these uneducated are employed in and own most of these individual businesses. All the government needs to do in this instant is to regulate and train them towards the modern way of doing work.

 Most advanced countries started the same way. The past was improved and built upon. When you look at politics in Africa, you see chaos and fight for power without any plan to improve the way of life for the majority. There is strong desperation in Africa in going abroad because of the notion that everything is nice and you do not have to work hard to be wealthy. Hard work is the grease of progress everywhere. The big difference between Africa and the western or eastern world is that government is there for the progress of the people.

Africans want better life than the ones African governments offer that is the reason thousands leave Africa to the West and East for the pursuit of a better way of existing. It should not be that way. Any serious leader dedicated to the improvement of basic modern existence for the citizens can do so with commitment and perseverance. It has happened in the East and West; it is unfolding again in China and India.

Africa has resources and hard- working people. What Africa lack are sincere, honest politician and visionary leaders. If African leaders stop the bickering and in fighting that has plagued politics; they would see around them and realize that they are living below human expectation. The people in the West still come to Africa just the way their predecessors did some six centuries ago. They come and find no difference in our way of life.

African people spend time fighting among themselves rather than face the reality of poverty, HIV, AIDS and many diseases like malaria that is curable but have been killing millions of people. It is high time African government change their way of governance and improves the life of the people. The first African Nationalist did better than the second generation of leaders. The second generation of African leaders after independence plundered the reserves the nationalist left. The plundering is still going without abate.

Africa does not need a revolution for changes. Africa needs good sons and daughters to come to her rescue. Africa has benevolent children in large numbers and they should come forward to do good deed for their father and motherland. Nobody will help Africa except Africans and black people all over the world. We should not leave development to government only every patriotic African should lend a hand and give Africa a facelift. How do you feel when all the negativity and sometimes lies about Africa flies around you? Most people discriminate against black people without any reason other than the color of the skin. There are many colors in nature why the discrimination on the color of dark skin. Everything in nature has purpose and a reason.

A lot of Africans and black people all over the world have riches but they have ignored the place of their ancestors. They can help Africa come from these predicaments of poverty, diseases, and haplessness by contributing their quota. Look around, each continent is awash with basic amenities but Africa. What Africa needs most are lights, portable water, housing, infrastructure, and clean environment. These issues should be the focus of government and entrepreneurs in Africa. You need to rebuild Africa from the ground up. Most countries are reaching the epoch of their development while Africa has not started at all.

We go abroad to live and enjoy the good things of life provided by the government and the people; does it occur to us that Africa can be developed too. We enslave ourselves overseas doing odd jobs to make ends meet despite our education. Europeans once enslaved and colonized Africans and they fought for freedom and got political independence yet nothing has been done to move the African people forward in the right direction. Africans need to wake up. We should stop rhetoric and endless speech and take action. The challenges facing Africa is enormous. Do you see any leader in Africa moving Africa in the right direction? None of the leaders has any plan in changing the faces of Africa from poverty and disease to affluent and healthy. These leaders dabble into issues that have nothing to do with governance and development of African people.

Look at the current financial crisis in the West right now, everybody is running around and working hard to find solution to the financial problems. The West is not pointing finger at anyone. They all have their hands on deck looking for solutions for the current quagmire, and are confident that there would be solution. The nations in the western hemisphere encourage one another and they have viable systems where the responsibility of everyone is the provision of good life and pursuit of happiness.

Africans need to start now and take charge of their destiny. Despite inaction of the West on the effect of their coming to Africa had on Africans there are good-hearted people among the West who would assist if Africans start moving in the right direction to lift themselves from the doldrums of poverty and disease. Man is naturally good but greed destroys the good nature of most people.

What African leaders have not realized is that a leader is like a father in a family. A father is responsible for everyone in the family. The well- being of every member of a family is the responsibility of the father. Likewise, the well- being of members of a community lies at the feet of their leaders. Leaders are in charge of the resources in their communities and it is their responsibility to allocate the resources to projects or endeavors that would benefit everyone in their community.

Leaders in African seems to be accountable to no one hence the unbelievable misuse of public funds and resources. Even where democracy is practiced, there has never been any free and fair election. Opposing parties always lay blame of the election rigging on one another. African politicians never accept the fact that in an election, someone wins and others will lose. If the intention of politics in Africa was to make life better for the people why then are there cries and woes after every election in Africa?

Politics in Africa is a means for people to take control of the public wealth and use it as they want. That is why losing an election becomes personal and party members kill one another. If the losing party has manifestos that would improve the way of life of people and their generation yet unborn then they should sell or educate people on how better they are to the populace instead of engaging in warfare.

The democracy practiced in Africa has the same three tiers of government just like the West: The executive, the legislatures, and the judiciary.   It is quite amazing that the same system works perfectly for the citizens of the West but has not worked for the citizens of Africa. Frankly, it is not the democratic system of governance that is not functioning in Africa rather it is the way Africans operates democracy. The incumbent would not transfer power after losing in elections. The country would rather be on fire than for them to relinquish power.   The peaceful transfer of power is the beauty of western democracy.

The majority of the electorates do not know their rights in Africa.   In view of that, African countries should have an independent body that would be responsible for educating people on the importance of their votes. In Africa, the elected officials act as if they are doing the masses favors by doing their duties. If there is increase in political awareness in Africa, the level of violence after any election will reduce. How long can the majority look on? Political parties act like cults in Africa. The parties are concerned about the welfare of the members than for the larger community. University students who graduate cannot find jobs unless they have connections with someone in the political party in power. Sometimes jobs are reserve for the children and grandchildren of party members. Should it be that way?

The winning party should let people know beneficial plans that would provide access to good drinking water, lights, good infrastructure, employment, education, clean and healthy environment, adequate health system, and decent accommodation. There should be accountability and

transparency in all their undertakings. Except for the first African nationalist who tried to provide some basic amenities. None of the policies that came after had the people as the reason to govern. There was no patriotism or love for country in the revolutionary soldiers as they called themselves. They governed iron handedly and took most of the reserve in their respective countries coffers.
Those leaders that came after the first nationalist leaders were nothing but looters. They have no idea of governance. Do you blame them? No. They were mostly military personnel who trained in the art of warfare. The responsibility of the military is to protect the territorial integrity of their land and people and not to govern.

In the 1970s, close to ten years after independence from colonial governance, most African countries came under military Head of States. Apartheid continued in South Africa where black Africans were never free on their ancestral land. The people yearned for change of government due to brutality of military men and disregard for ordinary people. The military era brought setback for Africa. They did nothing to improve the way of life of the people possibly due to lack of knowledge of governance and sheer irresponsibility.

There was a head of state, who proclaimed in the 1970s that his country has so much money that he did not know what to do with the money. Meanwhile, most of the people did not have portable water to drink, darkness at night in most places, no schools in most towns and no infrastructure in most urban areas let alone villages. The high demand of petroleum in 1970s brought unprecedented wealth to pockets of Africa but the then military leaders did not invest in critical area like water resources, health facilities, environment improvement and in the people. The governments could have invested in permanent infrastructures with the revenue derived from petroleum in 1970 required for nation building and that would have propelled Africa towards greatness.

Democracy returned to Africa in early 1980s. The peoples of Africa being tired of oppressive regime of military rulers demonstrated their dissatisfaction in many African countries and the military rulers had no choice but to listen to the people and democratic parameters were set up to go back to the democratic process of governance. The military head of states after tasting political power did not want to leave politics and sought political power instead of going back to military duties. Most politicians in West Africa are former military rulers. Recent events in Ivory Coast, Sierra Leone, Uganda, Zimbabwe, and Kenya demonstrate that politics in Africa is for personal aggrandizement and scoring grudges and not for the benefit of the people. Please take a look at Africa countries and you would still see people living in shanty towns not fit for animals.

Formal education has come to stay but has not necessary helped Africans to improve. The educational systems in Africa are what the colonists set up to educate Africans in European ways of live to their benefit. The educational systems continue to benefit Europe because Africans learn about Europe and learn to be good consumers of European products. If you are in African markets or stores all you find are products make from Europe. This is good for Europeans because their factories are busy manufacturing and the people productively engaged while Africans spend the meager money they have on European goods. The depended on imported goods and food is a debacle on Africans' neck. There are many items that Africans import from overseas that can be cultivated, processed and manufacture in Africa.

Rice is a staple food of all Africans and yet billions of revenue is spend on importation of rice every year. According to NERICA, an organization funded by African Development Bank to develop a new seed of rice solely for Africa, 240 million people in West Africa rely on rice and cost approximately $1 billion a year to import. Although, the

Africa rice does not yield much in comparison with Asian rice it is the rice favorable to African soil and good for the people. The African rice is rich in mineral and therefore healthy for the people. The Asian rice that is introduced into Africa through NERICA requires more water whereas the African rice does well in the arid environment. More investment in resources and large cultivation would be able to yield more rice production. If Africa is able to invest $1 billion in water provision and electricity this would be moving the continent towards better development than spend it on rice the continent can cultivate by itself.

Cultivation of large- scale rice farms and processing would create jobs and provide income for African people. African leaders should begin to look into areas that are affecting the progress of African people. Africans were feeding themselves before Europeans came to Africa. What happened that Africans are no longer able to feed themselves? This is a question African leaders need to be looking for answers for; and not over reliance on the rest of the world as if Africans are less human who needs help for survival from other people.

Africa is everybody's market; they do business in Africa and make profits without giving back by way of investment. They pay taxes in their home countries for government to spend in providing amenities but pay nothing to reward Africans for the money they make. The only thing these same people say about Africa is that they are backward people. Everyone find a way to make money on Africa due to inactivity of African leaders concern for the people they rule. By relying on other people to take decisions on how to do everything from living to death is a drag on the progress of Africans. We allow ourselves to be treated as sub-specie of the human race

Europeans manufacture many items solely for Africans. Who sets the standards for these things they manufacture and sell to Africa? There is nothing wrong in commerce but when it is lopsided, it creates problem for the weaker party, in this instance Africa. Foreign companies control African resources, therefore, Africa does not have negotiating power in the commerce arena. Nothing has changed. Changes will come to Africa if the leaders begin to realize that the purpose of governance is to provide vehicles or avenues that would make it possible for citizens to use their talents and creativity to realize their dreams.

The modern amenities like electricity, water, drainage systems, roads, hospitals, schools, security, and protection determine advancement of nations. These are too expensive for individuals to provide and that is the reason government, organizations, and companies are required to provide and individuals would pay for services when provided.
Educating people is continuous in all phases of life. Training young children on African vocation is education. These children could find a way to improve on these vocations. Africans should improve on the current educational systems that would favor development of Africa talents and not mimic foreign cultures. The mimicking of other cultures has become a way of life in Africa. The Chinese, Indians, and Jews have proved that you can be who you are and still progress economically. .

The West is always improving technologically. Whatever the West and East enjoy today was not built one day it took years of improvement on the basics to be where they are today that the rest of the world look up to them. America introduced mass production of automobile to the world and different countries copied and perfected to suite their own taste. The Japanese and Germans engineers are the best when it comes to automobiles but the idea did not start from these countries. African countries could start to make things that would suit their taste and environment instead of being over dependent and wasting the resources for building durable and tangible structures for the people and country on consumables they could produce themselves.

We should begin improvement on things that are natural to us and the techniques would come naturally. Even games, story-telling, poems, riddles, and foods of African origin have been abandoned for that of the West. Africans should retrace their steps back to the past and modernize some of the things their ancestors did that made them such a healthy and strong people. Africans are industrious; but over dependent on already made items from other places is destroying their ingenuity. I repeat the West and East depend on Africa for raw material for their factories and market for their products. The whole world depend on African resources but not ready to contribute to develop the area.

Our children would like to know who they really are instead of a bunch of mimics. Africans have similar cultures and they should take advantage of the similarity to bring people together. There are different people everywhere and they have been living peacefully with one another. Europeans do not look the same and they speak different languages and have diverse cultures. In Sudan, millions of people were slaughtered during the ethnic cleansing between people of Arab descendants and the indigenous dark skinned people. What is wrong with being dark skinned? Is it their fault that they are dark skinned? Is it a crime to be different? Have they not occupied that area of Sudan since time immemorial? Ethnic cleansing should stop in Sudan and anywhere they take place. Human beings are sacred and they should not be slaughtered like animals. As a matter of fact animals should not be slaughtered unless absolutely necessary. The leaders in the areas where this injustice occur do not care about the people they governed.

The situation of Africans at present does not require wars; but how the people of Africa can improve on their livelihoods and enjoy the good climate, environment, vegetation, and resources that nature gave them abundantly that are siphon and enjoy by other people. Black people and Africans look helpless in the current world and the only way to alleviate the situation is to be active participant in their own life instead of others dictating what is it and not to them.

All sons and daughters of Africa should be concerned about the future of the African continent in moving it forward. Africa is gradually turning into "no man's land." The countries in Central Africa are selling huge lands to foreigners again when African farmers do not have land to cultivate and graze their herds. There should be cooperation between the new foreigners coming to Africa to help Africans grow and not to use Africans as under paid laborers.

The Europeans came there in the 1400s and are still coming in the 21st century, now the Chinese are rushing to Africa to take resources. Recently India indicated its intention in getting resources from Africa, it is happening right before your own eyes. You cannot go to the western world and act without respecting the laws, and the constitution but when these people come to Africa, they behave in ways that are contrary to African laws and constitution and do things they cannot dare do in their own country. Why is it so? The answer lies with the African leaders who care about personal richness and least regard for the citizens.

Africans in Diaspora have come a long way. They are showing lights that the black man can. They should sustain the momentum. The progress black people in Diaspora have made should be carried on to the African continent. In the United States of America, many black people have made progress in wealth accumulation through hard work but a lot needs to be done in wealth creation in the black community so that people can start having their own businesses instead of being labeled workers. In black communities businesses are owned by foreigners who cannot live among us but make money from us. Why can't blacks be involved in providing for their communities? Blacks do have movie theaters and restaurants owned by blacks but we need to be involved in owning businesses instead of just working in businesses.

Workers life depend on investors and if for any reason the investors do not like the policies of the government in power they can withhold their fund and do not invest to create jobs for workers. If most of the people work towards becoming investors instead of consumers of products then the investors who stop investing would be losing value in their wealth since no one is buying but everyone is investing. Building wealth is the only way black people can get their dignity back. There are many opportunities in America to create wealth for the current generation and the next through systematic saving, investing in the stock market, bonds market, insurance, and spending less on things that do not add value to one's wealth.

Blacks spend a huge percentage of their income on consumables and less in creating wealth. If you look around us, you would see things that we bought that did not require spending money on but we did. You lose part of your wealth by buying things you do not have to have. A lot of your hard earn money is lost by buying junks make with the intention of taking your money away and perpetually keeping you in poverty. Think of building wealth by putting some money aside through buying life insurance with cash value, buying fixed income annuities, and owning a home that can build equity. Show interest in building wealth instead of spending money on your body only.

Too much negativity of our color has made us obsessed with our beauty and we spend most of our hard earned money to look the way society think we ought to be. Realize the beauty in you instead of what society dictates because you are beautiful the way you are. You are naturally beautiful the way you are.

Look at the Jews, despite what they underwent in the past have not stopped moving on. The Jews have become part of the richest and industrial people on earth despite their past and the perception other people have about them. The Jews have a small population but they ensure their people enjoy quality life. The Jews are close- knit people and work towards ensuring each other's security and happiness. They have a history that is similar to blacks but they have overcome all the hardship of the past.

Africans and blacks people allow the past dictate the future. The past has come and gone, but it looked like we have not learned any lesson from it. Nothing has changed our behavior and attitude to life. We should take life seriously and enjoy it. We only labor without enjoying the good things of life. We can channel our own path so that our future generations will be better than the present. Develop Africa and we will see how our pride and dignity will rise again. We should believe we can move Africa to greatness once again.

Chapter Seven

<u>Rebuilding the Continent</u>

We should rebuild Africa. The continent has suffered long years of neglect and it is time the continent got a face-lift. The Arabs occupied most part of Northern Africa during the propagation of Islam. The Arabs also engaged in slaves trade but not as massive as the Triangular Atlantic Slave. The Arabs have been part of African people but they hold onto their Arab identity than African   Due to long co-existence with the Arabs a sizable percentage of Africans people still speak a variation of Arabic as their first language. Most of these North Africans are Muslims. Since Islam is a way of life, the cultures of most communities in Africa have turned Islamic. Islam blended well with the traditional way of life of Africans and it became part of Africans communities. The Islamic influences are mostly in North Africa and Northern part of most countries in Africa.

While the Arabs were in the northern section of Africa, Christianity brought by European missionaries dominated the coastal part of Africa. Christianity also brought it way of life and changed the African way. The Christians tried to change everything African. While pretending to spread the Gospel of Jesus Christ, they had other interest and motives as well. The same people who introduced Christianity to Africa engaged in slave trade. They used their religion to justify the wrongs they did to Africans.

African people lived under kings in city-states and kingdoms before the arrival of these intruders. There were kingdoms and empires with various administrative positions and leaders. There were division of labor whereby families, clans and, communities specialize on what they have comparative advantage, and flourishing trade routes all over Africa. Africans then were trading mostly with the east in spices, gold, iron, and clothing. Commerce was flourishing and wealth was everywhere. There is nowhere in recorded

291

African history that there had been epidemic or endemic and diseases killing the Africans The black people were strong and healthy because they worked hard and lived well.

The Europeans started trading at the coastal cities in Africa and spreading Christianity as well. The Africans resisted the intrusion as much as possible.   The African people revered their kings and leaders because they symbolized gods on earth. The Europeans knew this so they began to kidnap the kings and these soften the Africans resistance. The kings and priests were the most powerful people so any harm to these groups meant harm to the whole community. The Europeans observed the Africans and saw that they work hard in everything they did, these Europeans coming from a warring nation understood the impart of changing a leader so they began installing new leaders who had their sympathy on African people and this erupted into series of warfare in most communities in Africa. This created confusion in once peaceful communities and mistrust ruled the day. Families, friends, and neighbors could not trust one another anymore.. People of lesser social status were installed leaders by the Europeans; the action angered people and hatred set in and betrayal followed. The Europeans craftily created the atmosphere of confusion and wars were breaking out in most communities hence the African people became enemies of one another.

 By this time, European explorers had discovered the Americas, and the Native Indians were dying from diseases and over work. The Europeans realized that the African was better suited to work in plantations so the most callous trade in human existence began, the Triangular Atlantic Slave Trade.   Millions of Africans as human cargoes were shipped to the Americas to work on plantations.

Fortunately, the black people are now free from physical slavery and can determine their own destiny but they have not done much to actualize that freedom and create economic freedom. The westerners are people who are never satisfied with what they have, and are always probing and exploring the world and wanting more and ignoring the concern of other inhabitants on earth.

These explorers do not tell all stories of their expeditions. They tell only what would ridicule and degrade other people in their encounters. There is no country on earth with perfect people. There were other civilizations before the present. The current civilization benefits some people more than others. The current civilization is more beneficial to the people who initiated it than those who have to learn and live in a system they were not involved in its decision. In particular, black people had to jettison their own culture and way of life and learn alien culture.

You can train people to learn but you cannot change their perception of things. Human adapt better when they are a part to what they do or contributing in creating what they do. It has amazed many scholars why Africa has not changed despite many years of association with other cultures. You are what nature made you to be and cannot be someone else. Despite many years of leaving the African continent, many Africans in Diaspora still long for Africa.

Africa is currently in dire need of development. The world knows what would bring development but they are standing on the side- line watching. They only see diseases and poverty in Africa. Nobody has been bothered to find out why Africa is still poor despite the leap in the world economy. The average African wakes up every morning working hard to provide for his or her family just like any other human on earth. The African is by himself or herself struggling to obtain the basic needs for survival amidst limited modern amenities at his disposal. The west is not to be blame for what is going on in Africa. The blame is right there at the foot- steps of Africans.

The resources used in the industrialized world still come from Africa and yet the supplier is poorer while the receiver gets richer and better. Why is the disparity in terms of human and environmental developments in Africa and the west so vast? The answer does not lie in human nature but the leaders who lead the people. The leaders of the west know that their main responsible is to the people and no one else. If African leaders imbibe the principle of making the citizens the reason to be in power, definitely there would be progress in Africa.

Africans operate the market economy but there are certain institutions that sustain the market economy that Africans have not put in place. Africa needs to establish institutions like commodity exchanges, stock markets, strong financial institutions-insurance, reinsurance, investment banks, venture capital markets, research centers, economic researchers, market analysis corporations, and legal systems where no one is above the law. Law and order is what creates stability and security in the west. Americans operate still on a constitution declared close to 250 years ago.

The most urgent need is a commodity and stock exchanges. The stock market enables everyone to have ownership in a company by buying shares of the company and enabling large accumulation of funds for big projects. The stock market is the heart of the west and east, it enables company to have easy access to funds and also helps in the dilution of ownership so that business risks is not bear by one person and in the same manner profits are so distributed to shareholders. The West is able to embark on large projects because the rich put their resources together by way of the stock exchange. This is what African should be doing in order to be able to embark on gigantic projects like provision of electricity, water, roads, and many large infrastructures. There are stock markets in African countries but they are subsidiaries of foreign companies who have businesses in Africa. Africa as the main suppliers of most minerals and cash crops does not have a commodity market.

There are five top commodity exchanges in the world:
- New York Mercantile Exchange.........USA
- Tokyo Commodity Exchange............Japan
- NYSE-Euro-next.............................European Union
- Dalian Commodity Exchange..............China
- Multi Commodity Exchange.................India

The last two established by China and India as recently as 1993 and 2003 respectively.

By the way, what is a commodity market? Commodity markets are markets where raw produce or products exchanged among buyers and sellers.   The raw commodities traded on Commodity Exchanges are-agricultural products, livestock, meat, energy (gas, electricity, coal, and oil), metals, and rare metals. Agricultural products are soft while minerals are hard. There is no differentiation in the commodities on the market therefore the price is usually the same. The commodity markets help farmers in advance economies to have access to funds to aid them in farming. The farmers in the west and east are encouraged by governments to farm by way of subsidies and low taxation.

Produce buyers and farmers enter into contractual agreement to produce certain produce at an agreed price, and the farmers receive money before planting, this is call future contracts. These contracts agreements are trade on the stock market.   The farmers harvest the crops and deliver to the buyer. This process enables the farmer to focus on production and increase productivity. In view of the continuous productivity of the farmer, there is usually no shortage of produce in markets in advanced economy.   This system creates employment for people who are the middle-men and in the distribution channel because the produce need to be taken from the farmer to places where they would be sold and process.

The system of pricing using 116 different commodities weighted equally has not been changed since 1818.. (Source Report 219171- Wharton Business School). It has not changed because, it favors the buyers and not the poor countries and the people who labor to produce the products. This is one reason developing countries would forever remain poor unless they begin to process their resources instead of selling them raw. Partial processing would add value and this would increase revenue and create employment for the people. The prices of processed commodities tend to be higher due to need and differentiation it went through to become a finished product, for example computer.

Developing nations in which most African countries belong, are currently suffering under the system where the prices of their commodity is established based on a system developed in the 1900s. The manufacturers set the prices of manufactured goods therefore producers of raw materials should also set their own prices basedon demand and supply principles..

The current situation is skew towards developed economies that buy low priced commodities from developing nations, add values, and turn around and sell the items made at exorbitant price to the developing nations. What is a developing country or nation? A developing nation is a nation with low level of material wellbeing. The bulk of the African continent falls within the definition.

On the other hand, "a developed nation is the one that allows all citizens to enjoy free and healthy life in a safe environment" by Kofi Annan former Secretary General of the United Nations.

The statistical indices for measuring a nation's development are- per capital income or standard of living, life expectancy, rate of literacy. This is the index the United Nations use to categorize nations. Quality of life is used interchangeably with standard of living in some writings. Quality of life measures wealth, employment, infrastructures, physical and mental health, education, recreation, leisure- time and social associations.

In view of the above criterion and for African nations to move forward they have to establish institutions the market economy thrives on. The establishment of joint commodity market among Africa nations is paramount to improve the revenue they get from the mono product their economy depends on. The commodity market would attract investors to participate and Africa can have funds to provide needed amenities. The existence of the market would create new areas of employment, open doors to new ideas and African farmers and miners would get value for their labor.

The cash crops like cocoa, coffee, groundnuts are exchange on the commodity market in Europe. The commodity market established by Europeans in 1888 when Africa was still under colonial domination has not changed the way it operates. Most Africa countries still depend on commodity as the main source of revenue and have not find a way of adding value to the cash crop before shipping them overseas. This way of doing business is what is holding Africa back. Europe and the rest of the western world depend on these commodities for their factories. People in cold climates are dependent on coffee and cocoa to keep warm in cold seasons. Chocolate is made from cocoa and chocolate was many years ago a delicacy only for the aristocrats but it is available for everyone now.

Everybody would benefit from the market since livestock, agricultural products, and minerals will trade on the commodity market. The Maasai and Fulani herdsmen would have standard market for their livestock and their live would improve. Since invertors from other nations would be involved there would be standard for the livestock sold and this would bring in more revenue and better productive animals. It would usher in better life for African workers because they would receive the same pay as any other producer of the same product around the world.

Local markets for livestock and agricultural products have existed in African communities for centuries but recent governments in Africa did not see them as a vehicle to bring about economic changes. The government could develop and assist the existing market, updating to current standards, providing infrastructure and overseeing the activities in the market. Many societies started the way Africa currently is but changed gradually over time with better technology introduced. Africa has not witnessed internal economic changes instituted by the people themselves. It is never late to start and now is the time for Africa to take internal stock and make drastic changes that would involve everyone both literate and illiterate. The people of Africa need to work together as it was in the past to move the people forward. Definite internal changes have to take place in Africa for the people to enjoy worthwhile existence. The continuation of the way things are currently would continue to retreat Africa to the background of development because the world is moving at leaps while Africa is crawling.

There is no structured commodity exchange on the continent of Africa. The existence of a commodity market is the fastest gate to economic development. China and India saw the importance of commodity exchanges for economic progress and established the Dalian Commodity and Multi Commodity exchanges n 1993 and 2003 respectively. Africa needs to establish a commodity market to develop the continent.

Ancient civilizations thrived on commerce in commodities. The empires that flourished then were those that traded and had security in the trading arena. The world has not changed it is the way of doing things that have changed. The modern commodity markets trades in forward and future contracts. A forward contract is an agreement between two parties to exchange at some fixed future date a given quantity of a commodity for a price defined today. The fixed price today is the forward price. That is, a farmer can sell a future contract on his corn that would not be harvest in months at a guarantee price. A breakfast cereal manufacturer buys the corn contract now at a guarantee price; the contract price will not change even if corn prices rises or falls in the future. This system protects the farmer from price drops and the buyer when the price goes up. Speculators and investors buy and sell future contracts to make a profit and provide money to the commodity market system.

Commodity market need to spring up in Africa to help farmers concentrate on producing with the assurance that their produce would be bought and not rot as the current situation in most part of Africa. Let African bring dignity back into farming so that the educated young graduates see farming as a lucrative venture. The things that Africa ignores are what make the western nations great. They invest and have interest in whatever the citizenry engages in. There is so much surplus liquidity around the world and Africa should attract investors by putting in place organized commodity market where legitimate and organized trading in commodities can take place on the continent.

If a commodity market is establish in Africa middle-men would buy what the farmer produces; manufacturers and processors would buy the products, process and quality products would be available, employment would increase and the society would be busy and hence a good life. People are ready to work to provide for their families and live productive lives. The black man is a hard working individual who knows how to enjoy living but because there are not many organized opportunities around him, he appears lazy to others.

Aside from commodity markets, Africa need investment banking, stock markets, strong financial institutions, insurance and reinsurance companies, strong legal institution, and credit rating companies to monitor the financial institutions and companies and a central bank with one currency for all African countries. Currently African countries do not understand the mechanics and significant of financial institution in the market economy. Strong lack of understanding of financial institutions and investment is one of the drawbacks in Africa's progress. African countries spend money on consumables rather than investing in durables that can generate more wealth. All the loans and grants Africa takes from external donors are return to the donors by way of purchases. Africa needs to establish a strong financial institutions a requirement for a strong economy.

The financial institutions in Africa are subsidiaries of European or American companies. These foreign institutions are in Africa to make profits for their home company and not to develop Africa. The central banks in African countries handle most of the financial transactions but other financial apparatus should evolve to handle the complex nature of the market economy. The central bank controls the money supply and currency value in a country. The mechanisms central banks use to control money supply in an economy are the open market operations, discount windows, reserve requirement, lender of last result and supply of currency in the economy.

Each of the above mechanism is apply to different situation in an economy. The open market is use to sell or buy government securities. Do you know banks create money? Banks create money by lending to customers using depositor's funds. In order to protect the depositor banks are required to keep a percentage of deposits as reserve before lending. The central in advanced countries are insurers for banks. Banks go to the discount window to borrow money at the lowest rate possible. The central bank is the lender of last resort mechanism is that central bank is lender to banks.

Africa needs to create investments banks that would source money for investments. Investment banks handle mergers and acquisitions for businesses. There are many individuals and businesses in Africa who have innovative ideas to improve the economy but lack of capital kill the ideas in the infant stage. If Africa has viable investment banking, venture capital market on the continent prospective innovators would be able to find investors who would be willing to invest in the ideas. There are many proposals developed by many universities in Africa but the ideas die on the university shelves due to lack of capital or avenue to source funds.

A viable investment bank would attract some investors who want to invest in Africa. Expanding the financial system to include commodity, investing banking, venture capital insurance and reinsurance would aid in propelling Africa forward. The financial markets when created by entrepreneurs should be accessible to everyone irrespective of education. If such markets exist in Africa some of the Africans in Diaspora would gladly buy shares in the land of their ancestors. African leaders should set in motion ideals of progress instead of fighting over power and ethnicity. Economic progress is what Africa needs not in fighting.

European nations used to fight among themselves for superiority but they stopped and concentrated on how to improve their lives and that led them to where they are today. It is time Africans think of progress for their children and grandchildren and stop unnecessary bickering on ethnicity and languages. The people of the world are improving on their standard of living and black people should join in the current industrial progress this time around. Africans should learn how to create wealth instead of looking for other people to come to their rescue. The continent produces what other people take and turn into wealth for themselves.

The following are the major investment banks in the world and none is of African.

301

- Bank of America Merrill Lynch, USA
- Barclays Bank , Britain
- BNP Paribas, Euro-next
- Citigroup, USA
- Deutsche Bank, Germany
- Credit Suisse, Switzerland
- Goldman Sachs, USA
- JPMorgan Chase, USA
- Morgan Stanley, USA
- Nomura Holdings, Japan
- UBS, Switzerland
- RBS, Scotland
- Well Fargo, USA

Africans need insurance and reinsurance in other to leave sustainable wealth for the next generation. The next generation of black people should not be just workers for other people but also owners of business and capital. Africans do not believe in insurance. Insurance is the means businesses, families transfer properties when unforeseeable events happen by means of payments called premium to insurance companies. In 2008 the premiums paid to insurance companies was $4.3 trillion. Despite the global economic meltdown in 2008 in the financial sector, insurance companies faired very well. The insurance companies in the world exist mostly in advanced countries and they account for the bulk of global insurance. The premium income of Europe was $1.75 billion, North America $1.35 billion and Asia $933 billion. United States and Japan accounted for 40% of world insurance, being only 7% of the world population in 2008. The leading insurance companies in the world are as follows:

- American International Group- USA
- China Life Insurance-China
- Met Life USA-USA
- AXA Group- France
- Travelers-USA
- Ping An Insurance Group-China
- Aviva – United Kingdom

- Tokio Marine Insurance-Japan
- Lloyds of London- United Kingdom
- GNP Assurance- France
- Geico, a Bershire-Hathaway Company- USA
- American Life Insurance-USA
- AEGON- Netherlands

Since the world is a Global Village Africans should be involved in activities that make the rest of the world better. Financial institutions are the bedrock and wonders of the modern world in which Africans have not been actively involved.

Another vital market in the modern world is the stock market. The stock market is an important source for companies and governments to raise money. Businesses publicly trade and raise capital and additional funds for expansion by selling shares of ownership of the company in a public market called stock exchange. Stock market enables investors to buy and sell securities in the stock market. Securities are certificates that represent ownership in a company. The stock market enables holders of the securities to sell or buy them as an investment or to source funds. The operations of the stock market in countries facilitate economic growth. The size of the world's stock market as of October 2008 was $36.6 trillion excluding derivatives that stood $791 trillion. The main potent stock exchanges in the world are:
- New York Stock Exchange- USA
- Tokyo Stock Exchange-Japan
- Euro-next- Europe
- London Stock Exchange-United Kingdom
- Shanghai Stock Exchange
- Hong Kong Stock Exchange
- Toronto Stock Exchange
- Frankfurt Stock Exchange
- Madrid Stock Exchange

There are stocks markets in some Africa countries, but most of the listings are foreign companies that colonist established in the colonial era. Most indigenous Africa businesses operate as sole proprietorship and have problems raising capital for expansion. Many established businesses in Africa die with the owners. Individuals with money could buy into viable businesses and turn the small business into a corporation so that the business survive after the owners die and the families would continue to receive income and live the life they are used to when the breadwinner was alive or even better.

African governments have a lot to do if they want to improve the life of Africans and improve the face of Africa. They need to educate indigenous businesses on how to keep records through public enlightenment programs. The importance of raising capital to expand business to create employment or educate others on how to operate the business should be part of public enlightenment program in African countries. This happened in the west when rebirth began in Europe. The public were educated on the new changes. Africa needs internal development in order to move away from the present situation of poverty and have not. The way forward is to emphasize on internal developments by way of improving existing local business structures ignored by successive leaders in Africa.

Iron making was indigenous to Africa. What happened to that ingenuity? The cottage industries in Africa are in neglect due to reliance on exporting of commodities to the west and east and importing items that African can make given the resources and environment. What happened to weaving, dyeing, gold, diamond, and copper smith, soap making, pottery, carving, herding and agriculture industries? The above listed are legitimate enterprises African governments can improve upon to engage more people productively. These small industries need improvement by using modern technology to make old things better. There is no way Africa can improve if it does not develop what it already has.

Economic activities of the people create growth and wealth for a nation. No amount of external aids can help Africa unless the internal economic activities of the people are improved. Everywhere in Africa, people are busy working but they are under compensated for their efforts Paying workers more wages would not create inflation if productivity increases in relation to pay. The value of a currency becomes stronger if there is productivity and demand for the products and services. The wages in the west and east are higher than wages paid to African workers by their employers and government. There is no basis to believe that the worker in the west and east work harder than workers in Africa.

Unfortunately, African leaders have not realized the effect of under employment and pay on their people. Inflation occurs if more money is chasing few goods and services. The currency of an economy loses value if the economy depends on other countries to provide more of its needs rather than producing them internally. People paid higher wages or salaries would have positive net balances to invest in the economy thereby creating more job opportunities. The world is a market economy and Africans need to participate fully and confidently.

Take a glimpse at the different vital economic commodities Africa supply to the rest of the world.

Angola-Crude Oil, Diamonds, Refined Petroleum Products, Coffee, Sisal, Fish, Timber, Cotton.

Benin-Cotton, Cashew, Shea Butter, Palm Products, Fish

Botswana-Diamonds, Copper, Nickel, Soda Ash

Burkina Faso-Cotton, Livestock, Gold, Mango Concentrate and Puree

Burundi- Coffee, Tea, Sugar, Cotton, Hides, Uranium, Nickel, Peat, Cobalt, Copper, Niobium, Platinum, Tantalum, Gold, Kaolin, Limestone

Cameroon-Crude Oil, Petroleum Products, Timber, Cocoa, Coffee, Cotton, Aluminum

Central African Republic-Diamonds, Gold, Copper, Cobalt, Timber, Cotton, Coffee, Tobacco

Chad-Crude Oil, Cattle, Cotton Gum Arabic, Camel, Fish,

Democratic Republic of Congo-Diamonds, Gold, Copper, Cobalt, Timber, Crude Oil, Coffee

Republic of Congo-Petroleum, Timber, Plywood, Sugar, Cocoa, Coffee, Cut Diamonds, Lead

Ivory Coast-Cocoa, Coffee, Timber, Petroleum, Cotton, Bananas, Pineapple, Palm Oil, Fish, Cocoa Butter, Oleic Acid, Fibers for stuffing car seats and mattresses

Djibouti-Hides and Skins, Coffee, Location for refueling and bunkering,
French and USA Naval Stations

Equatorial Guinea-Petroleum, Methanol, Timber, Cocoa,

Eritrea- Livestock, Sorghum,

Egypt-Crude Oil, Petroleum Products, Cotton, Chemicals, Metal Products, Processed Food

Ethiopia- Coffee, Qat, Gold, Leather Products, Oilseeds, Live Animals, Flower, Kaolin, Coal, Soda Ash, Tantalum, Salt, Gemstones, Iron Ore, Maize

Gabon-Crude Oil, Timber, Manganese, Uranium

Gambia-Peanuts, Fish, Cotton, Palm Kernels

Ghana-Gold, Cocoa, Aluminum, Fish, Bauxite, Aluminum, Diamonds, Manganese Ore

Guinea-Bauxite, Uranium, Alumina, Gold, Diamonds, Coffee, Fish

Guinea-Bissau- Fish, Shrimp, Cashew, Peanuts, Palm Kernels, Sawn Timber, Rubber, Beeswax

Kenya-Tea, Coffee, Petroleum Products, Cement, Soda Ash, Limestone, Sisal, Livestock, Fish, Gold, Salt, Pyrethrum, Fluorspar,

Lesotho- Manufacturing (clothing, footwear, road vehicles), Wool and Mohair, Live Animals

Liberia-Rubber, Timber, Iron, Diamonds, Cocoa, Coffee

Libya- Crude Oil, Natural Gas, Chemicals

Madagascar-Coffee, Vanilla, Shellfish, Sugar, Cotton Cloth, Chromite, Petroleum Products

Malawi-Tobacco, Tea, Sugar, Cotton, Coffee, Peanuts, timber

Mali-Cotton, Gold, Livestock, Kaolin, Salt Phosphate, Limestone, Cottonseeds, Deposits of Diamonds and Copper

Mauritania-Iron Ore, Fish, Gold, Copper, Petroleum

Mauritius-Textiles, Sugar, Flowers, Molasses, Fish

Morocco-Textiles, Electric Components, Chemicals, Transistors, Crude Minerals, Petroleum Products, Citrus Fruits, Fish, Vegetables

Mozambique-Aluminum, Prawns, Cashews, Peanuts, Cotton, Sugar, Citrus, Timber, Bulk Electricity, Sugar, Marble, Granite, Gemstones, Bauxite, Tobacco, Copra

Namibia-Diamonds, Copper, Gold, Zinc, Lead, Uranium, Cattle, Fish, Karakvi Skins

Niger-Uranium Ore, Livestock, Cowpeas, Onions, Cotton, Deposits of Gold, Phosphates, Coal, Iron, and Limestone

Nigeria-Petroleum Products, Cocoa, Rubber, Gum Arabic, Palm Kernels, Coconut Fats, and Oils

Rwanda-Coffee, Tea, Hides, Tin Ore
Coltan Cassitente, Iron Ore

Senegal-Fish, Groundnuts, Petroleum Products, Phosphates, Cotton, Iodized Salts

Sierra Leone-Diamonds, Rutile, Cocoa, Coffee, Fish

Somalia-Livestock, Bananas, Hides, Fish, Charcoal, Frankincense, Myrrh, Uranium Deposits

South Africa-Gold, Diamonds, Platinum, Coal, Machinery and Equipment, Concentrate Fruits and Puree, Ferroalloys, Stainless Steel, Motor Vehicles, Synthetic Fuels, Wine, Wool, Wheat, Dairy Products, Tobacco, Sugar Cane

Sudan-Oil, Petroleum Products, Cotton, Sesame, Livestock, Groundnuts, Gum Arabic, Sugar, Iron Ore, Copper, Chromium Ore, Zinc, Tungsten, Fish, Vegetable Oil, Flowers,

Swaziland-Soft drink Concentrate, Sugar, Wood Pulp, Cotton Yarn, Refrigerators, Citrus, Canned Fruits

Tanzania- Gold, Coffee, Cashew Nuts, Cotton, Sisal, Cloves, Pyrethrum,

Togo-Cotton, Phosphates, Coffee, Cocoa

Tunisia-Phosphate, Chemicals, Semi- Manufactured Goods, Textiles, Mechanical Goods, Hydro-Carbon, Electrical Equipments

Uganda-Coffee, Fish, Tea, Cotton, Flowers, Gold

Western Sahara- Phosphates

Zambia-Copper, Cobalt, Electricity, Flowers, Cotton, Zinc, Vegetables, Gemstones, Fruits

Zimbabwe- Platinum, Cotton, Tobacco, Gold, Ferroalloy, Textiles, Coal, Nickel, Asbestos, Copper, Iron Ore, Deposit of Chromite

Cape Verde- Fuel, Shoes, Garments, Fish, Hide

Comoros- Vanilla, Perfume Essence, Cloves, Copra

Seychelles- Canned Fish, Frozen Fish, Cinnamon Bark, Copra, Petroleum

Sao Tome and Principe- Cocoa, Coffee, Palm Oil

There is no reason based on the above resources that the people of Africa should be poor. The commodities above sustain the industrialized world. If the industrialized world is rich with healthy people, there is no justification for Africa to be poor. The receiver is rich while the supplier is poor. There is something intrinsically wrong with the trading agreement between Africa and the rest of the world.

African countries have the ace card but do not know how to play the game that is why they are losing in the world market. The countries of Africa are so distracted in infighting and political power such that they do not see the worth and power they have in the market economy. The world should catch cold when Africa sneezes, but alas, it is the other way round. The petroleum exporting countries began to enjoy the benefit of their petroleum when they form trade cartel. African countries with similar or same products could form trade cartel so that they could bargain for the right prices for their products. They do the hard work by planting and mining and the person who do the processing and manufacturing reap the higher profit. Africa Union should be concerned about the situation where their countries are drowning in debt despite their valuable resources and hard work of the people. Africa Union should include economic development as part of their program.

Africa leaders have no excuse not to revisit the trade arrangement that existed before independence and see how they can negotiate better for their people and country. It is the same world and sky and there is no reason Africans should be suffering the way they do now. It is a pity that, Africans have not learned to shed the colonial robe. The countries are independent on paper but tied to the aprons of their colonial masters. Europeans came to Africa to trade in the 1400s and that venture opened big ventures and opportunities for Europe than they envisaged. Africans have become dependent on Europe like father and child; this relationship is hindering the progress of African people. Africa is a grown child now and should learn to leave the father alone and develop its own economic future.

When America became independent from Britain in 1776 it began to develop internally. America isolated itself from global activities for over thirty years in order to develop the necessary infrastructures and put the necessary apparatus in place in order to prepare and overcome any challenges from Britain the former colonist. America was the commodities supply depot for Britain before American independence. It created its own factories to make all that they needed instead of dependence on Britain as a new nation. The plan worked well for America and now it is the most powerful nation on earth that all countries want to emulate. America through the sacrifice it made in the past has the strongest economy and the best military power.

African countries got independence from European colonists but forgot they could only thrive economically if they had economy independence as well. African leaders are looking for immediate gratification and not the future prosperity for their people and country. Most of these African leaders have been to the west or east and seen how people live and how the governments work for the people. It is over fifty years since the first black African country Ghana got independence from Britain and the situations of the people in Africa is deteriorating instead of progressing. If you ask any child in the west to tell you what they know about Africa, the response would be hunger, disease, and animals.

If Africa want to change its present situation countries producing similar commodities should form cartels. There are no substitutes for most of the commodities Africans exports to the industrialized world. If the international trade agreements between Africa and its traders had been fair then Africa should not be poor. Europe saw progress and advancement after the partition of Africa for the resources. The system established during the partition of Africa had continued for over five hundred years, and African leaders have never wondered why the people who receive their resources are rich and they continue to be drowning in poverty.

In order for the future generation of Africans to enjoy life like every other person on earth, they should change the way they trade their vital resources.

African governments need to establish commodities markets in order to be part of the decision in determining the prices of their sources of revenue. The inter trading between advanced economy and Africa would be fair if Africa decides the price of its product based on the market mechanism of supply and demand.

Before moving further, would you like to see the hypothetical cartels for various commodities and the participating countries? African countries would have strong bargaining power for their commodities if they create cartels and take decision of what to bring to the market how and when.

Commodities /Countries and Companies that depend on Commodity

Cocoa- Ghana, Cameroon, Republic of Congo, Ivory Coast, Equatorial Guinea, Liberia, Nigeria, Sierra Leone, Togo, Sao Tome

Cocoa/Companies- Nestle, Hershey, Cadbury, Lessonia, Bloomer Chocolate, Archer Daniels Midland, M &M Mars, Ben & Jerry, Fowlers Chocolate, Godiva, Kraft and many other small chocolate and cosmetic companies.

Coffee- Sao Tome, Angola, Burundi, Cameroon, Central African Republic, Ivory Coast, Ethiopia, Guinea, Kenya, Liberia, Madagascar, Malawi, Sierra Leone, Rwanda, Tanzania, Uganda, Djibouti, Democratic Republic of Congo

Coffee/Companies- Maxwell House, Folgers (Procter & Gamble), Starbucks, Sara Lee, American Coffee Company, American Coffee Incorporation, Aikana, Kona Coffee, Alaska Coffee Roasting Company, Carribou Coffee, and over thousands of coffee roaster companies

Diamonds- Angola, South Africa, Botswana, Central African Republic, Democratic Republic of Congo, Republic of Congo, Ghana, Guinea, Liberia, Sierra Leone, Namibia

Diamonds/ Companies/Countries- Global Rewards Investments, Right Jewelers, 3D Diamonds, 4Cs, A E Solomon, Eight Star Diamonds, World Diamond Congress, World Federation of Bourses, International Diamond Manufactures Association, Diamond Cutting Centers- Antwerp, Belgium, India, New York, Israel

Timber/Plywood- Angola, Cameroon, Central African Republic. Ivory Coast, Democratic African Republic, Republic of Congo, Equatorial Guinea, Gabon, Ghana, Guinea- Bissau, Liberia, Mozambique

 Timber/ Countries- China, Italy, France, Spain, Portugal, Germany, Japan, India, USA, Canada, International Tropical Timber Organization and numerous furniture and construction companies that sprang around the globe

Cotton-Angola, Benin, Burkina Faso, Burundi, Cameroon, Central African Republic, Chad, Ivory Coast, Egypt, Gambia, Madagascar, Malawi, Mali, Mozambique, Senegal, Sudan, Swaziland, Togo, Tanzania, Uganda, Zambia, Zimbabwe

Cotton/Companies/Countries- A leading exporter of cotton, USA subsidizes its cotton farmers therefore they produce more to the market and this lowers prices due to the law of supply and demand. This is hard on African cotton farmers. Despite their hard work, they live in deplorable conditions. These companies depend on cotton: Parkdale Mills, Franzonni, Nike, Armani Monsanto, Patagonia, Coop Schweiz, Hess Natur, Marks & Spencer, they should pay their own quota to these poor farmers who work hard on the cotton field to produce cotton on which they make billion of dollars by just making goods from cotton. Have they imagined what would happen to their businesses if these farmers do not work on the cotton fields?

Cashew/Peanuts/Sesame- Benin, Gambia, Guinea Bissau. Malawi, Mozambique, Senegal, Sudan, Tanzania.

The above countries have to compete with USA, China, and India in the sale of their major revenue earner thus peanuts. Definitely, they do not have the technical know how to differentiate their peanuts through processing to earn more on them. These countries sell their products to merchants who determine the price. These countries are among the poorest countries in Africa. They should not be poor because peanuts and processed peanuts are multi billion industry and the companies that depend on African peanuts should realize that the farmers on whom they make millions of profits from deserve a better bargain for their produce in other to achieve their aspirations as people.

Shea Butter- Benin, Burkina Faso, Ivory Coast, Ghana, Mali, Senegal, Nigeria

Most cosmetics and skin care companies depends on shea-butter as the basic base for their products but these vital resource which is peculiar to the Savannah and Sahel of Africa is taken almost free in view of the million dollars these companies make and the deplorable conditions the Africa farmers live in.

Companies should begin forming partnership with the supplier countries so that the producers can also have a better standard of living. Due to ignorance and lack of business education, these vital products in the cosmetic and skin care industries are sold at rock bottom prices and the country and people that produce them live like beggars. The following companies L' Occitane en Provence, Mystic Shimmer Skincare, Nilotica Botanicals, Shea Terra Organics, Jergens, Neo Strata, Bath & Body Works depend on Shea butter and should pay the producers the right market price.

Palm Product/Copra-Benin, Ivory Coast, Ghana, Gambia, Guinea Bissau, Comoros, Seychelles, Sao Tome

Palm Products/Companies- Archer Daniels Midland, Bunge and Cargill, General Mills, Kraft Foods, Kellogg, Nestle, Procter & Gamble, Unilever, Equatorial Palm Oil

Palm Oil- Uses- Soaps, Cereal, Bio-fuels, Margarines, Ice Creams, and many more

Copper- Botswana, Democratic Republic of Congo, Mauritania, Namibia, Zambia

Copper/Companies/countries-Equinox Copper Mining, African Copper Plc, London Stock Market (Copper Trading Exchange),Telcom, Eskcom, Trannet, China, Simpex, Societe Generale des Minerals of Belgium, Phillips, General Electric, At &T, Car manufacturers,

Copper uses- Military Hardware, Underground Cable, Thermal Conductors, Electrical Conductors, Building Material, metal alloys(Bronze-Copper and Tin, Brass-Copper and Zinc), Refrigeration, Air Conditioning, Household wares, Electroplating and many more

 United States and European companies own and manage most copper mines in African countries.   These companies declare millions dollar profits but have not proportionately contributed to the development of the land and people where they mine copper. They instead support oppressive governments in these areas. They make money on Africa to develop their own counties and people. European countries and America sell ammunitions to these countries instead of technologies on developing water resources, electricity and many modern technologies that would improve lives.

Soda Ash- Botswana, Kenya, Egypt, Uganda, Botswana

Soda Ash-uses-Glass, Fiberglass, Detergents, Medicine, Food Additives, Photography, Water Treatments, Oil Refining, Synthetic Rubber, Explosives, Toothpastes and many more

Livestock- Burkina Faso, Eritrea, Mali, Namibia. Niger, Somali, Sudan, Uganda

Hides and Skin-Djibouti, Burundi, Burkina Faso, Rwanda, Namibia, Nigeria, Somalia, Cape Verde, Mali, Senegal, Sudan, Zimbabwe,Gambia

Hides and Skin – Uses-leather, bags, shoes, car seats, furniture, wall covering, clothing etc

Many advanced countries export hides and skin and for the above African countries to benefit from this main source of revenue they should add value to the hides and skin through tanning or turning the hides into leather before exports.

Gold- Burkina Faso, Ghana, Democratic Republic of Congo, Ethiopia, Guinea, Mali. Mauritania, South Africa, Uganda, Zimbabwe

Gold-Uses-Gold is the most useful of all metals. Gold conducts electricity and does not tarnish, easy to work with although fragile. Jewelry, Coinage, Bullion, Electronics (Cell phones, Calculators, Global Positioning Systems, Television), Computers, Dentistry, Medical (Medication, Surgical Instruments), Aerospace, Awards and Symbol of Status, Climate Controlled Buildings, Domes

Tea- Burundi, Kenya, Malawi, Rwanda, Uganda, Tanzania, Mozambique,

Tea/Companies – Fauchon, Tea Gschwendner, Unilever, Tetley, Twinnings, Upton Tea, Lipton, Nestle, Luzianne, Brooke Bond, Lyon Tea, Bigelow

Uses – Tea is the most consumed beverage in the world. Kenya is the largest tea producing country in Africa but does not have processing factory to make tea bags for the consumer table. Adding value by means of processing tea would greatly increase revenue for Kenya and other countries named above.

Gum Arabic-Chad, Nigeria, Sudan, Senegal, Kenya, Cameroon, Niger, Tanzania, Eritrea, Somalia, Mali, Mauritania, Burkina Faso, Ethiopia

Gum Arabic/ Countries –Import and Re- Export- France, United Kingdom, India, Germany, Italy, Japan, USA. These countries by adding value make over 130% of the value paid for the import from the above African countries. France companies dominate the re-export market of Gum Arabic. Gum Arabic is from Acacia trees prevalent in the Sahel area of Africa

Gum Arabic- Uses- Food Stabilizer in the Food processing industries, printing and photography industries, glues, cosmetics, textiles industries, soft drinks syrup, gummy candies, shoe polish, adhesives for stamps, fireworks , carbonated beverages etc

Sugar-Burundi, Congo Republic, Malawi, Mauritius, Mozambique, Swaziland,

Sugar- Over120 countries in the world produce sugar and this affects the price of sugar in the world market. Most of the sugar producers in Africa export the raw sugar. The importers refine the sugar and make more profit than the farmer who toiled in deplorable condition to plant and harvest the sugar cane. Europe and North America depend on sugar from beets from local farmers.

Bauxite/Aluminum/Alumina-Ghana, Cameroon, Guinea, Mozambique,

Bauxite/Alumina-Companies- alumina is derived from bauxite and then smelted to make aluminum. The industrialized countries depend on aluminum to make automobile, planes, instruments, ships, buildings, railway coaches, and many other vital uses that bring revenues of billions of dollars. The discovery of this vital mineral has helped the modern way of life. However, the price paid for bauxite is peanuts compared to its uses and benefits. Bauxite is not traded on an exchange and the price is determined by demand and supply.

Guinea currently has the largest bauxite deposit in the world and the following companies Alcoa of USA, Alcan of Canada, Rusal of Russia, and GAPCO supported by Japan are the investors in Guinea bauxite deposits. Guinea with this important mineral is one of the poor countries in Africa.

Manganese-Gabon, Ghana, South Africa

Manganese/Companies-Steel Making, Cell Batteries, Aluminum Cans, Electronic Circuits, Pesticides, Weapons, Animal Feeds, Fertilizers, Cosmetics, and Plastics
There is no substitute for manganese mineral and the price should be higher due to its many uses and importance in manufacturing in the advanced economy.

Uranium-Namibia, Niger, South Africa, Gabon

Uranium Prospecting –Algeria, Angola, Botswana, Burkina Faso, Burundi, Cameroon, Central Africa Republic, Chad, Egypt, Gambia, Guinea, Libya, Madagascar, Mauritania, Mali, Morocco, Mozambique, Nigeria, Sierra Leone, Somalia, Sudan, Tanzania, Togo, Uganda, Zambia, Zimbabwe.

The prospecting companies are from the West and Russia. Every piece of Africa has suddenly become uranium enriched. The world is clamoring for non -proliferation of nuclear weapons but the search for uranium deposit has become astronomical on the Africa continent with greedy African leaders signing agreements without thought to consequences on the life of the people or land.

Rubber-Liberia, Nigeria, Ivory Coast, Cameroon

Rubber/countries- USA, China, European Union, Japan

Rubber- Natural rubber is indispensable in the modern world. It is use in transportation, industrial, consumer, and medical sectors. Tires making consume over 50% of natural rubber produced. Natural rubber is used in making transmission belts, hoses, tubes, industrial linings, and bridge bearings. Natural rubber is used to make golf balls, and other sporting goods, erasers, apparel and seismic material

Another way Africa can benefit from its vital resources is to form partnership with the major users of its commodities. These companies create jobs in their respective countries and are involved in community activities to make life better for their citizens. They do not offer the same assistance to countries and people that offer them the raw materials for their entrepreneurial activities. The current method of international trade has to change for Africa to move forward.

Rhetoric is the only thing Africa receives in abundance in the journey to improve its economic condition. Africans should realize that they are the source of the resources and market for the industrialized world. Therefore, there would not be any genuine effort to change Africa for the better. The moment Africans know the importance of their contribution to this market era the table would turn in their favor.

Africa is the only continent that has not make any effort towards industrial development and continues to depend on others for things it could conveniently produce or manufacture by its self. All the same, her bowel is opened every single day in mining, cultivating and digging for resources. The trained children of Africa due to lack of employment opportunities migrate to the western to work. Most of these Africans are under paid and under employed overseas.   If these companies that take African resources establish partial processing of the resources in Africa there would be employment for educated African and would not need to migrate to the west or east.

 Frankly, by establishing processing facilities companies in the countries they take resources from aside from helping the indigenous people are on the hand helping their home country by reducing the number of people who migrate there.   The amenities in their home countries are over stretch due to influx of immigrants; jobs would be available to the citizens and perennial problem of unemployment would be minimal. The world would be prosperous for everyone; human beings would respect one another irrespective of differences in skin color or location.

The following companies depend on cocoa to sustain their multi- billions businesses while the people who work on the cocoa farms live in poverty and hapless condition. Cadbury, Hershey, Nestle, and many cosmetics industries depend on cocoa and the by-products to sustain their businesses. They have been using cocoa for over four hundred years and have not bothered to look into helping the people who produce the main ingredient cocoa. Cocoa bean is cultivated in the tropical climate and it needs special care to grow and careful processing so that the dry beans would not be bitter. The cocoa tree takes about five years to begin producing beans and need constant clearing of weeds since it cannot withstand parasites. The cocoa trees are sometimes at the mercy of bugs that feed on the cocoa beans.   The demand for cocoa products are growing constantly but the price of cocoa is artificially pegged and this makes the cocoa farmer live in perpetually poverty.

The rapid industrial take off China and India is putting more strain on African mineral deposits.   The leaders at the helm of affairs in Africa are negotiating the resources away to the detriment of the next generation of Africans. The Africa of tomorrow is going to know his or her right in this world and would want to participate in the affairs of this world and not sit on the side lines like the present corps of Africans are doing. The current African is timid and does not assert itself in the world affairs. He or she is satisfied with hand- outs in the form of aids and grants from the industrialized world. The industrialized world uses African resources to create and manufacture the modern goods and turn back and look at the African as a backward person.

It is time Africans began to move towards industrializing. What is industrializing? It is the process of manufacturing human needs to make life comfortable and convenient. Africans worked to produce the commodities that usher in the current world. It is time Africans work to improve their lives and that of future generations.

 The population of China is 1,338,500,000, that of India is 1,182,880,000 and the population of the whole continent of Africa is a mere 840 million as of February 2009. These two countries, China and India are racing to be the next industrialized country and they are counting on Africa mineral sources. These natural resources are finite and replenishment would be impossible after depletion. African leaders should gear up to take Africa to the industrialized route. Africans deserves comfort and convenience just like any other human being.

The emphasis on this writing is a way forward for black people in Africa and in Diaspora. The black race has been spectators in the world and earth affairs for too long and it is time they plunge into the world and enjoy it like any other human being. Africa has what it takes to take the plunge; the only thing lacking are leaders who care about the people they lead.

 In Adam Smith's book "The Wealth of Nations", mentioned that, the main factors of production are raw material capital and labor. All these inputs are equally important for production to take place. However, in recent times capital and management have been recognized as more important than raw materials and labor because the rich and the affluent control the two, the providers of raw material and labor are grossly under -valued and this leave room for poverty to rise and the rich get richer.

Chapter Eight

Rebirth

The definition of rebirth is revival or renaissance. Black people should experience rebirth in other to move from the present predicament they face. The revival of black people is urgent. Black people have to begin a new life that would restore confidence and dignity to black people in Africa and Diaspora. Black people need a new life that would revive their consciousness to remember who they were and where they are.

Slave trade and scramble for Africa's resources by Europeans have had serious effect on the life of black people. The different cultures of the Arabs and Europeans imposed on black people during occupation have negative impact on the cultures of black race. Black people are versed in Arabic and European cultures but they are neither. English, French, and Arabic are the lingua franca of most African countries. None of the African countries has an Africa language as lingua franca. It is sad. Well some will say it is too late, but nothing is late if there is determination and perseverance on the part of the people and leaders.

Africans speak their mother tongue at home but officially, they jettison their natural language for foreign languages. As mentioned earlier, they are neither of the official languages they speak. The English, Arabs, French, and Portuguese know themselves. Learning in one's natural language aid learning and thought processing. Look around and one will find that countries that are leading the world speak in their own language. Some would say different nations formed America but they speak English. America developed its own style of English. It is American English not just English.

The black race needs discovering of self in order to progress forward. It appears black people are complacence in the way things are but a closer look at situation reveals most blacks are living in poverty, doing menial occupation and fighting all types of diseases in Africa gives a grim picture of the future of blacks. The industrialized world depends on African resources and yet Africans are the poorest among the human race. Most black people work hard without much recreation and yet they are poor and live in misery.

In view of the above predicament, blacks should re- examine themselves and check what it is that they are doing wrong. Look at the situation of black people all over the world, in Brazil, in the United States, in Europe, in Haiti and in Africa. Anytime there is a catastrophe black people bear the most brunt. Can you recollect the Katrina Hurricane, the landslide in Brazil, and the recent earthquake in Haiti? Fortunately, African countries do not experience many natural disasters like many other countries but Africans have created many manmade disasters for themselves like unhealthy environments(that breeds mosquitoes and many disease carrying insects), poor sanitation, lack of portable drinking water, and unnecessary wars among one another. The neglect to develop African environment is causing hazards to people, animals, and vegetation.

Africa has neglected its environments to such an extent that mosquitoes and diseases carrying bacteria survive. Malaria, guinea worm, tuberculosis, and many more illnesses are a menace to African people. Many of the diseases that currently plague Africans had been eradicated in most part of the world long time ago. These diseases survive mostly in filthy environment and dirty water. Keeping the environment clean and safe is very important because most disease causing organisms survives in warm and dirty environs.

The rebirth of black people is imperative and paramount if the next generation of blacks would be able to enjoy all the good things of this world just like anyone else. Modern civilization started in Africa and new renaissance has to start from Africa sooner. The dignity of black people is Africa and without giving the continent the best it deserves people would continue to look down on black race.

Renaissance of the12th century was a period of significant changes in Middle Age Europe. Significant transformations in social, political, economics, and intellectual revitalization of Western Europe in the 12th century ushered in the modern world. The rebirth in the 12th century led the way to Italian renaissance of the 14th century down to the scientific development of the 17th century. The 14th century renaissance affected literature, philosophy, arts, politics, science, and religion. People had the desire to study and imitate nature. Banking and commerce with other lands brought wealth to Italy in the 14th century.

Marco Polo an Italian explorer traveled to the Far East in the 15th century and his report brought awareness of other people and their way of life. Western Europe made contacts with the Islamic world and learned the work of Islamic doctors, philosophers, scientists, and mathematicians. The works of these intellectuals in Arabic and Greek were translated into Latin for people to read and study. Latin was the principal language widely used in Europe at that period. Europe developed universities that became the center of learning for new ideas and methods from other places of the world. During this period, the rate of new inventions increased and innovation in managing traditional means of production increased.

  In the 15th century rebirth spread from Italy to all Western Europe. In Portugal, it arrived by way of wealthy Italians merchants who invested money in profitable Indian commerce controlled by Portugal. Rebirth reached England in the reign of Queen Elizabeth I. Renaissance arrived in France in 1495 from Italy when King Charles VIII invaded Italy.

A Swiss historian Jacob Burckhardt summed up rebirth as removing a veil from man's eyes allowing him to see clearly. Some historians view rebirth as a movement from feudalism to individualism and capitalism leading to the creation of more wealthy individuals. The new wealth came from education, employment as distinguished from social wealth that one was inherited from one generation to the other. .

African leaders and elites have veil over their eyes and do not see clearly. Africa needs to learn to start on its own by coming together to develop economically. The formation of African Union is a good start for Africans but more needs to done in the area of economic development. The dependent on mono product for export is a serious hindrance for Africa. Africa should begin partial processing of the product before shipment to overseas thereby adding value. Economic expansion should be items African countries should be discussing when they meet. The world is a market and Africa is not a serious participant in the market.

Africa has the resources the industrialized world depends upon; Africa can dictate the terms of trade on their resources if the countries in Africa unite economically. Since the development of the western industries depended on resources found in Africa during colonization and there is no substitute to these resources, Africans have good chance of negotiating value for their resources. The western world processes these resources from African countries and make billions upon billions of money but do not contribute to development of Africa the way partners should do. African countries are partners in the world development but have not been receiving fair share of their contributions. It is time Africa countries stand firm and get what is rightly theirs so that they would be able to develop their countries and people.

Every nation wants the citizens to enjoy the fruits of this life. Leaders all over the world thrive to make basic things of life like electricity, housing, water, accessible roads, and recreation within reach of most people with the exception of most African leaders. African leaders act as if they are answerable to the former colonists and do not act to protect their people or initiate programs that would be beneficial to citizens.

The environment and living condition of most people in Africa is deplorable. African cities have more shanty- towns and slums than anywhere in the world. Life is dynamic and changes in societies bring improvement and a better way of life. People could resist changes in the way they eat and live but not on the environment that belongs to everyone. It is the responsibility of leaders and elites to bring changes to the environment and their communities.

African leaders are the custodians of Africa people and any bad perception of African reflects on their leadership. Leaders and elites bring changes to the people. Slum and shanty –town dwellers in Africa are waiting for the leaders to make good changes to make African environments decent, healthy, and attractive. The above action does not require complex technology; it requires caring and desire to bring better live to the people. The improvement in the environment can create thousands of jobs for people. In the western hemisphere, millions of people make their livelihood through working to keep the environment clean and beautiful.

Africans have not inculcated good maintenance culture. Takings care of properties could save African governments lots of money. Old buildings are not taking care of and they become dilapidated where as some gallons of paint could make them new. Historical monuments need refurbishing to attract tourist and generate revenue. The streams that run through African cities have been turned into trash dumps and sewage instead of beatifying the banks with trees and clean water flowing.

A clean environment breeds healthy people and incident of diseases would reduce. Africans need to plant flowers and trees around cities instead of surroundings streets with littered thrash and filthy stagnant waters. The stagnant waters and open drains aid the breed of mosquitoes that transmit malaria parasites. Millions of Africans die yearly from malaria and they could be saved by just keeping the environment clean and covering gutters and spraying drains with insecticides. The covered pavements could become pedestrian walk instead of people competing with motorists and motor cyclists in most Africa cities streets.

Aesthetic was part of the African people. The African's belief in beauty made him/her adorn the body and face with beautiful paintings and marks. In African villages, floors were painted with fresh clay and herbs each day to make them beautiful and fresh. What happened to the aesthetic instinct of African people that Africans now live in *slum* in the cities without concern? Many beauty aspects of the body came from Africa to the West. Ear piercing for earrings originated from Africa. Africans should revive the culture of beauty in Africa and be proud of themselves and culture. The body and environmental grooming are vital to keep the spirit alive. The brain works better in a clean body and beautiful environment.

African governments should invest in Africa environment to make Africa beautiful. Entrepreneurs could invest in the environment and make profits. The entrepreneurs could build houses that people can buy and pay mortgage over time. The houses should have amenities and the environment beautiful with flowers. In Africa, individuals still build houses by themselves; it takes a long time to complete and this disfigures the environment. The ability to keep the environment clean and safe for people is a vital part of the 21st century world.

If the buildings or residential properties in Africa cities are valued and given monetary values as is done in most advanced countries the per capital of Africans would increase and this would translate to wealth for the nation and people.   African societies, particularly in traditional areas do not put monetary values on residential property they live in. Properties are valued in Africa only if the property is being used as collateral for a loan from the bank.   In view of this, the value of African's wealth is grossly under- valued. African societies know the importance of owing property so everyone tries to build without governmental assistance.

Transportation sector is an area where Africans need to improve upon. Efficient transportation is vital to economic development and growth.   Africa needs integrated transportation system linking all countries together. This would link towns and cities and movement of people, cargoes freighting would become easy. Africans can move freely and not tied down with the artificial boundaries created by colonization. Every community has a competitive advantage over one another and allowing people avenues to move freely would improve relation among people and they will learn to appreciate one another.

  In most African cities, proprietors dominate the transportation sector with limited government involvements. Transportation is chaotic in most urban centers in Africa due to limited road network.   Let us take a glimpse at common mode of transporting people and cargoes use through the continent of Africa.   I am using the transportation system in Nigeria as an example.

Nigeria- is one of the populous countries in Africa but the transportation system is inadequate to serve the teeming population and aid economic improvement.   The rail system is not efficient due to lack of maintenance. The roads are nightmares riddled with pot- holes. The country was once a proud owner of fleet of airplanes operated under the name Nigeria Airways. The air transport in Nigeria is currently in the hands of private and foreign carriers. There is no public transport system in Nigeria that can meet the requirement of the population.   A country with a population of over 300 million and in rich resources should be able to have a vehicle assembly to meet part of the automobile requirement.

Nigeria roads and streets are full of vehicles that would not meet emission requirement of many countries. These are vehicles off the road in many industrialized countries that are imported to Nigeria. It is Africa and it does not matter. These vehicles emit pollutant into the atmosphere that creates smog around most Nigerian cities. These entrepreneurs could team up to fund a vehicle assembly instead of gradually destroying life in the name of making money. Poverty is a terrible thing; people drive in these death trap vehicle and they are happy because there is no other alternative.   There are limited inland waterways in Nigeria but has over ten seaports.   Nigeria transportation system mirrors public transportation problems in Africa.

If there are expectations and consequences for over stepping bounds, people behave better. The fear of consequences when rules or laws are broken make people conform.   The western world thrives on the rule of law. Laws bring order, peace, and respect. Traditional African societies lived under laws and regulation and everyone lived by respecting the laws. The occupation of foreigners in Africa destroyed the existing societies and everything changed for the worse. Africa can go back to live by way of laws that are fair to everyone irrespective of social leanings.

African countries need pools of innovative and creative ideas to be able to compete in the world.   The peoples of Africa are not united and this does not augur well for the progress of any people. After all, Africans are perceived as one block of people outside the African continent. The outside world, see the color of the skin pigmentation and nothing else. Africa has a multitude of intelligent and educated people all over the African continent but there is no connectivity between them. Institutions for researches on African issues need to be encouraged and established. The educated elites and the wealthy Africans, instead of finding solution to

African problems through connection with other contemporaries sit on the fence and subscribe to nepotism just like the politicians.

If Africa invests into food production, processing, packaging, and marketing, they could create great enterprises all over the world. There are foods of different nations all over the world but Africa has not got into the business of promoting what they eat. There are people of African origin in Diaspora who are proud of their African heritage, and would love tastes of Africa.

Famine has been a constant problem in Africa and one wonders why because Africa has vast arable lands, rivers, and lakes. The subsistence type of farming practice cannot feed the future generation of Africans. African governments should employ agriculture extension officers to work hand in hand with farmers. Mechanical agriculture can work in the Sahel and Savannah areas of Africa because the land is flat without big trees but entrepreneurs have not invested in agriculture in these areas.

African entrepreneurs rely on importation of finished products from the west and that yield quick profit to the detriment of their own people and country. Food production is not a very profitable undertaking and this is the reason governments in the industrialized countries subsidize farming heavily. The governments of Africa should subsidize farming to encourage and attract the young generation. The money spent on importation of food crops that grow successively in Africa, could be channeled to support farmers. Food would be cheaper and create jobs for Africans to do.

Most sub Saharan Africans depend on rice as staple food. Nigeria alone imports over 1,000,000 metric tons and pays $300,000,000 on rice alone every year. Rice can be cultivated in all the arable lands in Nigeria and yet a tiny portion is devoted to rice production. The difference between African rice and imported rice from Asia is in the processing method. There is nothing stopping Africa governments from investing in rice production on a very large scale to meet local demand. A nation should be able to sustain itself from its resources.

Uganda has taken the bull by the horn. It has encouraged local rice production and rice importers are investing in rice cultivation. If the trend continues, Uganda would soon become an exporter of rice instead of importer. These are actions other African countries should emulate in order to improve the continent and the people. If Africans cannot explore the universe, at least they should be able to feed themselves.

The whole sub- Saharan Africa spends over $2 billion a year on rice importation. The money use in rice importation can be used to help African farmers improve on rice cultivation and the finished product. Another staple of Africa is maize. The maize grows all of Africa but African entrepreneurs have not invested enough in maize production to meet demand and reduce famine on the continent Africa. Of the three basic needs of man outside air are water and food. Air is free from nature but food has to be cultivated and processed. In view of environment pollution in recent times, water has to be purified before drinking and for other uses.

African governments invest heavily in ammunition but little on food production. Food production and processing is one of the main stay of developed countries and the governments subsidizes heavily and invest in researches. Industrialization evolved around providing basic needs, convenience and comfort to man.

Why have African leaders not seen the need to improve on the economic and human situation in Africa? These leaders should stop fighting for political power and make efforts to improve life and the society. Internal rift and conflict in Africa would disappear when most people are comfortable. When people are busy and enjoying the comfort of life, achieving their aspiration, and providing for their love ones there would be little idle time for conflicts. Most conflicts in Africa would not happen if there are employments to engage people. Africans are being educated but there are no jobs for them to practice what they have learned or investment funds for them to create their own businesses. The young educated people in Africa are frustrated because after spending many years acquiring education there are no jobs.

The western world is relatively peaceful because most people are able to achieve their aspirations and able to have a productive life during most part of their lives. Europeans used to fight one another but have stopped and united to concentrate on keeping the life style they created during renaissance era for generations yet unborn . The western world always look ahead, the financial problem they are currently facing is not for the present generation but for the future generation. They continue to make sure their people are ahead of everyone else and they live in comfort and enjoy all that the world can offer. The western world does not fight each other anymore but they side opposing sides if other countries are fighting themselves. The focus of governance in the West is the progress of the citizens; to create and maintain comfort for their people.

African governments it is time you take a leaf from the West, because they have perfected the art of living on earth.

Agriculture provides livelihood for nearly 80% of Africans but it is the least developed sector. The government focuses more on crops that yield foreign exchange than food consumption. African leaders have neglected their farmers that work to provide the bulk of revenue for most African countries. African government should provide amenities in the farming communities to boost the living standard of farmers

Angola imports over 50% of the food consumed due to 27 years civil war that destroyed most of farm-lands. It also receives food donation from the international communities, however it recently banned genetically modified organisms food. Why should Africa continue to depend on external forces for its needs? Human beings wherever they are located on earth need the same basic things and fight for the same limited resources on earth. It is high time the black race learns from the past and be independent politically and economically.

African scientists and Agriculturalist should research into ways to increase food productivity. It is a fact that International Institute of Tropical Agriculture is all over African countries, their goal, agenda are to improve upon, and increase production of crops that feed the factories of the west and not on food consume by Africans.

It is time Africa governments realize that every government is there to protect and provide safe environment for its citizens and not to cater for other countries citizens. The governments of Africa should unite to fund a food research institution that would focus on how to improve and increase food production. Most Africans consume similar food crops, creating a common research institutions where African scientist would be involved would easy the perennial famine situation in Africa. There are research institutes for the commodities African exports to the West like cocoa and coffee, but there is none on rice, maize, sorghum, yam, cassava, millet that are staple food for Africans. Drought is a serious problem facing most farmers in the savannah and Sahel lands in Africa. What are the millions of mechanical engineers of African origin doing concerning irrigation? Rain has not been falling as expected, what about creating irrigation systems from watershed in the ground. Africans should realize that everyone problem is everybody's problem.

Livestock production is an area that Africa has an edge but unfortunately government have left everything to the traditional nomads. These nomads deserve a decent way of life. They can be shepherds without having to travel distances to feed their herds. Ranches can built for the raising of animals with the families living on the ranch. Africa needs to make changes and stop living in the past. The young generation of Maasai, Fulani, and nomads over Africa should be taught the modern way of herding. They should be shown the benefits of living on ranches and the benefits to their animals and themselves. A cattle, is a cattle whether in Africa, Australia, or Argentina. It is always disheartening seeing on television dead herds of cattle of African nomads due drought and starvation.

Africa needs to move with the world because they are part of it and not a separate entity. All people have a past they cherish dearly, and changes that improve the glorious past should be imbibed while the remnants of the past are kept in museums for remembrance or historical archives for future generations. The nostalgias of the past can be alive when necessary through plays and movies. This is what the West had done. They have not forgotten their past despite living the present life in modern technological advancement. Societies are not static they are dynamic. The elites and wealthy Africans should show the families that raise animals that changes would only make life better while they continue in the occupation in the family for generations.

A case in point on the plight of the Fulani herdsmen happened in Ghana in April 2010, where a Fulani herdsman and his 700 cattle were arrested for crossing the border from Togo to Ghana. However, this arrest was against the Economic Community of West Africa Protocol on Trans-Human. The Fulani supply meat, cheese, cottage cheese, hides and skin to most part of West Africa. The Fulani are in Niger, Mali, Burkina Faso, Nigeria, and Cameroon. African governments should allocate grazing lands to the nomads to raise their herds. The usual conflicts that ensue between the nomads and crops farmers might be eliminated.

There are herdsmen in advanced countries but they raise their animals on ranches. African leaders could do the same to breed healthy animals and bring lasting peace to the communities. Raising animals on ranches would yield bigger and healthy cattle. Africa can start meat processing business like making corned beef and other meat products and limit importation of same. These are business opportunities African governments can tap into to create employment. Australia and Argentina thrives partly on animal raising. Young men and women are fleeing African due to lack of employment opportunities. The highly educated Africans are under- employed in foreign countries; when African countries could better use their knowledge to develop Africa.

Moving forward, neighboring African countries can pull resources together to improve on food production and processing. Despite insufficiency in food production most of the harvests of African subsistence farmers rot or perished due to lack of transportation, refrigeration, and storage facilities. Countries and people have always come together to solve common problems. Europe did that in the 14th century during the Black Death epidemic. Russia and United States are working together on space programs. African Union is helping to stabilize Sudan and war torn countries in Africa.

Africa Improvement Union as an arm of the African Union to deal with food problem that is common to all African countries. Agriculture is the key for changes in Africa. Since there is abundant land and the people are hard working all that is required is encouragement and assistance from the governments and wealthy individuals. Let the people of Africa show the rest of the world that they are capable of solving their food problems. People flee their communities whenever there is drought in Africa and women and children suffer the most at this period. It is about time African leaders worry about feeding the people instead of creating unnecessary sentiments about the differences in languages and cultures to divide people.

One common area of engagements in Africa aside from farming is petty trading or street trading in all sorts of imported goods from the industrialized world and China. Most street traders are illiterate or semi educated who do not have formal education or vocation. Street trading is an informal and unregulated commercial activity condone in most African cities and towns.
The governments in Africa are not involved in the welfare of the people as such people endeavor to do petty trading to keep body and soul alive. There is no help from the government to the people in Africa and people have to find ways to survive.

Street trading is a way for many African people to make money to get a nest egg for investment in retail trading. Street is very dangerous because they move between cars when there is traffic hold up. This way of making money sometimes turns fatal as some street traders are run over by cars every day. Africans lack organized retailers and therefore depend on small family retailers. Very few of these family retailers survive after the demise of the founders.

African entrepreneurs should take up the challenge to create job opportunities where they employ people. The government of Africa should realize that like a father in the house the welfare of people in their countries is in their hands. Welfare is part of the system in market economy of Europe and United States. In the United States of America government assist the poor by way of food stamps and subsidized housing. European nations help their poor by providing universal health system, low cost housing, and free education. African leaders cannot continue selling African resources without helping the people who jointly own the resources with them. The people of Africa are being short changed by their leaders in this modern time. The citizenry and the government need to work hand in hand to create a productive and peaceful nation. Africa is yearning for an atmosphere of peace, productivity, and progress.

Leaders all over the world are changing their people to live better and worthwhile lives; and African countries could do the same if the leaders believe and care for the people they govern.

Another employment avenues in Africa are artisans, automotive mechanic, tailors, seamstresses, cooked food seller, masons, carpenters, traders of food crops, taxi drivers, weavers, sculptors, electricians and many blue collar occupation done by individuals that are not organized. They learn their trades without formal education. They acquire the knowledge require for the occupations through observation, demonstration, and practice. They turn up to be very good in what they do. The same processes enumerated in the paragraph could be employed by African leaders in equipping Africans on new technologies that would aid faster development for the African continent. Japan and China learned the technologies from the western world through copying, altering and improvement.

The automotive mechanics are the most amazing they can fix any car no matter the make. These are the geniuses of Africa but they are not recognized. They accept any payment the seeker of their services pays. Recently however due to the influx of semi educated people into the trades they now form unions where they fix prices but still very low compared to what such services would cost in the developed economy.

The government and wealthy Africans should set up organized environment where these people could render their services and receive at least living wages. Raising the living standard of people raises the living standard of the community. Standards need to be set and everyone would have expectation of what is expected. If African leaders set standards of living that they want people to live in decent accommodations, work in safe and clean environment, have functional educational system it would happen because the people want these but could not do them on their own without governmental or entrepreneurs involvement. In the western society the governments, entrepreneurs and people work together, respect each other's contribution and that is the reason they have been able to maintain such enviable position in the world.

African countries that produce same commodities should form cartels in order to be able to negotiate fair prices for the commodities. Scarce products should be highly priced due to demand. The commodities grown in the tropics like cocoa and coffee have no substitute and their demand is high so countries producing them should be making good revenue but unfortunately they are not making the deserve revenue. Companies like Nestle, Starbuck and many others that add value or process the cocoa and coffee are making huge profits at the expense of the growers of these commodities.

There should be some partnership agreement between the supplies and users of commodities where profit sharing will be the mode of payment. The present systems where Africa sell their commodity without adding value would continue to make Africa and its people poor. Land that should be devoted to food production are used for cash crops but the African is not gaining proportionately in the profits from the cash crops. The current situation in the commodity markets favors the end producers; the famers, who sacrifice their time and labor to plant, harvest and process the coffee and cocoa beans are being short changed in the current commodity trading. The manufacturers reap the profits that should go to the producers, that is, the farmers. (insert an African on his cocoa farm)

The way Africa countries have been trading the commodities has not helped in generating required revenue for the growers and the condition of living of the growers is very deplorable. These companies should rethink how they take these valuable resources and pay close to nothing for them. The African farmer deserves a decent life from his labor and those who make millions of dollars profit should share part of the profit with the producers if they want them to improve on their current state of living. The world is becoming a global village and everyone should enjoy in the input and output of their contributions.

 Manufacturers set prices of manufactured goods and similarly producers of commodities should be able to set prices for their commodities. The users of the commodities would not make any changes to prices until Africans realize the importance of service they render to the world and adjust prices to improve their own economy. Africa may not need most of the things they import if they are able to improve on arable agriculture, animal raising and set up food processing factories. African leaders need to be concerned about the welfare of the people and their undeniable rights as people to enjoy life that is available to any human on earth. Rural areas in Africa have not seen the light of modern amenities despite increase in the sale of African resources in the world commodity markets.

A vital amenity in most modern society is electricity, the engine of technological advancements. Africa should reinvest in all sources of electricity generating technologies to meet current and future energy demands. Availability of electricity would create avenues for industrial take off. South Africa was able to host the 2010 World Cup because they have efficient electricity.

Most African countries are still in the middle ages where candles and oil lamps are in use at night for illumination in communities. Electricity supply is erratic and power shortages rampant in most cities. The few hydro- electric power stations installed in the colonial era and small additions after independence are in operation without adequate maintenance. Lack of maintenance culture is an endemic problem in Africa.

According to an article in the Economist August, 2007 African population of close to a billion generates only 4% of the global electricity. A World Bank article in the Economist estimated that building a series of dams along the Congo fast flowing water could supply 30,000 megawatts of electricity to power the entire continent of Africa. What is stopping Africa from embarking on the project? This is an area where unity among Africans is critical. African countries should put their hands on deck and work towards electrifying the continent.

Africa should shed the label of Dark Continent and become a Continent of Brightness. The time to do this is now. African leaders should join hands to electrify Africa to let the next generation be proud of their predecessors. It is possible. This should be a priority of African leaders now. China is moving fast, and India is trailing behind. When is Africa joining the ride for a better life for their people?

Africans have been relying on small generating plants to supply their homes and small businesses with electricity, but the carbon monoxide these plants exhaust have killed thousands of Africans. It is very pathetic when Africa has the resources to generate electricity from hydro, sun, geothermal, winds, natural gas and nuclear yet live in darkness. The main problem would be capital but there are natural resources to support any investment. In finance theories, a project can pay for it self but allocating cost to the revenue that the project generates.   If Africa receives fair prices for its resources from the west and east there would not be any need for African countries to be borrowing money.

The western world established the current world financial system to assist western nations to rebuild after the world wars. In other for African countries to move, forward in the current dispensation they need to know how the world financial system works in other to benefit. The African nations have not been involved in the world financial system as such they do not understand the mechanisms of how it works in order to benefit from it.

Provision of electricity to most parts of Africa should have been the first priority after independence from colonial rule. The development of pipeline to carry gas that is flaring away in petroleum exporting countries can be diverted to generation of electricity. Solar panels would be additional means of providing electricity in Africa. Tapping into geothermal energy on the Great Rift Valley from Eritrea to Mozambique and wind power could provide the African continent with needed electric power. Efficient management of existing power plants and pooling resources together to creating power grids across the continent is imperative. North and South Africa are relatively sufficient in electrical energy, the main problem areas are West, East, and Central Africa.

There have been many talks and symposiums on electricity for these areas, but action is what is required. Progress is in the pipeline to create regional power based on reports from the World Bank. The proposed regional power points would be as follows:
1. The Southern African Power
2. The East African Power
3. The North African Power

An article in Newsroom Jersey in July 2009 reported that, twelve German companies are proposing to install thermal power in North Africa to meet European Electricity demand for 2020. The major planners in the project are Deutsche Bank, Siemens, Muenchener Rueck- an insurance company, and RWE German largest power supplier. The proposed project would cost $560 billion to install and connect European grids to receive electricity across the

Mediterranean Sea. They would supply power to The North African countries and the Middle East as well.

What happens to the rest of the countries in Africa who need electricity more than Europe? Almost 920 million Africans live in complete darkness at night. Being black, nothing has changed. It is always about Europe and Europeans. The Germans are employing divide and rule tactics to set up electricity in North Africa to augment their own supply and provide for North African and the Middle East and neglect the rest of Africa.   Arab descendants have been ruling North Africa since they conquered the areas in the 1500s and the people mostly speak Arabic.   External forces continue to take vital decisions for Africa without involvement of the African people. Tapping the sun's energy to develop electricity for Germany without providing benefits to other countries on the continent of Africa is not adequate. What are black African leaders doing? African leaders should not sit and watch again this time while Europe determines black people's fate. Nothing has changed on the perception of Europe on Africa. Just like they bounced on the continents to divide it among themselves in the 1800s and sold the people as slaves. Being black nothing has changed.

It is time African scientists, engineers, investors, planners got together to come out with solution to light up Africa. The educated and wealthy African cannot continue fleeing Africa to live in developed economy. The people in the developed economy created the comfort and convenience for themselves. The citizens in the west are tired of influx of people into their countries as employment opportunities are limited in recent times and had to compete with others in the job market. The western world does not want many immigrants anymore and they are closing loopholes to restrict numbers of immigrants that enter their countries.

African leaders need to view the negative effect emigration has on the various countries. The educated Africans who have the knowledge and means to develop their countries are fleeing to another country to offer services that Africa needs. The argument is that these immigrants remit funds home and it helps their home country. No, it does not help their respective countries as much as it helps the country of their migration. These immigrants increase the productivity of their host countries and pay taxes for the governments. Most of these immigrants are well educated and tend to be under- employed in their host countries. African countries have to under study the developed countries; and learn how they have been able to consistently created employment for their citizens after they became a republic.

Lack of good drinking water is the cause of most water borne diseases in Africa; yet not much have been done to provide good drinking water. Africa has the following water sources- The Congo River, the Nile, the Zambezi, the Niger, Lake Victoria, Volta, Lake Chad, and many tributaries. African countries particularly in the Sahel have droughts most of the time that destroy crops and animals. Irrigation of crops had been part of Egypt's agriculture since ancient times and one wonders with the modern technologies and the water sources Africa has the continent has not been able to have effective irrigation systems in place. The governments of Africa are obsessed with political power such that they do not plan for things that can make life better for their citizens. Good leaders do not require protection from other nations but their own security apparatus.

Water is the second vital needs of man and majority of people in Africa do not have access to clean water. What is the use of governments if they cannot make life healthy, convenient, and comfortable for the people they rule? If you look at Africa, particularly sub Saharan Africa you wonder whether the leaders understand governance or what governing entails.

African leaders should make provision of clean water a priority and monies invested in ammunitions to stay in power can be diverted to water and electricity provision. The leaders of Africa do not need to coerce people to vote if they were governing as governing should be. Electorates vote for leaders that satisfy their needs and aspirations. In Africa, elections are nightmarish for the voters because politicians go to politics to enrich themselves and become aggressive and violent when they lose.

African countries should have a joint project to develop water sources and provide water for the teeming citizens. There should be collaboration and cooperation among Africa countries to move the continent forward. Eastern and Southern part of Africa have over 75% of the water sources in Africa and joint efforts by African governments would be the solution to extend water to the Sahel and parts of Sahara.

Safe water is not free in most countries around the world, and Africans do not expect it to be free either. They need clean water to reduce diseases, to have a long life, and to swim in clean water and enjoy water sports. The money spend on individual bore hole wells could be combined to develop a lasting solution to the water problems in Africa. The colonists left some legacy of pipe borne water why have African leaders not improved or expanded the infrastructure. This is the 21st century and one would think Africa would have moved forward but sadly, the continent and people are retrogressing.

Staple food crops like sorghum, maize, wheat, pulses, and many African staples do well in the Sahel but due to perennial drought, they are unable to grow food- crops to their capacity. It is time African leaders change their strategies and tactics and be concerned about the progress and growth of their respective countries and people. Food is very important for human survival and African leaders have lost sight of this important factor. Africa should not have famine and people of Africa should not go hungry because there is vast land and hard- working people. Entrepreneurs should invest heavily in agriculture instead of leaving farming to subsistence farming. Africa should move from the past and do what other leaders are doing now to increase food production. The reliance on World Food Organization and World Health Organization would not change situations in Africa. Africans are part of the human race and they continue to allow other people to guide them through the world as if they are strangers. The basic needs of man are healthy environment, food, water, electricity, and shelter. These are the basis for other requirements and Africa lacks the former. It is good to communicate if you have the basic needs of life in place then communication and other modern way of life would follow.

Very few states in America are the bread- basket of the rest of the states. If Africa countries that have water reserves could help those with dry lands with water, hunger would become something of the past in Africa. Unless Africa countries get together to assist one another in areas where they have comparative advantage, progress would continue to elude the continent and people as a whole. African entrepreneurs should be involved in big projects like water and electricity development instead of selling imported wares from overseas countries to Africans.

Health Delivery is very poor in Africa. Most things the rest of the world take for granted are luxuries in Africa. Even getting a clean place to ease oneself in transit is a problem. What have the leaders of Africa being doing with all the revenue they receive in selling African minerals and commodities? The following disease, malaria, tuberculosis, dysentery, cholera, guinea worm should have been eradicated from Africa. These diseases are caused by unsanitary environment and drinking unsafe water. Africa should be able to handle prevention of these diseases but unfortunately not.

. According to the World Health Organization 40% of Africans are illiterate that means 60% are literate. The essence of education is to improve one's life and be able to apply knowledge acquired to everyday life. A great play writer, William Shakespeare said that knowledge gained and not applied is a waste. The educated 60% Africans should know the importance of good health, and should have been able to impact knowledge on healthy living to the less educated. Public health education is very vital particularly in a society where the environment is not cleaned and hygienically maintained. The majority literate Africans should make the health of the people in the society everyone's concern. Healthy people are wealthy people.

There is strength in unity and that is what Africa needs now. Africans should set aside language differences and geographical location and move the continent forward. People who came from different places in Europe that spoke different languages were able to form a nation that is the greatest nation on earth today, the United States of America. Africans have lived with each for long and it is ironic that the differences in language and vocation have become the weapon they use to destroy themselves nowadays. The diversity among the different group of people in Africa should be their strength and pride. There is economic benefit in large scale. The countries that are leading the world now are the populous countries; China and India.

If African leaders can join hands to together to set up state of the art health delivery centers in Africa it would benefit everyone. When leaders are ill in Africa they have to travel to Europe or Asia for health treatment. It is time African leaders have faith in their own people who are physicians. If you do not have faith in the people you lead then it does not make sense being their leader. African physicians work in hospital overseas and it is the same medical education the whole world uses with the difference that African doctors are not given the technology they need to work with in their home countries.

347

Primary care delivery has improved significantly in the urban centers in Africa but the rural areas where the majority of Africans live are in serious deprivation of health care. Preventive health education should be a priority of African countries. People should not get sick before they know the importance of living in clean environment. You do not have to be literate to understand the importance of good health. The onus lies on the educated and wealthy Africans to participate in making the next generation of Africa healthy. If leaders care about their people, other people would care too. If leaders do not care about the people they rule, no one would.

If any of the African head of state is sick, they go overseas for treatment at public expense. These leaders should be ashamed of themselves. What is good for the goose is good for the gender. These leaders are Africans and if they think the health delivery system in their respective countries are not good enough for them then it is not good for the populace as well. It is time African leaders put the African people first, before the leaders. In a democratic system of government, it is the people then the leaders.

Every place on earth is moving fast in terms of development but Africans keep on fighting one another for political power and ethnicity differences. How do Africa leaders feel when they travel to another country to be treated? Do they feel secure? No nation's leader apart from Africans would leave their country and seek treatment abroad when they have physicians. If the leaders think African doctors and health practitioners are not good enough then they should re train and equip the hospitals.

The countries in the Middle East have excellent health delivery system because they believe it is the responsibility of a country to provide accessible health system for the populace. African countries cannot continue depending on World Health Organization to solve its health problems. Africans are human and they should learn to be responsible for themselves and drop the dependency syndrome that has become a fabric with African leaders.

One area that calls for immediate attention is trauma care. There should be well- equipped trauma centers in African cities. Introduction of information and communication technology into the health delivery system is vital in this day- and- age. The stressful nature of urban life is the same anywhere in the world but it becomes too stressful in Africa due to lack of modern amenities and individuals have to provide everything for themselves. Sedentary occupation is creating another wave of health issues in Africa. Diabetes and hypertension are very common among African elites. The new diseases are killing young African elites in record numbers.

These diseases are silent killers, and with the situation in Africa where superstitious beliefs are high, often sudden deaths are therefore, attributed to witches instead of looking for the underlining cause of death. In view of the superstitious nature of African societies, autopsy is very rare when someone dies suddenly. Exercise as a preventive way to relieve stress should be introduced everywhere in African countries. In Japan, factories workers perform light body exercise before work commences. Most African women who are retailers are getting obese because they sit in their stalls all day without much movement. Africa leaders should create an encompassing society where everyone belongs, cares and contribute their best to the society while at the same time realizing their individual aspirations.

If Africans were responsible for themselves, they would have caught
HIV/AID when it started before it reached the proportion it is now. According to statistics from the World Health Organization over 40million in sub-Saharan -Africa live with HIV/AIDS. Africans count on other people to take care of their responsibility for them. It always takes outsiders to tell

Africans what is happening to them. Is it not time African countries become independent? African countries got independence on paper not in reality. The invisible hands of the colonists still direct African affairs.

Despite inadequate health delivery, the few trained-personnel are leaving the health sector in drones in most African countries to seek greener pastures in the industrialized world. The problem with Africa health delivery is not personnel but the countries themselves. The salaries structures in most African countries are not geared towards providing comfort, improved way of life and comfortable retirement. Salaried paid to workers are not adequate to meet their personal needs and the society lack many basic amenities like safe water, housing, electricity, and road infrastructure.

In other to broaden awareness of happenings to people there should be improvement in media and communication facilities and apparatus in Africa. In most African countries, the government controls the media and information the public receives is bias. Public education is very vital due the dynamics of the modern world that is changing faster and people should be in constant aware of events happenings. Dissemination of information is part of democracy but African leaders and journalists do not see eye to eye. There is information censorship in Africa than anywhere one can think of in the world. If African politicians are doing right for their people, why should they be bothered on what someone writes or utters.

The African journalist and media have been doing a good job on dissemination of information but more still needs to be done in the area of public education. Information on everyday living and improvement are very vital in African community where ignorance feeds on superstition. Movies on ways people are improving their lives despite the odds should be common so that people can learn and take away from it. Television has great effect on people so issues to change life better dominate television presentations and reports.

Public communication has improved in some African countries with private ownership of radio and television stations. The internet had opened avenues for Africans to see the rest of the world clearer instead of relying on abstracts from books.
The mobile phone technology has really improved interpersonal communication tremendously. The zeal that informed the huge investment in mobile phone technology in Africa should be geared towards provision of electricity and safe water in Africa. Africans spends a very high percentage of their earning on mobile phones and it is good business for the companies.

In order for Africa countries to experience rebirth the leaders have to make the people the reason for governance. Who stands for the black person?. The black man must tell himself I deserve some dignity because I am human. The situation where majority of African countries now depend on aids and foreign food donation when they have lands and people is very pathetic. Africans are very lucky because they do not have to start from the scratch to develop technology for most modern amenities. In most instances foundations for amenities are already in place in African countries, what is required is an undertaken by investors and government to expand and build more amenities where they are lacking.

The leaders of Africa would have to make some sacrifices by forgoing the way they presently govern and adopt a new method where everybody counts. By embracing all people, the government would sow the seed of patriotism. People builds a country, therefore if the African leaders lessons their autocratic behavior and any body feels welcome, many sons and daughters of Africa and other investors would come to invest. There is cliché that is around lately, 'the world is Global village'. If the world is truly a global village majority of

Africans would not be sleeping in darkness at night, infected with HIV/AIDS, drink unsafe water and infected with curable diseases, live in over- crowded slums, have, no access to health care and the system of education does not arouse innovation and creativity. Millions of dollars go to waste each day in the industrialized world through abundance of material acquisitions that are not necessary for survival and this is money that could be channel to develop the continent that supply the industrialized world with raw materials. Everybody points to Africa's under development forgetting the fact that without African resources most things people cling to would not be possible. The phone technology gets most of its input from resources from Africa.

Africans are currently spectators in this world they accept anything the rest of the world throws their way and the best thing they do is to fight one another with weapons made by other people. Africans have been humiliated throw slavery but have not used the lesson to improve on the people and be economically independent. Africans rely so much on the rest of the world for everything, while the world depletes African resources. This needs to stop for Africa to move forward. Africans have to become active participant in the world community.

The reliance on world institutions like the United Nations and its agencies, the World Bank, International Monetary Fund, and other agencies would never help Africa from the current situation unless Africans know what they want and move towards the goal. To these institutions, the status quo in Africa is in order because it fulfills the agenda of the United Nations. The initial purpose for the establishment of the United Nation was to bring peace to parties that fought one another in the Second World War. The second reason was to rebuild Europe that was devastated in the War After Second World War, the UN has been involved in many aspects of restoration of peace, keeping peace, rendering economic assistance, and advising countries on how to manage their countries particularly the countries that were former Europeans colonies with the exception of the United States of America.

 Majority of the United Nations dependents are all under developing nations. The time- frame for the developing countries to become a developed nation depends on United Nations.   No developed country depended on anyone for development aside from the determination and aspiration of the citizens of that country.

The economic structure the UN advocates under the structural adjustment program did not yield the expected results of economic improvement and stability in Africa. The structural adjustment program failed in most of these countries mainly because these countries did not have an established economic system and the leaders in these countries do not have the same aspiration of making life better for their citizenry. The requirement of the program was harsh on the people but made way for the providers of funds to make more money on the poor countries. Requirement of the structured adjustment program on borrower countries:
- Reduction in government spending (education, health and sanitation and other programs that the government provides for the people)
- Monetary tightening (high interest, devaluation of currency, decrease access to credit)
- Elimination of government subsidies (food and other items)
- Privatization of governments own companies and enterprises
- Reduction in barriers to trade to foreign investment and ownership

Just a look at the above restrains shows that the program was not meant to benefit Africa but to continue the status quo of foreign domination on Africa.

All the African countries that participated in the program created more foreign debt burden for their respective countries. The short-term borrowing creates more revenue for the lender, because the turn- around is very fast   Interest on borrowed money grow exponentially and the borrower would forever be paying back money to the lender. Credit is good only if feasibility study on the project indicates repayment of the credit is certain   Most African countries do not have experts on finance but they have accountants whose job is not on finance, investments, and budgets.

African countries that took the International Monetary Fund loans and strictly followed the structured adjustment programs were worse off.
 Several economic indicators stimulate the western economy and not only government. In most African countries the government control most of economic capital and there is no welfare for people to fall back if they lose their jobs. African countries do not have unemployment program, or voluntary agencies that assist families in hard times in the west.   The IMF structured adjustment program actually benefited the lenders because African countries are indebted to loans that did not change anything but worsen situation. No outsider can have the best interest of a people but the people themselves. If you know the history of Europe, you would recollect that, the domination of other nations on other nations created most wars. Everyone always put their interest first and this is a fact of human nature.   .

A way out for African countries is to encourage internal productivity. A country does not need to borrow money from outside to meet the internal need. Governments should provide grants to entrepreneur and encourage research into new ideas. The citizens of a country and investors are all that a country needs to progress. The leaders of African should encourage all citizens to be part of the governance and great changes would come to Africa. African have the resources to be great it lacks great leaders who are dedicated to the course of the citizens.

Why should a country borrow money to meet its internal needs? A country is not a business enterprise that makes money from business operation. The productivity of the citizens of a country is what creates their wealth. The wealth of a country is the gross domestic product and services less all external liabilities. Africa needs to stimulate internal growth. The countries should encourage the best minds of Africa to generate ideas on how to move the continent forward. Outsiders are benefiting more from African resources that Africans because the leaders in charge of African do not have trust in their own citizens. They are not ruling with honest intentions or else Africa should developed better than it is at present. The people of Africa are yearning for a better life.

By encouraging the citizen in their endeavors, investing in the country instead of foreign lands and appreciating the people they rule Africa would be able to come from the doldrums of poverty and haplessness. African should take advantage of the diversity it has and exploit the goodness in the diversity. Who bred African leaders that they turn to despite the people they rule?

This book concludes with the note that black people all over the world is part of this universe and have contributed immensely to make it what it is today. Black people for a fault or no fault of theirs have moved to a lower status in human society. In most nations were black people live, black people are workers and do not own the factors of production and it is entrenched in those societies that a black person has to work for someone and not own their own business and employ people to work for them. Education that taught people how to create wealth were never provided in black communities. The few black people in foreign lands, who risk the consequences to own properties and business were demonized by other people.

In Africa, the leaders do not rely on the expertise of their own citizens and construction, and major public projects are assigned to expatriates. African leaders are lured with elaborate entertainment when they visit foreign lands, when the visiting countries know very well that they would not treat their people the way their friend is treating his people. African people are adversely portrayed on western television as sick and poor or not to be trusted. Amazingly, without African cheap resources the world would not have reached the current milestone.

The new emerging powers India and China are buying African mineral resources to develop their respective countries and the money receive has less value than the finite resources. African leaders should be asking for developmental partnership instead of selling resources that cannot be value with paper currency. Countries that need African resources should help provide Africa with what Africa needs like good roads schools and hospitals. Despite the evil of colonization, they gave Africa countries the infrastructure most African countries have today. If the colonial powers could do that, why have Africa leaders not demanding for projects in exchange of resources. Through this type of exchanges, we are giving back to the land that gave up the resources.

The belly of the continent of Africa must be hollow due to the mining of resources from the colonial period to the present day. It is time Africans demand tangible things that would benefit everyone instead of the paper currency for exchange of commodities and mineral resources that are finite. We can mint paper currency, but the finite resources in Africa cannot be replenished in millions years. The payment with paper currency creates room for corruption and embezzlement; these two are cankerworms in African Countries. The money received from selling Africans valuable resources are siphon to the west and east instead of investing them in Africa. There is no change in Africa the way the colonialists left them after independence. The soldiers who took over power in 1970s distorted Africa than anyone in African history. By the way, where will Africa get resources when the time arrives; and the time has arrived for African's renaissance.

The leaders of Africa should endeavor to let development spread to the rural areas of Africa where majority of Africans live.   The farmers of Africa work very hard to produce, coffee, cocoa, cotton, sugar, gum Arabic, peanuts, bananas, frankincense, myrrh, vanilla, tea ,tobacco, cashew, and many more to the world and they are the poorest while the processors of the produce make millions of dollars.   There is no value given the labor of the African farmer in the commodity market, he works hard and get paid money that makes him perpetually poor. This has been the cycle of life for most African farmers and when are they going to get real value for their input. No body talks about the dedication of African farmer to work and produce products that has increased life expectancy for the world while his own is shortening year in year out.

The hazards of the African farmer is even less compared to African miners, who go in the belly of earth to mine diamonds, gold, iron ore, tin, salt, uranium, platinum, copper, bauxite, nickel, cobalt, zinc, gemstones, soda ash, tantalum, manganese, lead, and many more. These miners are not even paid living wages when their efforts make millionaires of other people. They risk their lives to go underground to bring resources to the surface of the earth. It is time leaders of Africa take the circumstances of their people seriously because the powers they wage belong to the people. If the leaders improve Africa 's environment Africans in Diaspora would be eager to come to Africa for vacations in the same way people of European origin invest in Europe through tourism.   The bane of Africa is the leaders, the citizens of Africa have been doing their best and the leaders have mortgaged their own people for personal wealth.

End Notes

- Jared Diamond- :Guns, Germ, and Steel, The fates of Human Societies, 1999.

- Website-: unmuseum.mus.pa.us/Henson.htm

- H.J. de Blij, Peter O.Muller, Geography Realms, Regions and Concepts, American Journal of International Law Vol. 14 #4. 2003.

- Hahn Steven-: The Greatest Slave Rebellion in Modern History: Southern Slaves in the American Civil War.

- About.Com-: African-American History

- Steve Goldman-:The Southern Slave Revolt.

- Basil Davidson-: Western Africa before the Colonial Era,1998.

- Robert Appleton Company-: Life of Prince Henry of Portugal, London 1868.
- Barbara Tuchman-: Distant Mirror the Disastrous 14th Century.

- Richard Hooker:- World Civilization, 1996.

- PBS online Article-: Slave Revolt of 1712.

- Quintard Taylor-: Black-past Organization Haitian Revolution, 1791-1804.

- Herbert Aptheker-: American Negro Slave Revolts; New York 1993.